THE Art AND Practice OF Home Visiting

THE Art AND Practice OF Home Visiting

Early Intervention for Children with Special Needs and Their Families

by

Ruth E. Cook, Ph.D.
Professor
Department of Education
Santa Clara University, California

and

Shirley N. Sparks, M.S., CCC-SLP
Associate Professor Emerita
Department of Speech Pathology and Audiology
Western Michigan University, Kalamazoo

·P·A·U·L·H·
BROOKES
PUBLISHING CO ®

Baltimore • London • Sydney

Paul H. Brookes Publishing Co.
Post Office Box 10624
Baltimore, Maryland 21285-0624
USA

www.brookespublishing.com

Manufactured in the United States of America by
The Maple-Vail Book Manufacturing Group, York, Pennsylvania.

The individuals described in this book are real people whose situations are masked
and are based on the authors' experiences. Names and identifying details have been
changed to protect confidentiality.

Library of Congress Cataloging-in-Publication Data

Cook, Ruth E.
   The art and practice of home visiting : early intervention for children with special
needs and their families / by Ruth E. Cook and Shirley N. Sparks.
   p.   cm.
Includes index.
ISBN-13: 978-1-55766-885-1
ISBN-10: 1-55766-885-X
1. Family social work.   2. Social work with children with disabilities.   3. Children
with disabilities—Services for.   4. Parents of children with disabilities—Services
for.   5. Children with disabilities—Family relationships.   6. Home-based family
services.   7. Social case work.   I. Sparks, Shirley N. (Shirley Nichols), 1933–   II.
Title.

HV697.C667 2008
362.4—dc22   2008017835

British Library Cataloguing in Publication data are available from the British Library.

2012   2011   2010   2009   2008

10   9   8   7   6   5   4   3   2   1

Contents

About the Authors

Ruth E. Cook, Ph.D., is Professor of Special Education and Director of Early Intervention/Early Childhood Special Education, Santa Clara University, California. Dr. Cook earned her doctoral degree with an emphasis on developmental psychology and two related master of arts degrees from the University of California at Los Angeles. She focused her interest on young children with special needs while serving as Director of the Early Childhood Center at Southern Illinois University at Edwardsville and the Child Development Center at Mount Saint Mary's College in Los Angeles. Daily involvement with families of children from highly diverse backgrounds convinced her of the importance of fully involving families in all aspects of their children's development.

More than 25 years ago, Dr. Cook recognized the value of providing practical training based on evidence-based practices designed to facilitate inclusion of young children with special needs in natural environments. To this end, she initiated the publication of the co-authored *Adapting Early Childhood Curricula for Young Children with Special Needs* (Prentice Hall, 2007). This pioneering text is now in its 7th edition. In addition, she is a co-author of *Strategies for Including Children with Special Needs in Early Childhood Settings* (Thomson Delmar Learning, 2000). She has directed several federal training grants that provide tuition assistance to prepare students to work with young children with special needs both in their homes and in center-based programs. Dr. Cook consults widely and presents often in the areas of family–professional relationships and strategies for effective inclusion.

Shirley N. Sparks, M.S., CCC-SLP, is Associate Professor Emerita, Department of Speech Pathology and Audiology, Western Michigan University, Kalamazoo. While at Western Michigan University, Ms. Sparks spent a sabbatical year with the department of public health in Battle Creek, Michigan, doing home visits with public health nurses. More recently she was an adjunct faculty member in the Department of Early Childhood Education at Santa Clara University, Santa Clara, California. She received her bachelor of arts degree in speech pathology and audiology from the University of Iowa, her master of arts degree also in speech pathology and audiology from Tulane University, New Orleans, and completed all but her dissertation in the Ph.D. program in the School of Public Health at the University of Michigan, Ann Arbor.

Ms. Sparks is a pioneer in early intervention, working with families, home visiting, and giving numerous presentations throughout the country. She has felt strongly that it is necessary to remain a practitioner in the field to experience real problems that early interventionists encounter. Until very recently, she served as a consultant to HOPE Homestart in San José, California, a home program for children with special needs from birth to 3 years. A fellow of the American Speech-Language-Hearing Association, Ms. Sparks has authored training modules and many articles and chapters on early intervention and the family in addition to a book on genetics in speech-language disorders and a book on the effects of prenatal substance abuse on speech and language.

Foreword

I can think of no more significant or timely topic to address than the subject matter of this book. Early interventionists representing a wide array of professional disciplines will be indebted to Ruth Cook and Shirley Sparks for their depth of clinical insight, personal experience, and familiarity with the professional literature that they have brought to bear in this volume.

After 30 years of providing services for families of infants and toddlers with special needs, and interacting with professional audiences in venues around the world, I have come to see that one of our most glaring omissions is the dearth of preservice training early intervention professionals have available to them. This is particularly true as it relates to the unique opportunity professionals have in making home visits. I am pleased to suggest that this will no longer be the case, due in large measure to the efforts of Cook and Sparks. Those headed toward a career in early intervention as well as veteran clinicians will profit from this material.

Experienced early interventionists are aware that the efficacy of the services they provide is largely dependent on the degree to which the parents/caregivers are full participants in the process. Stated succinctly, those children whose parents/caregivers are engaged in the process generally do better overall. The current practice of early intervention mandates that the initiation of services takes place in the context of the home. Hence, a direct linkage exists between what takes place in the home setting and the overall effectiveness of the services provided. This further underscores the timeliness and importance of the material contained in this text.

Perhaps the opening sentences of Chapter 2 best summarize the purpose of this book:

Given that the field of early intervention has shifted from direct intervention with the child to a focus on the family as a whole, it has become extremely important for the home visitor to thoroughly understand how stress affects parent–child interactions and overall family functioning. Without this understanding, home visitors cannot provide the support or develop the relationships necessary to empower the family to meet the special needs of their child.

In my estimation, it is about time that someone has provided early interventionists with clinically relevant information enabling them to "thoroughly understand how stress affects parent–child interactions and overall family functioning."

This is an exceptionally well-written book, one that will assist early interventionists for many years to come. It is easy to read, clinically germane, and professionally accurate, and most important, it will benefit the children and families we serve. I recommend it without reservation. Someone much wiser than I once wrote, "Do you see a man skillful in his work? He will stand before kings." I'm not sure about standing before kings, but I encourage you to join me in congratulating Cook and Sparks on a job well done. My only regret is that this material was not available to me 30 years ago.

Louis Rossetti, Ph.D.
Professor Emeritus of Communicative Disorders
University of Wisconsin, Oshkosh

From a Mother
to Her Home Visitors

Four years ago today, Chase was offi-cially diagnosed with autism. At that time, Chase was 20 months old and had zero receptive language (couldn't follow the simplest of directions), had zero expressive language, didn't point, was barely walking and couldn't get from a sit to a stand without pulling up on something, didn't interact with  *Natalie (his twin sister) at all, couldn't eat most solid foods, made sporadic eye contact, flapped nonstop, stimmed on anything he could get his hands on, didn't play appropriately with anything, and didn't know his own name. He also cried almost constantly. I could hardly take him out of the house even for the shortest periods of time. He had chronic runny poop and fluid behind his eardrums that would not drain. Chase was diagnosed with severe autism that day.*

I want to take this time to thank everyone who has been involved in Chase's life since that time. Because of all of you, Chase is no longer plagued by the worst parts of autism. He is still autistic but can now be con-sidered high functioning. In some instances, he is indistinguishable from his peers! Just yesterday, a therapist said to me, "I was trying to find the autis-tic kid at preschool and I couldn't!" That sums up how far this kid has come!

He is social, makes great eye contact, plays with his peers, has age-appropriate language (with some social pragmatic challenges and obses-sion with some subjects such as Mario Kart and Nicktoon Racing games!), can read, has an amazing memory, plays with Natalie, charms the pants off most adults, has an IQ that is borderline gifted, has normal poop (trust me, if you are a parent of an ASD kid, this is a HUGE feat!), and attends typical preschool and many typical activities such as swim lessons, gym class, and music class. He has great joint attention and truly wants to please those around him.

When Chase was first diagnosed, I didn't know what the future would hold for him. Thinking about the future really scared me...but today, while I am sure Chase will continue to have challenges and need support, I am confident he will be able to live on his own and hold a job. Thank you to each and every one of you for loving my kid and providing him the best of YOU!

Lori Yurtin

Preface

In the not-too-distant past, children identified with special needs did not typically receive public intervention services until they reached the age of 3 years. Laws such as Education for All Handicapped Children Act of 1975 (PL 94-142), Education of the Handicapped Act Amendments of 1986 (PL 99-457), and Individuals with Disabilities Education Act (IDEA) of 1990 (PL 101-476) changed that forever in the United States. The Individuals with Disabilities Education Act and its reauthorizations mandate that children with special needs receive a free appropriate public education beginning at birth. Furthermore, that education is to be in a least restrictive environment. For children younger than 3 years, this most often means providing services in the home with the family.

The mandates from these laws created a pressing need for more home service providers: early interventionists, infant educators, developmental specialists, speech-language pathologists, occupational therapists, physical therapists, psychologists, and social workers. This book is designed to encourage and guide all early intervention home visitors—students, seasoned veterans, generalists, specialists, and even supervisors—as they strive to provide effective in-home intervention services for children and families.

For those of us who previously provided early intervention services in clinics and centers, complying with the new requirements called for a rapid transition to providing services in the home. In the clinic, we were used to having a consistent environment tailored to our liking. We had little tables and chairs for evaluation. Materials were in orderly cubbies on our walls. Parents brought their children to us, and they might or might not have been able to observe what we were doing. Under the new requirements, we had to change our way of doing things: We must go to the home, create an environment for functional assessment, and help children learn to live in the real world. What's more, our services are supposed to be *family centered.* Although that term invites interpretation, we know with certainty that it means we are no longer in complete control of the agenda. Parents are to be consulted about what they want for their child. We aren't the directors of the process anymore. We are expected to work collaboratively with caregivers to facilitate achievement of outcomes for them as well as for their children.

The mother's letter at the beginning of this book arrived unsolicited by e-mail as we were finishing the manuscript. Is there a better illustration of the success of early intervention? This mother is an excellent example of collaboration between parent and service providers in the home. She was in every way a team member and team leader. She was an informed and a strong advocate for her child.

How does one learn to be a home visitor? Has anyone done this before? Yes, as you will find in Chapter 1, home visitors have been on the job since the early 1900s. Our models were social workers and public health nurses. Shirley Sparks remembers well visiting a family along with a public health nurse in the mid-1980s with the purpose of finding out what was done on a home visit. She sat with growing alarm as this first visit with a family progressed almost like a social occasion. An older child was watching television. The nurse said things like, "Tell me about Robert," "What's it like to live with Robert?" and "What would you like to see happen in the next few years?"

Then, she sat back and just listened. The mother had lots to tell—about her pregnancy and Robert's premature birth and how tiny he was. She told how her mother was afraid to touch such a tiny little thing. She told about how her husband still wouldn't hold the baby because he cried so much. As she talked about problems, it seemed that the time was right to give her some advice. There were solutions for some of the things she mentioned. Wasn't that what we were there for? It seemed that we should give Robert a good evaluation. Was this what should be going on in a home visit?

Finally, the nurse weighed and measured the baby and asked about what Robert generally ate. Then she said, "We need to see that

Robert gains weight. Are you worried about anything else?" Now the mother really got talkative. She was worried that her husband might lose his job and they would have to move away. She was worried about her older daughter and how she was acting like a baby again. And she was worried that she wouldn't be a good mother to both children. The nurse nodded her head, made some notes, and made an appointment for the next week.

In the following weeks, all of this mother's concerns were discussed. Some could be problem-solved together. For some, she needed specific advice. And for some, she needed to talk and be heard. After she was heard, she was ready to listen. This was what *infant mental health* really meant.

In the early days of crafting early intervention home visits, mistakes were made that provided opportunities for learning. We learned about complicated and diverse families, collaboration, listening, siblings, sick kids in the house, teen parents, parents with addiction problems, managing our time very differently, and cultures different from our own. But after 2 decades of mistakes and successes with hundreds of families, certain truths and patterns have emerged. Those are the lessons found in this book.

It seems that after years of home visiting, we think we have seen everything that one could possibly see of child needs, parent needs, family configurations, and coping mechanisms. And then we visit another new home and encounter a whole new situation that calls for new approaches and new solutions. Nothing, it seems, is the same. But what is constant in these homes, almost without exception, is the resilience of parents. No matter what is asked of them for the health and well-being of their child, they will attempt to do it. Also constant are the demands of the outside world. There is work to be done for income. There are frustrations with the intervention system that is supposed to help them. There are other children, older parents, and spouses to care for. Parents are exhausted by the demands of life. We must take care to lighten rather than increase those demands. We must not forget to tell them how well they are doing.

Home visiting is not like any other early intervention service. Home visitors are alone with the client child and family. No one is watching to say whether the home visitor has done a good job or has made a misstep. It is hoped that there is a helpful supervisor or someone to go to for guidance, but they are rarely there in the moment. Home visitors have opportunities to be change agents not only with children but with their families as well. May we learn from our mistakes and develop mutual respect with families.

Acknowledgments

Without exception, the examples cited in this book are personal, true stories of families receiving early intervention services, although most of the names have been changed. Without those stories, this book would not be authentic and it could not have been written. We are grateful beyond words to those families who have taught us the meaning of collaboration, cultural values, empowerment, and unconditional love. Caregivers have wellsprings of energy and resources, and we can only stand in admiration as we are privileged to be admitted into their lives.

Shirley Sparks would like to express appreciation to Margaret Briggs, Ph.D., and Gail Donahue Pepin, Ph.D., colleagues from the early days in early intervention training for the American Speech-Language-Hearing Association, for having benefited from their wisdom. Hours of brainstorming about difficult cases were invaluable.

Both authors are also grateful to colleagues at HOPE Homestart in San José, California, where Shirley was employed as a home visitor: Kitty van Keulen, who supplied a steady stream of new references for us to consider; Carmen Ireta and Anastacya Tillman, who supplied pictures; and Director Christy Tall, who facilitated their participation. We are also grateful to Carole Osselaer, M.A., for allowing us to share her keen insight into the needs of young children with visual impairment and what it takes to manage the health care system.

Louis Rossetti, Ph.D., a pioneer and leader in early intervention, has been an inspiration, teacher, and friend. We are honored to have his Foreword in our book.

The editors and staff at Brookes Publishing are to be commended for their patience and dedication. Particular praise goes to Sarah Shepke, Acquisitions Editor, and Amy Kopperude, Production Designer, for their efficiency and the care they have taken to be true to the spirit of our book.

Both authors are very thankful for the friendship and spirit of collaboration that developed between them while both were serving as faculty at Santa Clara University. It made the writing of this book a pleasure. Of course, this project would not have been possible without the total support of our husbands, Curtis Cook and Richard Greif, who helped in countless ways. We hope they perceive our mostly unspoken gratitude.

1

An Overview
of Home Visiting

"The test of morality for a society
is what it does for its children."

–Dietrich Bonhoffer

Home visiting is not a new profession. Historically, educators, along with other professionals such as doctors, nurses, and social workers, have used home-community visits as an effective tool to provide support and services to children. Home visiting can be documented as being in operation during the reform era (1870–1920). Mary Richmond (1912) recognized it as an arduous profession and wrote a handbook on how to seriously, systematically, and scientifically conduct friendly visits among the poor. Some early history of home visiting is included here because 1) we can draw parallels between the challenges of those early home visits and what we find today, and 2) we can learn from the successes of those early pioneers.

Pioneer home visitors recognized the unique feature of home visiting: that the visitor's willingness to enter a family's home and neighborhood signals a less formal, more relaxed relationship between visitor and parent; thereby equalizing the balance of power between the two. Bhavnagri and Krolikowski (2000) found similarities in societal conditions then and now. A brief look at the similarities to the present time in each of these societal conditions may hold some surprises for modern home visitors.

Photograph courtesy of Visiting Nurse Service of New York.

Eradication of Poverty by Changing Environmental Conditions

During the reform era, many believed that poverty could be ameliorated by positively transforming the crowded urban environment (providing adequate health care, housing, parks, playgrounds, support services, and public welfare). Child advocates today also believe that the United States needs to improve the status of its children. Like children living in poverty during the reform era, children living in poverty today are precariously housed, suffer from impaired health, and have higher rates of school failure. Then and now, poverty and welfare, the role of communities, and government and individual responsibility are the subjects of intense debate.

Massive Arrival of Immigrants

The United States Immigration Commission reported that in 1909, 57.8% of schoolchildren in the nation's 37 largest cities were of foreign-born parentage. In 2007, 20.2% of the school-age population had one immigrant parent and 22.6% of young children birth to 4 years had one immigrant parent (Center for Immigration Studies, 2007). Dealing with myriad cultures and languages is not unique to modern home visitors.

Rapid Transformation of Society

During the reform era, American society was rapidly undergoing transformation from a rural agrarian society into an urban industrial society. As we make the changes necessary for a technologically literate nation, families face new forms of instability (e.g., mothers must work and find child care, families are fragmented and relatives are not close by). Today, American society continues in the process of transforming itself from an industrial society into an information society.

Promotion of Volunteerism

The early home visitors were volunteers who visited the homes of people living in poverty—mostly immigrant families—to promote the importance of education. Long before Bronfenbrenner (1979) called a child's multiple settings microsystems and linked them together to form the child's mesosystems, these volunteers visited not only the child's home but also the whole community. They knew the children as individuals by intimately knowing the families and the neighborhoods in which they were raised. Their dedication was extraordinary as is the dedication of the home visitors of today who are paid for what they do.

Lessons from the Past

These dedicated pioneers achieved some major successes; for example,

1. They were able to help parents view play as an educational activity and not as frivolity and a waste of time. Parents reported a transformation in their child-rearing practices (Bhavnagri & Krolikowski, 2000).

2. They became experts in networking and helped families by effectively using the community and welfare services as resources. They helped to change child labor laws and to start kindergartens. Klass (2008) recommended that the modern

professional visitors should network with community agencies, institutions, and organizations to reduce barriers to services for children and families. This networking is exactly what the early visitors were doing, and we can learn from their efforts. Unhampered by restrictions of confidentiality and legal missteps, they saw a need for a service and they moved to implement it—from health care to social service agencies. They were able to provide true wraparound programs, or family-centered, community-based, integrated, and full-service education.

3. They established rapport with families and were welcomed into the families' homes. Wiggin articulated how she used multiple strategies (e.g., flexibility, respect, sensitivity, empathic identification) as she built relationships during home-community visits:

> I never entered any house where I felt the least sensation of being out of place. I don't think this flexibility is a gift of especially high order, nor that it would be equally valuable in all walks of life, but it is of great service in this sort of work. Whether I sat in a stuffed chair or on a nail keg or an inverted washtub, it was always equally agreeable to me. The "getting into relation" perfectly, and without the loss of a moment, gave me a sense of mental and spiritual exhilaration. I never had to adapt myself elaborately to a strange situation in order to be in sympathy. My one idea was to keep the situation simple and free from embarrassment to any one; to be as completely a part of it as if I had been born there; to be helpful without being intrusive; to show no surprise whatever happened; above all, to be cheerful, strong, and bracing, not weakly sentimental. (1923, pp. 112–113)

4. They worked with families of non–English-speaking children and with families whose cultures did not value education or democratic values. One of their goals was to help these families adjust to their new country.

5. They established standards of professionalism. The pioneer home visitors were well-educated professional teachers, social workers, and nurses. As discussed in two special issues of *The Future of Children* (Gomby, Culross, & Behrman, 1999; Gomby, Larson, Lewitt, & Behrman, 1993), research has shown that

trained teachers, social workers, and especially nurses with expertise in child development and health had more effective outcomes with children and families than did paraprofessionals who had limited education and expertise in the field. Furthermore, research reported in those issues indicated that high frequency of visitations and intensity of contacts positively affected results. From all accounts, the pioneer home-community visitors worked with missionary zeal, and their home-community visits were of such high frequency and intensity that they often moved into given neighborhoods to devote their entire lives to their work (Bhavnagri & Krolikowski, 2000).

The pioneer home-community visitors implemented recommendations that we consider to be modern. It was their foresight and innovation that contributed to their effectiveness. They taught us how to serve children and families by providing multiple individualized and customized services. They laid the groundwork for our present-day philosophy and approach to home visiting discussed below.

HOME VISITORS TODAY

Families may be served by a number of providers representing different services. Multiple agencies such as developmental services, public health, school districts, and other public agencies also may be involved. The roles of these home visitors may vary. Some home visitors have very specific therapeutic roles (e.g., speech-language pathologist, physical therapist, occupational therapist, vision specialist, teacher of the hearing impaired, social worker). We have designated these professionals as *specialists*. Others may interact with the family primarily as consultants or as monitors of a child's progress; these are called *generalists*. Most often, a family will be served by an early interventionist or early childhood special educator whose focus is a comprehensive view of the family as a system. There may or may not be specialists who also visit the home. Someone on the team acts as team coordinator and may be differentiated as the service coordinator for this family.

The interest or expertise of the primary service provider should coincide with the family's major concerns about their child. If the major concern is delay in motor function, an occupational therapist or physical therapist may be the primary service provider, or he or she may serve as a consultant, visiting the infant educator and family in the home. A specialist may provide intensive assessment, make recommendations, and model interventions and then "back off" (McWilliam, 2005). In this context, the specialist may not have the time to let a relationship with the family take root and blossom. Developing a relationship always takes time. Collaboration between the generalist and the specialist is thought to be the best way to serve the family (McWilliam, 2005).

Nature of Children Served

Who are the children being served in early intervention? The programs are designed *to serve children who are at risk for poor development because of delays and disabilities* (Scarborough, Hebbeler, & Spiker, 2006). *Risk* refers to preventing any developmental problems from occurring; indeed, some children go on to have no problems. *Developmental delay* means that problems have occurred, and *early intervention* is about remediation. Again, some children do catch up to their same-age peers and no longer have a delay by the time they are eligible for kindergarten.

The National Early Intervention Longitudinal Study (NEILS; Hebbeler et al., 2007), begun in 1995, studied the outcomes of early intervention for 10 years in 20 states. Although there is no "typical child" who is served by early intervention or who is served in the home, the NEILS study gives us an overview of the children and families served by early intervention programs. There is broad variation across states in definitions of eligibility and, consequently, in who is served, and there is a lack of consensus on established conditions (especially low birth weight). There is also much variability within "developmental delay," "diagnosed condition," "established condition," and "risk condition." For example, low birth weight is considered a risk condition in some states and in others it is a diagnosed condition. According to the NEILS study (Hebbeler et al., 2007), the most frequent reasons for eligibility for early intervention are noted in Table 1.1.

Table 1.1. Reasons for eligibility for early intervention

Speech/communication delay or impairment: 41%

Prenatal/perinatal abnormalities: 19%

Motor delay or impairment: 18%

Global delayed development: 12%

Congenital disorders: 9%

From Hebbeler, K., Spiker, D., Bailey, D., Scarborough, A., Mallik, S., Simeonsson, R., et al. (2007). *Early intervention for infants and toddlers with disabilities and their families: Participants, services and outcomes. Final report of the National Early Intervention Longitudinal Study (NEILS).* Menlo Park, CA: SRI International; reprinted by permission.

NEILS also found that children in early intervention are in poorer health than the general population of infants and toddlers and are more likely to have been born at low birth weight. They are also more likely to be boys, minorities, and poor.

Nature of Families Served

Children in early intervention come from all types of families. With the changing demographics in the United States, we must expect family structures to vary in composition (two parents, a single parent, grandparents raising grandchildren, two parents with no other children or with children from different relationships) and to be from a variety of cultures. Table 1.2 lists the family characteristics found in the NEILS study (Hebbeler et al., 2007).

PHILOSOPHY AND APPROACH TO HOME VISITING

As home visitors, our philosophy of early intervention provides the overarching framework for how we interact with children and families in their homes. It encompasses how we believe a child learns and how the child's nature and environment interact in normal development. As we learn from studying, from mentors, from exchanges with those we admire, and from our own experience, we develop a personal philosophy of early intervention. In addition, agencies are also driven by philosophical principles, and conflicts can arise when agencies and home visitors differ in philosophy and approach.

Table 1.2. Family characteristics

91% of children live with biological/adoptive mother.
69% of children live with biological/adoptive father.
Ten times more children are in foster care than in the general population.
15% of children live in single-parent households.
20% of children in early intervention have another child with special needs in the household.
53% of children in early intervention have two or more sociodemographic risk factors (e.g., economic, mental health, single parent).

Source: Hebbeler et al., 2007.

APPROACHES TO INTERVENTION

Approaches to early intervention and home visiting have undergone huge changes in recent years. The sciences of neurodevelopment and intervention have converged and brought about changes in the law to make early intervention family-centered. The family's needs and points of view must be considered in intervention planning. No longer does the home visitor assess the problem (although perhaps with the input of a multidisciplinary team), set goals only for the child, and proceed to tell the family how to move the child toward those goals. In that earlier child-centered approach, the family worked with the child on tasks assigned by the interventionist. The parent reported each week on progress made, and the interventionist set new goals for the following week. This approach seemed natural to home visitors who were used to the clinic or school model of intervention. The environment and intervention were controlled by the home visitor, at least for their sessions in the home. Today, the two competing schools of thought about the target of intervention are loosely categorized as child focused and family focused.

Child Focused

Many families choose intervention programs that feature child-focused strategies for their child with special needs. For example, parents may choose to have their child participate in intensive behavioral approaches for children who have established disabilities such as autism. These approaches are carried out primarily by specialists such as speech-language pathologists, occupational therapists, physical therapists, and behavioral specialists. Child-focused programs do not totally ignore family needs; however, family involvement is primarily enabling family members to meet the child's needs while at the same time meeting some of their own needs (Cook, Klein, & Tessier, 2008).

Family Focused

Family-focused early intervention is defined as concentrating intervention equally on the child and on the child's family; each member of the family is considered to be equally important. All family members have needs and wants and those of the child with special needs do not have priority over those of any other family members. In the child-focused approach, the "tutoring" task assigned to the parents has higher priority than the need for the husband and wife to have time together or for a typically developing sibling to have time alone with his or her mother. If a half hour is set aside to work on particular goals with the child with special needs, then is a typically developing sibling given equal time? Can both children participate in an activity (e.g., rolling the ball back and forth, going to the park)? Families may feel that they need permission to act as a family, with the normal push–pull of family life, without feeling guilty that they are not "teaching" every minute.

A family-focused approach gives high priority to family empowerment, defined as enabling families to help themselves. Family empowerment recognizes family members as capable individuals who are asking for guidance from a knowledgeable interventionist in order to solve their own problems (Cook et al., 2008).

Collaborative Team

A collaborative approach, with the family providing information and goal-setting priorities in collaboration with interventionists, is now the preferred approach. Everyone's viewpoint is considered—parents, grandparents, child care providers, and anyone else who interacts regularly with the child—and goals are established together. Instead of assigned tasks to meet the goals, the family is given guidance on their child's next developmental steps. Everyone decides together how best to provide an experience that will facilitate a desired behavior. Everyone who regularly interacts with the child must be informed of the decisions so that the child's environment is kept as consistent as possible. There is no therapy time set aside for family members to work on specific goals.

A cautionary note: As the pendulum has swung from child focused to family focused, there is a risk that the proverbial baby can be thrown out with the bath. Home visitors who subvert their better judgment in favor of a family member's alternative and, perhaps unrealistic, goal are not serving as equal members of the team. Intervention is not the sole purview of the home visitor, but decisions should not be made solely by the family either. It is the home visitor's job to know what is developmentally next and to show the family how to get to that stage. At the same time, however, the home visitor must take into account the family's priorities, readiness for intervention and change, and cultural values. Home visitors are neither dictators nor servants. Likewise, family focused does not always mean that direct therapy should not be given as intervention. For example, a child who will soon make the transition to preschool and who runs around the room and shows no interest in play materials may need direct therapy such as being put in a high chair to get him or her to focus attention and engage in a task. By doing this, the parent observes that the child can pay attention to a book or a puzzle. The child does not always need to be the leader in the interaction.

Natural Environments

At the very core of our work is the premise that natural environments are the best environments in which children with special needs can learn. As stated in the regulations to the Individuals with Disabilities Education Act Amendments (IDEA) of 1997, "Early intervention services must be provided in natural environments, including the home and community settings in which children without disabilities participate." An extensive review by Dunst, Trivette, Humphries, Raab, and Roper (2001) of the natural environment literature found that natural environment proponents differ considerably in how this provision has been conceptualized and operationalized. Furthermore, Dunst, Bruder, Trivette, and Hamby concluded from their review of the literature that

> Despite a rich research base for using everyday activity as sources of child learning opportunities, the delivery of early intervention services (special instruction and physical, occupational, and speech therapy) in natural environments has been increasingly emphasized as "best practice" to the exclusion of other natural learning environment interventions. And this has occurred in the absence of evidence indicating that implementing early intervention services in natural environments is effective. (2006, p. 4)

In short, service in natural environments is the law, although sufficient research verifying that it is evidence-based practice is lacking. For the time being, we will provide intervention in the home and at the same time not overlook opportunities to have children experience what the community has to offer (e.g., parks, libraries, play dates, restaurants, shopping).

Evidence-Based Practice

Personal philosophies and implementations of those philosophies are also shaped by what is now called evidence-based practice. Contemporary approaches to evidence-based practice can be traced to evidence-based medicine (Cutspec, 2004). Education is becoming part of this paradigm shift, however, by favoring research-based intervention and encouraging the use of evaluation instead of relying solely on common sense (Coe & Priest, 2002). In concept, research should inform an interventionist about what he or she can do when interacting with a child (or family member) to improve functioning or achieve a specific outcome. But, as Dunst, Trivette and Cutspec (2002) pointed out, research papers are typically written for other researchers, not for practitioners. That is, they do not state in clear terms how an intervention X influences an outcome Y. Furthermore, practitioners generally do not read research reports, and when they do, they find them minimally useful. Dunst et al. (2006) suggested that practitioners avail themselves of what they term *practice-centered research syntheses* (http://www.researchtopractice.info), which are written specifically for practitioners and parents. Findings from research syntheses describe the characteristics of the practices that can be expected to produce specific outcomes or benefits.

Core Principles that Shape Philosophies and Approaches

More than 40 years of research on parenting, parent–child relationships, and the state of intervention have been synthesized into evidence-based principles. *From Neurons to Neighborhoods* (Shonkoff & Phillips, 2000), the report of the National Academy of Sciences, evaluated the current science of early childhood development and the current state of intervention research. According to the report, the course of development can be altered in early childhood by effective interventions. The large effects of intervention will likely result from the aggregated impact of numerous, usually relatively small, but successful interventions. Each bit of information acquired by families, each reduction in social isolation or family distress, each well-designed child-focused educational intervention, each additional resource used by families, and each increment in confidence regarding the parental role can begin to alter developmental trajectories. The following sections relay core principles, based on the Shonkoff and Phillips (2000) report, that can shape our philosophies and guide us in our approach to practice. Each includes examples of implementation of that principle.

Human Development

Human development is shaped by a dynamic and continuous interaction between biology and experience. The nature versus nurture debate is scientifically obsolete. The adage, "neurons that fire together, wire together" (Wolfe, 2000) is another way of saying that experience changes the brain. Neurons or networks that are used over and over get accustomed to firing together and eventually get hard-wired and fire automatically; thus, they are wired together. If we practice something incorrectly, our neurons don't know the difference and make the permanent connections incorrectly, as anyone who has tried to master a skill without coaching can attest. A young child's environment is both physical and social. Its impact on development is mediated through the quality of the experiences it offers. We help families to provide those quality experiences.

> *Clancey was overdue for his first appointment with a dentist. Jeanine, his mother, told Jessica, the home visitor, that he would need to be sedated because he would probably work himself into a syncopal episode (hold his breath and lose consciousness) based on his previous experiences with the unknown. For several sessions, Jessica played dentist with Clancey, using a dental mirror for the pretend play. They acted out the sequence and then Jeanine took over for seemingly endless practices: Getting in the dentist's chair, looking in his mouth with the mirror, rinsing with a cup of water, and so forth. Clancey and Jeanine took turns playing the dentist and the patient. When Clancey went to the dentist, he knew what to expect and did not need anesthesia. It was just like his pretend play.*

Home visitor sessions can be forays into other natural environments in the community that offer a world of new experiences; these, in turn, create new neural pathways. Our intervention leads to functional outcomes; that is, there is a naturalistic reason for a child's action or response to the stimulus provided by the intervener, whether parent, home visitor, or someone else. For example, children learn to communicate because they want to interact with another person on an emotional level. They learn to walk because they need locomotion, and they develop fine motor skills because they need them to explore and manipulate materials they find interesting.

Children As Active Participants

Children are active participants in their own development, reflecting the intrinsic human drive to explore and master one's environment. We allow the child to learn in her or his own way, and we provide developmental guidance to families in order to facilitate learning. Often-asked questions for the home visitor are, "Is my child on track?" "Is she doing what she is supposed to be doing?" "What's next?" Perhaps the most important service the home visitor can provide is this developmental or anticipatory guidance: a hierarchy of what is next in the child's development. Such a guide, as included in the appendix, can help parents have realistic expectations and can be used to set new goals for behavior. Rather than age, the guide in this book depends on motor development as the benchmark for other milestones. So much cognitive development depends on motor milestones that we look at motor development first and then at what to expect at each stage of development, from raising the head to standing and cruising, to testing and doing. If a child exhibits language abilities with first words even though he or she is not walking, this is a pleasant surprise. If a child is sitting without attempting to crawl or stand and is still in the babbling stage, the chart shows that this is expected behavior and the caregivers may be relieved. The caregivers will appreciate having a copy of this chart to refer to especially when other family members push for behaviors that are beyond the child's capabilities at his or her developmental stage.

Equally important is the responsibility to inform the caregivers about the impediments to development that are the reasons for the home visitor to be in the home and working with the child and family. Following the diagnosis, parents have a high need for obtaining information with regard to the disability characteristics, treatment options, services, and resources available for their children (Mc-

William & Scott, 2001). Many families do their own research on the Internet, and assisting them in finding the most accurate sites is incumbent on the home visitor. Finding information on the Internet is addressed in more depth in Chapter 3.

> *Millie, a home visitor, visited Clifford, who has Down syndrome, and his mother Vanessa for the first time. Vanessa was most concerned about Clifford's speech and what she should be doing to help him. He made noises but there was nothing that she could call real communication. Millie showed Vanessa the developmental chart and noted that Clifford was in the crawler-creeper stage. Communication expectations at that point were minimal. Millie pointed out how well Clifford was doing in all areas with some exceptions; for example, in "Understanding the World," where he was not responding and imitating. Millie showed Vanessa some techniques for imitating what Clifford did and then waiting for him to repeat those actions that established eye contact and interaction. Vanessa changed her interactive style to facilitate Clifford's self-exploration with toys. Vanessa commented that now she knew where Clifford was going next in his development.*

Child Development

The development of children unfolds along individual pathways whose trajectories are characterized by continuities and discontinuities, as well as by a series of significant transitions. Brazelton and Sparrow (2006) called these bumps in development *touchpoints,* a predictable time or event in development at which a child's behavior seems to regress or fall apart. These touchpoints typically precede a growth spurt in a particular area of development and are often accompanied by parental frustration and self-doubt. We reframe and normalize the touchpoints and use them as opportunities to make a difference in the lives of children and their families. Normalizing behavior is closely allied with developmental guidance, but it differs in that behaviors that are construed by parents as regressions or aberrations are put into context for the parents.

José and Frances had three children who were nearly grown. They thought their family was complete when they had Peter, who was born at 32 weeks' gestation. Peter had a developmental course that was not unusual for a premature child, but José and Frances began to see Peter as their fragile child. Peter ate and slept on a demand schedule until he was nearly 3 years old. His three older siblings were also very careful with him. Frances saw to it that Peter was not "set off" (having a tantrum) by roughhousing with his older brothers, with the result that the older children began to give Peter a very wide berth.

Peter slept with José and Frances. Frances complained to Mary, the home visitor, that she would like Peter to sleep in his own bed. Mary asked about their bedtime routine and a pattern emerged: Each night after the bedtime ritual, José carried Peter into his own room and put him in his bed. Peter screamed when they entered the room and continued to cry until José picked him up and put him in the parents' bed. Mary asked the parents what had worked with their older children and was told that they had been put in their own beds from the beginning and it was not an issue. But Peter was different, they said. They had almost lost him and were still fearful that "something would happen" to him. Mary asked the following questions: "What do you think will happen to Peter if he cries?" "Do you think your older children would have reacted the same way if they had also been in your bed for nearly 3 years?" "What would you do for them?" Frances and José began to see Peter as having a normal reaction to a change in his comfort status. Having him sleep in his own bed was a touchpoint of development. Together, the parents and Mary worked out a plan where José lay beside Peter's bed until Peter fell asleep; then José moved back into his own room. If Peter followed, he was put back in his own bed with no exceptions. They were prepared for the usual pattern of Peter's increasing the amount of protest and they held firm. Mary reinforced their resolve and the normalcy of this parent–child conflict. She empowered the parents to move their child from external motivation (them) to self-regulation in an emotionally laden experience. She also talked with the older children and explained that Peter needed their interaction and how they could gradually take the small steps to physically play with him. Instead of throwing him up in the air, they could start with a give-and-take game of ball, until Peter trusted them to not surprise him.

Human Relationships

Nurturing and dependable human relationships are the building blocks of healthy development. Relationships depend on emotion, and the role of emotion in learning cannot be overestimated. Those relationships are optimal when there is a high level of "goodness of fit": The child performs in concert with the parent (Greenspan, 2002). Our role is to preserve and nurture all relationships within the family. We must also be aware that the mere fact of our presence in the home changes the dynamic of those relationships.

*Melanie complained to her home visitor that her husband Brad avoided their child, who had undiagnosed developmental delay. "If he would just play with Patrick while I'm getting dinner, it would help," she said. Instead, Brad delayed coming home, and when he did appear, he turned on the TV and tuned Patrick out. The home visitor asked if Brad had any experience playing with children. Did he know what to do? Melanie insisted that he "just play" without telling Brad how. It was unlikely that Brad would become an expert in floor time with Patrick, but he didn't know how to begin to have an interaction with a child of 2. Using the principle of **start from where you are** (see Chapter 4), the home visitor scheduled a visit when Brad could be home. She asked what he liked to do with Patrick and found that he liked to take him on errands in the car. He felt most uncomfortable at home when Melanie was listening to them (and, he thought, judging him). The home visitor suggested that he might take Patrick to the park while out doing errands and spend about 15 minutes trying out the swings or sandbox or feeding the ducks—whatever Patrick found appealing. Brad spent some time sitting beside Patrick while he played in the sand. Then he introduced Patrick to the ducks. This afforded some interaction as Patrick had to ask for some bread to feed them and then ran to his father for protection when the ducks approached. The next time they went to the park, Brad took a toy truck and some sand toys along. Whatever teachable moments ensued were spontaneous and natural and unknown to the home visitor, but the interactive bond between father and son had begun. A further step would have been for the home visitor to accompany father and son to the park, but Brad felt better when he was not being observed.*

Parents' Expertise

The parent is the expert on his or her child. One size does not fit all. All parents have strengths and want to do well by their child. Parenting is a process built on trial and error. Home visitors build relationships with the parents by asking them about their child. We ask parents to tell us what works with their child and what doesn't work. We know children in general, but they know their own child. We must be prepared to abandon our own agenda to accommodate dynamics within the home and new priorities of the family. Intervention demands an individualized approach that matches well-defined goals to the specific needs and resources of the children and families we serve.

> *Linda, a single mother, lived in a halfway house for women recovering from alcohol addiction. Her son Spencer was delayed in many domains and was prone to frequent ear infections. Spencer's home visitor, Lois, suggested that Spencer showed signs of middle ear fluid after his latest infection and arranged for Linda to take him to a free clinic that was open on Thursday afternoons. Linda's sponsor, however, pointed out that Linda's 12-step meetings would conflict with the clinic hours. Linda reported to Lois that she could not take Spencer to the clinic because her own recovery was more important. Lois swallowed her frustration at the prioritizing she thought was in error and began to look for an alternative medical facility for Spencer. She enlisted Linda's aid in finding that alternative, even though she could have done it more quickly herself. In this way, she empowered Linda to be responsible for herself and also for her child.*

Cultural Influences

Culture influences every aspect of human development and is reflected in child-rearing beliefs and practices. Being aware of another culture and its practices is not enough. Home visitors must be aware of any tendencies they might have to change a family's cultural practice to fit their own, which would only set the stage for mistrust. Throughout this text, we offer illustrations on to how to practice this cultural sensitivity, which is critical to a home visitor's success.

Home visitors are guests in the homes they visit, and the culture of those living in the home and the home visitor's sensitivity to that culture play a large part in the acceptance and development of trust in the home visitor. Shoes are not worn in the homes of people of a variety of cultures, so the home visitor would do well to always wear shoes that can be slipped off at the door. It is customary to offer refreshment to a guest in many cultures, and to refuse that refreshment is considered rude. If refreshment is the custom, a few minutes of drinking tea or coffee and exchanging polite conversation or catching up on the past week can reap rewards. A seasoned home visitor will be acquainted with the diet of the various cultures with whom she or he works, particularly if feeding is one of the issues for intervention. Cultural differences play a large role in the next scenario. Because Melissa, the home visitor, was sensitive to the Asian Indian culture of the family, the visit went smoothly, even though Melissa was perplexed by what she observed.

Melissa, an African American home visitor, is assigned to visit Sanjay, a 2-year-old who has a history of hypotonia. His pediatrician recommended him to the early intervention program because he was not walking at 15 months. His history also included low weight gain and little interest in food. His parents' main concern was his eating.

Melissa left her shoes at the door, presented her card, and asked if she might wash her hands (a part of every home visit). Sanjay's mother Radha offered a cup of tea, which Melissa accepted. Melissa entered the family room where Sanjay was sitting on the floor. His grandmother was rocking in a chair close by. Melissa approached the grandmother and presented her with her card and offered her hand, which the grandmother shook. Radha said that her mother-in-law was visiting from India and did not speak English. Melissa made it a point to glance at the mother-in-law occasionally and smile, which was returned.

Melissa inquired about a typical day for Sanjay, including everything he ate, how it was delivered (fed by his mother or grandmother or self-fed), and how much he ate. Radha said that Sanjay drank whole milk from a sippee cup, which she held for him while holding him on her lap. Sanjay fed himself oatmeal with a spoon for breakfast, but Radha fed him with her hands for lunch and dinner without utensils. Sanjay held his own cup with a straw for water. He would not tolerate any texture other than puréed food and gagged and vomited if any lumps were in his food. The diet was nutritious with rice, vegetables, and whole grains that were puréed in a blender. At the end of the chronology of the day, Melissa asked if anyone other than Radha fed Sanjay. Radha answered that her mother-in-law often fed him lunch or dinner. She force-fed him by holding his hands with one hand and keeping his jaw open with the other. Then she or Radha would insert a spoon into his mouth. Radha said this was a fairly common practice in India. Her husband had been fed this way by his mother when he did not eat. She reported that when that happened at night, Sanjay was often so upset and crying that they put him in the car and drove around until he fell asleep.

There are many unanswered questions in this brief scenario, but we want to focus on the cultural aspects of eating and feeding children. It was obvious that Radha was not willing to give up holding Sanjay on her lap while he drank his milk, and she was concerned that he would not accept any food that was not perfectly smooth. Melissa did not comment on any aspect of Radha's chronology of the day, but she asked Radha why she thought Sanjay did not show more interest in eating. Radha said that he had always been this way and that she had probably done something wrong to make him that way. Melissa was shocked to hear about the forced feeding. She did not want to contradict the parenting skills of the mother or the authority of the grandmother. For this case, where there was conflict with her values of child rearing, she needed help and advice from her supervisor.

Melissa and her supervisor, Patricia, looked at all the behaviors surrounding eating and separated them into physical and cultural. Physical factors included Sanjay's hypotonia and suspected sensory-based eating aversion. Cultural factors were the diet, hand feeding, forced feeding, and dominance by the grandmother. Not cultural was driving Sanjay around to help him sleep. Melissa felt strongly that several things in the home needed to be changed and change immedi-

ately: Of primary importance was to stop the forced feeding and to help Sanjay have more control over how he was fed to reduce his mistrust and aversion to unfamiliar foods. Patricia helped Melissa to see that the ways of feeding this child were embedded in culture and were nearly impossible to change, certainly not by telling the family that things should change to the American way. There was no need to change the diet, which was healthy, but Melissa would need to be informed so that all new foods that she suggested be introduced were acceptable as part of a vegetarian Indian diet. In this way, Melissa would make some changes in herself. The grandmother would need to be involved in all planning and she would need to see success. If Sanjay ate without being forced, there would be no need to continue that method. So Melissa and Patricia compiled information that addressed the physical difficulties, beginning with explaining sensory-based feeding aversions and pointing out how well Sanjay did eating with a spoon and drinking using a straw. Melissa asked if Radha and her mother-in-law would like to help Sanjay try a new food, and she offered to show them how to introduce it.

Daily Routines

No intervention will be effective if it cannot fit into the daily routines of the family. A longitudinal study by Bernheimer and Weisner (2007) built on an ecocultural (ecological + cultural) approach underscored the importance of remembering that progress is dependent on the child functioning within the context of his or her family and their daily routines. Bernheimer and Weisner's study gives credence to what home visitors quickly learn: "What happens between home visits has a critical impact on children's learning" (2007, pp. 199–200). By getting families to describe what they do all day, every day, it became clear that only interventions that could be slotted into daily routines had any impact. Home visitors, then, must recognize the importance of daily routines in planning interventions with families. By fitting interventions into everyday life, home visitors can be truly supportive through their efforts to create family-sensitive practices that can be sustained over time.

SUMMARY

Personal philosophy built on principles of the sciences of neuro-development and intervention guides us as we serve children and families. The trajectory of development can be altered by effective intervention. Whether we are child focused or family focused, we are obligated to consider the child's family in all we do. We can and must provide opportunities for learning, give developmental guidance, and respect culture and the parent–child relationship. We must guide and help parents negotiate the transition from external to self-regulation in their child, including learning to regulate emotions, behaviors, and attention. We must promote the acquisition of capabilities that are prerequisite to communication and learning. We must help children to relate well to other children and form friendships. We must expect change, and we must expect that as we coach the parents to effect change, parents will attribute the change to what they have done, not what we have done. That is the outcome we strive for, and it is called *parent empowerment.* We must always strive to provide evidence-based intervention. As new evidence of neurological behaviors emerge, research on how best to effect change follows. This is a tall order for the home visitor profession, but with a solid foundation of a philosophy to guide us, and with the experience of mentors to help us, home visitors are up to the challenge.

2

Understanding Families as Systems

"[B]oth clinical rigor and good science require us to assume that we do not know a child unless we know his or her family."

—Trout & Foley

Given that the field of early intervention has shifted from direct intervention with the child to a focus on the family as a whole, it has become extremely important for the home visitor to thoroughly understand how stress affects parent–child interactions and overall family functioning. Without this understanding, home visitors cannot provide the support or develop the relationships necessary to empower the family to meet the special needs of their child. The Individuals with Disabilities Education Improvement Act of 2004 (PL 108-446) provides for services in the home. This provision attests to the recognition that the family is the critical component of the caregiving environment that influences and is influenced by the child, resulting in varying outcomes for both the child and the family (Zeanah, 2000). Families not only are viewed as the constant in their child's life but also are recognized as being the experts when it comes to raising their children.

Clearly, no family member functions in isolation from other family members. The family is a dynamic system. Any change involving one family member automatically involves all family members. For early interventionists to understand the impact of stress on each family member and how they can best enrich the quality of caregiving, it is helpful to understand the family as an entity that operates as a system (Turnbull & Turnbull, 2006). It is a system guided by family rules or norms that organize and facilitate interactions.

The family systems approach is founded on three basic principles: 1) input/output, 2) concepts of wholeness with subsystems, and 3) boundaries (Smith, Gartin, Murdick, & Hilton, 2006). Inputs as discussed by Turnbull and Turnbull (2006) are the individual and collective family characteristics, including the special needs of the child with the disability. These characteristics or inputs are the resources that the family puts into its system of interactions. Outputs (fulfillment of family functions) result from the process of family interactions within and between the family's subsystems. The interactions work together to serve individual and collective family needs.

Boundaries are created by interactions within the family as well as between the whole family and people outside of the family. Families differ in how willing they are to share their thoughts and feelings with nonmembers. The degree of boundary flexibility affects how much the family will be willing to collaborate with outside professionals and agencies. Boundaries also help define members' roles with respect to one another and to extended family members.

When home visitor Noreen first visited Judy and her daughter, Mary Beth, Judy said that the main problem was the family's sleeping arrangements. Mary Beth woke several times during the night and stayed awake, so Judy and her husband Stanley decided that Judy and Mary Beth would sleep in the family room downstairs so as not to disturb Stanley's sleep. Mary Beth slept on a pallet on the floor and Judy slept on the sofa. Judy was 8 months pregnant and exhausted. Noreen probed the family dynamics as to Stanley's willingness to take some responsibility for Mary Beth at night to allow Judy to sleep. Judy made it very clear that Stanley's participation was off limits. Stanley worked and needed his sleep. Noreen recognized this family boundary and whatever suggestions she could make could not involve Stanley, no matter what the cost to Judy.

FAMILY REACTION TO VULNERABILITY AND CRISIS

Although often unprepared emotionally for the unique challenges of raising a newborn, most parents find giving birth to be a joyous experience. Even seasoned parents must readjust their style of living whenever another child enters their family system. Adjustments must be made in the way any family functions in order to meet the needs of all family members. It is important for home visitors to keep in mind that all families experience stress and crisis in the course of their lives. Nevertheless, all families have strengths and the potential ability to accommodate to change when necessary. With this understanding, we will focus on the nearly 4% of parents whose anticipated joy turns to confusion and anxiety resulting from being told that their child has a serious chronic medical illness, disability, health defect, or cognitive impairment (March of Dimes, 2000). What about their stress and despair? How will they adapt to their child's condition? How can home visitors provide the support necessary to increase the likelihood that families will, indeed, be their child's best resource?

Figure 2.1 was contributed by Carole Osselaer, whose young adult son and daughter-in-law were surprised to find their hopes and dreams shattered with the unexpected birth of a son with Down syndrome. Carole, herself a home visitor for Hope Infant Services in San Diego, California, compared her family's experiences with the life-altering events brought on by other natural disasters.

Increased Stress Levels

Research indicates that stress levels of parents of children with special needs are generally higher than those of parents of children without special needs (Smith, Oliver, & Innocenti, 2001). Parents of young children with chronic conditions not only cope with the usual stressors accompanying the birth of a typical baby but also must face "uncertainties about their child's health and prognosis, frequent medical appointments and procedures, and the additional workload of caring for a child with special needs" (Barnett, Clements, Kaplan-Estrin & Fialka, 2003, p. 185). In addition to the extraordinary demands of raising a child with special needs, parents may experience stress and disappointment when their child does not fulfill the hopes and expectations that often accompany pregnancies.

The Challenge of Coping

San Diego during the 2007 wildfires, New Orleans during Hurricane Katrina, and New York City on 9/11. What do these normally exciting destination cities have in common? They all share unplanned life-altering events that impacted people's lives in a variety of different ways. These cities experienced crises. The people involved, along with their friends and families, suffered physical, personal, and financial losses; stress; upheavals; anxiety; depression; and sleeplessness.

People who booked vacations to these cities had expectations of fun times and taking back home good memories. There was no option of going to another city; the plane just landed. Upon arriving in one of these cities during this period, there was no chance to think, thrust in an instant into a crisis mode. Fear and uncertainty added with a lack of sleep and lack of knowledge made it impossible for them to comprehend the magnitude of what was happening. They were bombarded with bad news on all fronts. It was hard to know what to believe and what to hope. How could this all be happening?

A majority of parents who have children born with special needs can look back after 2–3 years and describe the first year as feeling like being dropped "in a war zone or a disaster zone," as described above. Planning for a new baby with all the hopes and dreams parents have of shared sports, driving lessons, play dates, etc., not only seem to suspend in time, they come crashing to the floor, leaving nothing in their place but shock and grief when the information sinks in that something is wrong. The familiar is no longer recognizable and the future is filled with unknown fears. Each parent will process their own "natural disaster" in his/her own way and time, depending upon strategies developed for coping with grief, loss, pain, stress, and inevitable hardships.

Figure 2.1. The challenge of coping. (Courtesy of Carole Osselaer, home visitor and grandmother of a grandson with Down syndrome)

Jared described his feelings when his son Chance was born:

We had no idea that he was going to have Down syndrome. When I heard that, all I could think of at first was that we wouldn't be able to do all those things I had dreamed of doing with my son. Playing baseball, sports, and father–son things. It was as if my dreams died on that day. Of course, it doesn't stay that way forever, but everything is so new and unknown. He was in the NICU for the first few weeks. You don't know from day to day what is going to happen. Nothing is like it was, even if you've had a child before.

Even though the literature has long discussed stages or phases of emotional adjustment, it is important that we look beyond the stages of grief that have often been described. Normal emotional reactions such as anger, guilt, shame, discouragement, and denial come and go. It is critically important to realize that emotional responses depicted not only occur at the time of identification of a disability or chronic illness but also may reoccur throughout the life of the child and his or her family. In fact, it is easy to overestimate the impact of the initial crisis of diagnosis and underestimate later reoccurrences of grief. As discussed later in this chapter, transitions can be especially difficult times for families. It is also essential to understand that stress does not affect all family members in the same way. Fathers may experience one set of emotions whereas mothers experience another. Careful evaluation of levels of stress and strategies of coping available to families is a major step toward improving the effectiveness of any intervention or treatment (Lessenberry & Rehfeldt, 2004). Therefore, home visitors must be adept at listening, expressing empathy, and being patient and readily able to offer information and resources at a pace in keeping with the family's expressed needs.

Denial Can Be Positive

If parents do not seem to be listening or following the suggestions of professionals, it is easy for the professional to just categorize parents as being "in denial." It is essential for home visitors to understand that feelings such as denial and anger are normal and should be viewed as internal coping strategies. In fact, a team made up of parents and professionals has strongly urged us to shift our perspectives on the role of denial in the lives of families who are facing lifelong challenges (Gallagher, Fialka, Rhodes, & Arceneaux, 2002). Denial often allows families to pause and gather the strength necessary to cope with their changing circumstances. Home visitors, who understand that their role is to accept such feelings while they encourage families to explore their hopes as well as their fears, will be better prepared to be more supportive and less judgmental over the full course of early intervention.

Table 2.1 offers a summary of emotional reactions commonly experienced by families of children with special needs as well as some helpful ways home visitors might respond. This table should be viewed with caution, given increasing evidence that the process of

Table 2.1. Family/interventionist reactions to a disability

Family reactions	Feelings	Interventionist responses	What the interventionist can do
Shame, guilt, unworthiness, over-compensation Disbelief "He's just like his father." "Don't worry, he'll grow out of it." Shopping for a diagnosis Research mode (seeks all information/shuts down from communicating with others)	Shock Disbelief Denial	Frustration or concern that parents are not doing enough or moving fast enough for the child Discomfort Feelings of inadequacy	Listen with acceptance. Employ active listening. Work together on behalf of the child. Be patient. Provide resources, if appropriate (e.g., referral for parent-to-parent support). View denial as a necessary internal coping strategy.
Transferring anger to provider or other caregivers Verbal abuse Blaming others Resenting others who have healthy or typical children or not wanting to be around typically developing children	Anger and resentment	Feeling hurt that parent is taking it out on you Concern that family may display anger around child "Get over it" attitude Easily provoked by parent	Encourage patience in small steps. Get parent busy; give resources. Support and model positive parent–child interactions. Give suggestions for what works. Be caring and compassionate.
Delaying acceptance of the inevitable Working with determination or vengeance "Let's make a deal. If I do this, then this will happen." Can lead to depression when things don't go well	Bargaining	In an effort to help the parent, it is easy to get hooked into his or her state. You can't "fix" the child, make him better, or help him progress faster; you can increase your own frustration.	Show family empathic understanding; accept their feelings. Help parents understand that their feelings are normal and okay. Communicate with honesty: "It must be very frustrating."

	Depression and discouragement	Potential to do too much for the child and family	Focus on the positive; help parent identify the child's strengths, not weaknesses.
Feeling of "What's the use?" or "Why bother?"		Setting up unrealistic expectations: "He'll be walking any time now."	Help parents feel confident in their parenting skills.
Helplessness and hopelessness		Guilt that you can't fix it	Provide referrals for professional counseling or other support services.
Mourning the loss of the "perfect" or healthy child			
	Acceptance	Relief	Encourage comfort from other parents; link families to support systems.
Realization that something can be done		Fear of the unknown, that you may not be able to meet the child's needs	Encourage patience.
Adjustment in lifestyle			Model positive interaction techniques.
Adaptation to the child's needs			Praise parents when child shows progress.
Willingness to do practical things			Maintain open, regular communication with family.
			Encourage family to request your presence at individualized family service plan or individualized education program meetings; get copies of information.

From Cook, R.E., Klein, M.D., & Tessier, A. (2008). *Adapting early childhood curricula for children with special needs* (7th ed.). Englewood Cliffs, NJ: Prentice Hall; adapted by permission.

adaptation and acceptance should not be seen as linear phases or stages. Instead, home visitors should realize that feelings come and go at expected and unexpected times. Table 2.1 offers a sampling of positive professional reactions that are appropriate whenever such feelings are expressed.

VIEWING THE FAMILY AS A WHOLE

The reciprocal nature of the relationship between young children with special needs and significant others in their lives becomes clearer when viewing families as whole, interacting entities. As stated earlier, no family member functions in isolation. Even though the targets of intervention may vary, as discussed in Chapter 1, it is always assumed that any intervention with one family member will affect other members and interactions within the family (Hanson & Lynch, 2004). The needs of each family member are viewed within the context of the entire family as it functions within a larger societal system (Bronfenbrenner, 1979). Thus, a more ecologically based approach to understanding the most effective way to provide services to families is encouraged.

Initially, the home visitor must be concerned with immediately learning who the family identifies as members of their family. Traditionally, families were considered to be anyone living together under one roof. Such families were made up of a mother, father, children, and perhaps, an extended family member. The Waltons or the Simpsons of television fame easily come to mind as do the more current Incredibles of Disney lore. To better understand family dynamics, home visitors should consider families to be made up of anyone the family considers to be a part of their family.

Given the uniqueness of each child and the extreme variability in family *structure* (characteristics), home visitors must leave any preconceived notions based on past experiences at the door. Effective home visitors must be open to accepting and understanding increasing variability in family composition. This variability makes it impossible to generalize in any way from one family to another. The stresses created and process of adaptation for a single-parent family with several siblings living far from grandparents is likely be very different from that of a two-parent family with an only child who lives in the same town as grandparents. Clearly, the *family's natural resources* are very different in each of these situations. An essential task for the home visitor is that of determining what natural resources are available to assist a family in coping with their particular situation.

> *At the transitional individualized family service plan (IFSP) meeting (to manage Evan's transition from home visits to preschool), Georgia and her husband Frank's primary concern was continuing the respite service that the birth–3 program had provided. They really valued having a night out, together, now and then. Evan needed someone trained to handle his fragile status, which included feeding by gastrointestinal tube. The team began to brainstorm resources for the couple: How about an extended family member? A trusted friend? Neighborhood retired nurse? Georgia and Frank acknowledged that two of the suggestions might be possible: her father (who spoiled Evan) and an elderly nurse who was fond of Evan and would probably come sometimes. These solutions were pursued because a health provider was too expensive for the family.*

Family Structure

Family structure is a term from family systems theory used to describe those people whom family considers to be its members and the characteristics of the members. It includes such characteristics as cultural orientation, ethnicity, age, educational background, health status, and socioeconomic and employment status. Family structure and, thus, family life have changed dramatically in the last 2 decades. There are not only more single-parent families but also more children living in poverty. Increased mobility often separates families from their extended families. Even if families do not move from place to place, do not change their marital status, and remain in good health, families are dynamic entities that are ever changing. Just when a home visitor thinks she is beginning to understand how best to work with a family, something changes. A parent gets laid off from work or the eldest daughter, who had always been available as a babysitter, goes off to college.

Any change in the family structure requires an adjustment within the family system. Just as family characteristics affect the degree and nature of stresses within the family, they also help determine the most satisfactory approach to be taken by the home visitor. Consider a couple of extremes: one family with a mother who is highly educated and a second with a mother who has cognitive limitations. The first might expect the home visitor to be prepared to teach her about her child's disability and to help her gain access to research and the most effective interventions related to that disability. On the other hand, the second mother may necessitate a home visitor who is effective in promoting good parenting skills and in helping to prevent child abuse or neglect.

Cultural Orientation

Cultural orientation is an extremely broad concept. It can include factors such as geographic location, religion, language spoken, socioeconomic status, and sexual orientation. These factors help to shape each family's internal patterns of interaction as well as their willingness and ability to participate in collaborative relationships. In urging us to become culturally competent, Turnbull and Turnbull stressed understanding two basic cultural factors: "1) individualism versus collectivism, and 2) system-centered versus relationship-centered approaches" (2006, p. 14).

The field of special education focuses on the individual as evidenced in IFSPs and individual education programs (IEPs). Home visitors with European American backgrounds have probably been raised to pursue achievement and self-reliance. By contrast, the cultural orientation of many Asians may value the group more strongly than the individual. They may be more interested in how their child's disability affects their style of living than they are in enhancing the individual progress of their child. A home visitor might be expected to be as interested in the progress and development of siblings as she is in the young child with disabilities.

Although, traditionally, special education has stressed a system-centered approach to intervention, we are seeking to foster a more relationship-based approach in keeping with the orientation of many diverse ethnic/racial groups. We believe that to be effective as a home visitor, one must take the time to build trust through the establishment of genuine relationships. Some home visitors will have to make an effort to quell their desire "to get to the agenda." In many cultures, it is rude to appear to be in a hurry. In some homes in Hawaii, for example, "talk story" is expected prior to discussing any problems. Beginning by talking around a subject helps to build rapport and develop trust before "getting down to business" (Sileo & Sileo, 1996).

In addition, by nature, home visitors are likely to be the take charge type; otherwise, they might not have the confidence to go into the homes of strangers in an effort to be helpful. They value change and developmental progress. Some cultural traditions, however, accept the status quo and may see outside intervention as being too pushy. Some families are much more likely than others to accept events over which they feel they have little control. Although home visitors are trained to encourage family empowerment rather than family dependence, it is essential that home visitors develop the understanding of any family's cultural orientation in order to generate the respect so necessary for success.

When we realize that each family system functions according to its own values and experiences, which may be very different from ours, we can plan much more effective interventions. When planning, home visitors must constantly be tuned into each family's beliefs about child rearing. Those beliefs may be very different from what the home visitor may have experienced. Therefore, we have included several examples of differing child-rearing practices throughout this text. Whatever the family's beliefs or station in life, all families of children with disabilities are asked to cope with multiple agencies and professionals. All have increased demands on their time. Home visitors are put in the unique position of supporting families as they go through the complex day-to-day physical and time demands required of them.

FAMILY SUBSYSTEMS

Each family system is made up of relational or interactive subsystems. Turnbull and Turnbull (2006) described four such subsystems: marital (parent–parent), parental (parent–child), sibling (child–child), and extrafamilial (extended family). Within each subsystem, family members play differing roles. For example, a woman acts differently when she is being a mother than when she is being a wife. It is through the interactions of these subsystems that families fulfill the *family functions*—the work of the family. Given the variability in family structure mentioned above, a family may not have a marital subsystem if it is a single-parent family with no connection to the absent spouse. Such a family, however, may have more than one person fulfilling a parental role if extended family members are actively involved. To provide optimal support to caregivers, it is imperative that home visitors immediately seek to develop a trusting relationship with anyone in the family constellation who has caregiving responsibilities. It is not the role of home visitors to make judgments about the quality of relationships within and between the subsystems, but it is their responsibility to offer whatever support they can to enhance coping mechanisms and, thus, resiliency within families. Although we will often discuss the additional stresses and strains that having a child with disabilities places on a marriage, it is very important to realize that, as Berry and Hardman (1998) so clearly pointed out, "Having a child with a disability does not automatically mean the marriage is in trouble" (p. 35).

Family Dynamics

Family dynamics refers to *patterns* of interactions between and among family members. Each pattern is established before the home visitor comes on the scene. (We must also be aware that our very presence in the home alters the family's interactions.) Guralnick (2005) has identified three family patterns of interaction that can produce a substantial impact on the intellectual development of young children. As we have already discussed, families who have children with special needs are subject to stresses that other families are not. We will look at each pattern that occurs in all families with children. We will also note how patterns are influenced by a child with special needs.

Sensitive Responsiveness

The first pattern is the quality of parent–child transactions, which can be characterized as *sensitive responsiveness*. Embedded within this construct are the familiar parent–child patterns of contingent responsiveness and scaffolding that most parents do naturally. Contingent responsiveness can be illustrated by the "dance" that a parent does with a baby, in which the baby makes a sound and the mother imitates the sound, which makes the baby repeat the sound while maintaining eye contact. Scaffolding is providing a series of cues to assist a child through problem solving (Cook, Klein, & Tessier, 2008). For example, a mother helps her child to undress by partially removing his clothes and shoes and letting him follow through with the task.

As expected, children at biological risk (such as those born prematurely) or those with an established disability pose considerable challenges to those optimal family patterns of interaction. It can be extremely challenging for many parents to match their interactions appropriately to their child's developmental level and to establish joint attention routines so essential for optimal child development when the child does not initiate or react in expected ways. For example, a child who is 6 weeks premature may not be able to establish the eye contact with her mother that the mother longs for. Only when the child's maturity reaches that of a full-term infant will she be able to look into her mother's face. Unless her mother knows this, a feeling of rejection can result. (See more on establishing positive parent–child interactions in Chapter 5.)

Family-Orchestrated Child Experiences

The second pattern is referred to as *family-orchestrated child experiences*. During the early childhood period, parents take responsibility for organizing home and community experiences that can substantially influence a child's development. These experiences include seeing that home environments contain appropriate toys and materials, that the language environment is diverse and stimulating, and that community activities such as child care have many developmentally enhancing features. Numerous barriers to providing the best developmental opportunities exist—for example, those related to actually finding proper child care for a child with special needs or experiencing family vacations and excursions. The child's behaviors may limit taking the child shopping, to the amusement park, or out to eat.

Health and Safety

The third pattern of family interaction is *ensuring a child's health and safety*. Providing proper nutrition and maintaining preventive health regimens, such as immunizations and well-baby care, are two of the dimensions that fall into this family pattern of interaction. Protecting children from violence or witnessing violence is essential for maintaining optimal child development. Thus, children are more likely to develop vital competencies such as those related to self-regulation and exploration and to develop highly productive strategies that foster learning and development when they are safe and healthy.

Fragile children and those with multiple disabilities pose risks in their vulnerabilities to diseases. Exposing a child to other children at day care or in natural environments may pose a setback in that child's developmental progress, and parents understandably may want to limit access to other children. Children who have feeding problems and problems with regulation (e.g., sleeping) also strain the family dynamics.

Siblings

Siblings often imitate their parents' emotions. In fact, it appears that the most powerful predictor influencing sibling acceptance is parental attitude (Moore, Howard, & McLaughlin, 2002). In addition, siblings may have their own specific fears and misunderstandings, which change as they mature. It is not uncommon for young children to be afraid that they might "catch" the disability of their brother or sister or that they may have caused the condition by wishing that Mom would not have another baby. It is also not unusual for toddlers and preschoolers to experience jealousy as a result of the attention being given to a sibling with special needs. In Chapter 3, we discuss ways that home visitors can help siblings feel that they are important. School-age children need information to answer their own questions and those posed by their curious peers about what is wrong and why. Older siblings might be embarrassed by the behavior of their younger sibling or they might be cast into a caregiving role more often than they would like. Home visitors must reach out to siblings and include them in the fun that should be part of their visit. In so doing, they can help educate siblings as a means of increasing tolerance and acceptance of the sibling with a disability or an illness. Parents should be encouraged to make special time for the other children so that they feel valued and loved and don't always come in second.

It is important, however, to acknowledge the positive characteristics exhibited by siblings that might be derived from being raised with a brother or sister who has a chronic illness or disability. Lavin (2001) found siblings of children with special needs often to be more mature and accepting, to have a deeper understanding of life and the ability to advocate for individuals with disabilities. These siblings often choose to become helping professionals.

Extended Family

Of course, extended family members have their own needs and reactions. Grandparents have a double hurt because they not only experience pain for their grandchild but also grieve for their children. It is difficult to watch even a grown child struggle to cope with long-term problems. Grandparents know that being there when requested or writing a check won't ease the sorrow that their son or daughter must work through. Even so, grandparents and other extended family members can be helped to realize what an important role they play when they are a part of the family's natural resource system. Often,

relatives are the major source of babysitting relief for parents. It is this provision of relief or respite from daily caregiving duties that may make all of the difference in sustaining a marriage or fulfilling essential needs for recreation and relaxation.

Critical to effective intervention with families is the understanding of who, within the family, are the primary decision makers.

Josephina was a very active 24-month-old who had been referred for a rather obvious delay in expressive language. Her family did not readily acknowledge the concern because Josephina's gestures were communicative and they could understand everything she was trying to say. Although the home visitor had encouraged the family to have Josephina's hearing tested, it just hadn't happened. The child's parents would appear to listen intently to the home visitor and agree with her when the benefits of hearing aids were discussed, but they did not follow through even after they had been referred to agencies that would provide financial assistance. It wasn't until Josephina's maternal grandmother happened to be in the home at the time of the biweekly home visitation that a breakthrough occurred. After carefully explaining the need for and benefits of hearing aids to the grandmother, within a few weeks, Josephina was wearing and enjoying her new hearing aids.

In this case, the home visitor had not realized that Grandmother (Abuela) was the primary decision maker in Josephina's family, and previously Grandmother had not understood why hearing aids were needed because Josephina seemed to be communicating so well within the family. Decision making is often culturally determined, and so it becomes critically important to ask open-ended questions such as "Who in your family might like to help us determine the best way to work with Josie's hearing problems?" to ensure that primary decisions makers are included when important decisions about services are being made.

FAMILY FUNCTION

Family functions are fulfilled through family interactions. For example, family members share affection, plan together, resolve conflicts, teach new skills, and accomplish daily tasks. From the family systems perspective, the quality of *family function* results from the quality of the output of the interactions within and among the family subsystems. Hanson and Lynch (2004) combined the basic family functions into seven components essential to the development of young children. These include 1) love and affection, 2) daily care and health maintenance, 3) economic support, 4) identity development, 5) socialization and guidance, 6) educational and vocational development, and 7) recreation and recuperation. Home visitors will be more effective if they recognize and offer support specifically designed to develop the cooperative interactions necessary to fulfill these essential functions.

> *Jane, a home visitor, visited Kyle and his father Jack. Kyle, a bespectacled and bright little boy, had a serious motor problem with apraxia. According to Jack, Kyle's mother used "every drug there is" during her pregnancy except for alcohol. Jack was in recovery and was living with his elderly mother while he obtained sobriety and got a job. Grandma Ernestine was warm and loving and spent time with Kyle reading and talking. Jack admitted that he was not good at spending time with his son, saying that he had no patience for it. Jack*

was, however, an excellent advocate for his son; he was very involved in getting the appropriate early intervention services and attended all IFSP meetings. He also got a job with flexibility so that he could attend to Kyle's needs. Kyle's mother visited at times but always under supervision because she was still using drugs. When Kyle turned 3 and left the home program, Jack and his mother divided the family functions, but Ernestine was becoming frail. She could not drive Kyle, and cooking became harder for her. Predictably, this family was headed for stress as Ernestine's role became more and more limited. Jack's sister helped sometimes and Jack was courting a new girlfriend whom Kyle was fond of. The three of them went on outings together. Kyle's world was precarious at best, but for the time being they were managing all family functions.

Again, the family systems perspective helps the home visitor to remember that problems in any one area of family functioning affect other areas of family functioning. For example, because Kyle's grandmother could not drive Kyle to appointments, Kyle's father had to figure out another way to fulfill the function of providing transportation. Of course, economic difficulties will affect the family's choices in each area of functioning. There may be fewer choices in medical care, daily care services, and recreation and social activities, to name a few. Each family member's characteristics will affect functioning. Berry and Hardman (1998) discussed some of the characteristics that tend to be associated with greater and less stress. For example, children with conduct disorders or autism tend to create greater stress than do children with Down syndrome. Higher maternal education is related to increased stress whereas decreased stress comes with greater emphasis on religious beliefs. No matter what the individual family characteristics, it takes the voice of a parent to express the true nature of the stress experienced. In retrospect, Elisa's mother had the following comments:

> Parents of children with delays must endure many types of stress. We live with financial stress, and we worry about governmental budget cuts and changes in the laws protecting children with disabilities. We are responsible for selecting schools and therapies, but when our children are receiving such a vari-

ety of services, how are we supposed to determine what's working and what's not? . . . I often wished I could hire a full-time advocate to deal with all these external stresses so that I could just focus my energies on raising my daughter. (Cook et al., 2008, p. 35)

One of the areas of family functioning that is receiving considerable emphasis today is that of affection or the development of bonding between caregivers and infants. Home visitors are expected to observe and model for parents how to respond in ways that are sensitive to and contingent on their child's responses to his or her environment. Chapter 5 goes into more detail on ways to help parents match their interactions appropriately to their child's level of development even when their child does not initiate or react to adult attempts at interaction in typical ways.

Perhaps, the area of functioning that home visitors most often address is that of daily care and health maintenance. Not only do parents of children with special needs have to be concerned with meals, clothing, maintaining the home, and safety, but they also may have additional burdens related to medical tasks such as catheterization and tube feeding. Feeding itself is often an issue of primary focus, and we discuss this subject more thoroughly in Chapter 6.

It is essential that home visitors become tuned in to whether the family is able to fulfill its critical functions. Without this understanding, which comes from hours of listening and observing, home visitors will not be able to provide the support that defines how effective they are at their job. If families are not involved in recreation or do not have opportunities to socialize, home visitors can offer information on how to obtain respite and other forms of child care to give parents time to themselves. In fact, the provision of short-term respite care appears to have a considerable positive impact on the well-being of caregivers (Rimmerman, 1989).

One of the expectations of home visitors is to provide linkage to parent support groups. It is amazing how much comfort families receive from being with other families that have been there and know what they are going through. Federal and state funding has been provided throughout the country for the establishment of what are often known as family resource centers. These centers provide information, workshops on a wide range of topics, and support groups for siblings as well as caregivers for all types of disabilities. (See the Appendix for ways home visitors can help families take advantage of this vital resource.)

STRATEGIES TO FACILITATE FAMILY EMPOWERMENT

One of the keys to creating a respectful relationship with families that will lead to facilitation of family empowerment is to understand the difference between empathy and sympathy when entering into the home visitor–family relationship.

Developing Empathy

When families perceive empathy rather than sympathy, they know that the home visitor is not just feeling sorry for them; rather, she or he can truly identify with what the family is going through and can therefore better assist them as they face their daily challenges. Ciaramicoli and Ketcham (2001) considered empathy to be an active process in which the home visitor tries to learn all she can about the family rather than being content with superficial awareness. The home visitor tries to listen carefully and nonjudgmentally in an effort to see the world and the situation as the other person sees it. On the other hand, sympathy is thought to be a passive experience built on involuntary feelings of sharing another's fear, grief, anger, or joy. Steps toward developing true empathy are much like those developed by truly reflective listeners who use an active approach to perceive and respond to another's thoughts and feelings. These basic steps for achieving empathy, as adapted from the work of Ciaramicoli and Ketcham (2001), are outlined in Table 2.2.

Asking Questions

Questions typically are either closed-ended and can be answered with one-word responses or open-ended requiring a more involved

Table 2.2. Achieving empathy

Slow down and listen. Tension will be eased, and emotions are more likely to be calmed. It is more likely that rational thought may be expressed, allowing home visitors to encourage expression of the family's whole story. In truth, sometimes the best way to become an effective listener is to stop talking.

Listen actively with reflection. Reflect back to the speaker both the feelings and content of the message being heard. By repeating back what has been said and waiting for confirmation, messages will more likely not be misinterpreted. If necessary, repeat any point made, point by point. By actively concentrating and giving their undivided attention, listeners can keep their minds from wandering.

Ask open-ended questions. By encouraging full expression, speakers will not feel manipulated and are more likely to see that the home visitor is really trying to understand and get beyond superficial awareness. Such questions encourage dialogue that can lead to real communication and trust.

Avoid snap judgments. Listeners must avoid jumping to conclusions built on past experiences and the natural tendency to stereotype. It is easy to assume that similar families may have similar reactions. Remaining unbiased and shedding previous biases at the door require vigilance and self-awareness but are critical to the development of trusting relationships.

Avoid quick solutions. It is the tendency of anyone in a helping profession to want to offer immediate solutions that will alleviate pain, emotional or physical. Families deserve and usually desire to solve their own problems. By doing so, they can develop the self-confidence and skills necessary to seek resources to solve their problems once there is no longer a home visitor.

Source: Ciaramicoli and Ketcham (2001).

response. Closed-ended questions are useful to acquire specific information such as how old the child is or how many siblings he or she has. If too many closed-ended questions are asked, caregivers may feel like they are being interrogated. Such questions should be used minimally and wisely.

Open-ended questions invite families to share and be heard. Well-phrased questions asked with genuine interest and a willingness to listen acknowledge that parents are the experts on the subject of their own children. Respect is conveyed. Questions and invitations to mutually problem solve empower families. Families realize how important their opinions are and that they are expected to share in finding solutions to meet their own needs. Turnbull and Turnbull (2006) suggested that open-ended questions can be developed in the following ways:

Asking a question. "How is Katie getting along with her new hearing aid?"

Giving a polite request. "Please give some examples of what makes you uncomfortable during dinner?"

Using an embedded question. "It would help if I could learn more about Jordan's bedtime routine."

Even after we have encouraged thoughtful questioning, however, there are cautions to be considered. Special educators have a tendency to focus on deficits, problems, and concerns. It is easy to start off a home visit by asking, "How can I help you?" or "What problems are you having with Pedro?" Immediately, attention is drawn to what might be wrong or that we feel families need to be helped. Instead, we encourage home visitors to use open-ended questions to draw out the positive because the negative usually has a way of presenting itself. How much nicer it would be to ask, "In what ways have you enjoyed working with professionals in the past?" and, "Please tell me what you would consider to be a good day with Pedro?" Strive for an atmosphere of informal conversations rather than what might be perceived as an interview.

Listen Attentively and with Reflection

Attentive, active, and reflective listening is not only essential to the establishment of empathy but also critical to the development of relationships that are respectful and trusting. Gillespie (2006) broke active listening down into four easy-to-recall steps as follows:

Stop—Stop in order to pay attention. When this happens, the speaker knows you are focusing on him or her and that you think what he or she has to say is important.

Look—Face the speaker and make eye contact. Watch for nonverbal cues to help you understand what he or she is feeling and thinking.

Listen—Listen to what is being said by paying close attention to the content of the message as well as the emotions being expressed either verbally or nonverbally. Several messages may be communicated at once, and the content may not always be what is important.

Respond—Confirm your attentiveness through nonverbal head shaking, nods, and murmurs. Once the speaker appears to be finished, reflect back the content and feelings that you have perceived. Be sure to pause to give the speaker a chance to confirm your reflection. The speaker then knows that he or she has been heard and understood. "It sounds like you are afraid that Matthew will really hurt himself when he bangs his head against the wall." Acknowledging the mother's feelings before jumping in to help her learn how to respond to Matthew lets her know that you care about her, that she has been heard and that you are there to support her as well as prevent Matt from injuring himself.

Avoid Jargon

Home visitors must be careful to avoid using terms and acronyms that might be unfamiliar and misunderstood by family members. Not only can such terms lead to misunderstandings, but also parents can be intimidated by their use. Some parents are reluctant to ask what such terms mean. The responsibility to offer clear communication belongs to the home visitor.

Phrase Negative Information Carefully

Home visitors must get into the habit of always beginning a conversation with something positive and keeping the conversation as positive as possible. Even negative information can be phrased in a positive manner. For example, when Jamie's parents were disappointed that Jamie hadn't begun walking independently, his home visitor said: "It seems that you are very concerned that Jamie has not yet begun to walk by himself. However, you might have noticed how much less he stumbles when cruising around the furniture."

Respecting Family Preferences

Moore and colleagues, after an extensive review of the literature, stated:

> In place of intrusive interventions that, by nature, focus on individual abnormality with presumed family dysfunction, advocates and professionals in the field could better serve fam-

ilies of children with disabilities by protecting and strengthening the integrity of the family unit, and by validating the family's right to autonomy and efficacy. (2002, p. 60)

We have come to understand how important it is to develop intervention services that are family driven. By listening and truly hearing what families need and want, we can provide information and services built on families' concerns and priorities. Although some families may want information to read and assistance in obtaining community resources, others may seek therapeutic services or appropriate educational placements. And, there are some who just want more time to work through denial and grief!

Many moms would like to be just that—moms! When a child's condition requires that he or she be involved with a number of professionals, parents can easily feel that they are not in control and have little to say about their child's daily life. It is up to the home visitor to reassure them that they are the only ones qualified to be their child's parents and that they are the true experts when it comes to making decisions about what happens to and with their child.

Bethany was clearly at the end of her rope when Kate, the home visitor, came for her weekly visit. "I can't do one more visit from anybody or to anybody!" she said to Kate. At the IFSP meeting the week before, the team suggested that Valerie, Bethany's daughter, could profit by going to a remedial swimming class. Bethany, a single mother who had to leave her job to pick up Valerie at child care and take her to swimming class at the 1:00 specified time, had to make up the time at the end of the day. On the last visit to the swimming class, the swim therapist was not there and no one had called Bethany to cancel her appointment. Bethany wanted to cancel the classes, but they had been on a waiting list for a long time and she felt guilty about possibly jeopardizing Valerie's developmental progress. Kate affirmed Valerie's frustration and the difficulties she would experience by continuing the swimming therapy. When Kate suggested that Bethany discontinue the swimming therapy, Bethany expressed relief and gratitude. Bethany could use the time saved to relax with her daughter at the end of the day.

It is important for home visitors to understand how the quality of their relationship with the family may help determine how the family perceives their child's disability. If home visitors do not carefully listen and honor families' preferences in terms of what services are desired or the degree to which the family wants to be involved in early intervention services, they can contribute to feelings of helplessness and bring on greater insecurity. When home visitors are not tuned in, parents may become overwhelmed and begin to doubt their own abilities as caregivers. In their hurry to provide specialized services, home visitors may overlook the potential of the natural resources that can be provided by extended family, friends, and neighbors. The more families are treated as atypical, the less likely they are to realize that they are more like other families than they are different from them. "Adaptation to change and challenges brought on by a child with a disability can bring (and has brought) renewed strength, energy, and competence to individual family members and to family units as a whole" (Moore et al., 2002, p. 59).

Finally, it is necessary to remember that in some cultures, children are accepted and loved as they are. Parents and other family members may accept the circumstances of life and do not wish to interfere with what they perceive to be fate (Sileo & Sileo, 1996). Such families may not want early intervention services. If this is the case, then home visitors must accept the parents' wishes even though they may disagree. It would be natural for a home visitor, who has worked hard to arrange for services, to be disappointed if a family rejects the services and, thus, her efforts. In addition, the early interventionist might be tempted to accuse the family of being in denial or just not caring.

In such instances, it is important to remember that the parents' emotional responses may be influencing their behavior. Processing and integrating whatever information they have been given may take time. If the referral you were about to make is not a medical urgency, it is appropriate to be supportive and allow the parents to proceed at their own pace. Backing off gracefully, you, the home visitor, must let the family know that you—and the information you possess—will be available if they change their mind. What is critical is that home visitors avoid letting their own emotions interfere with their ability to respect families and their wishes.

Virginia, the home visitor who visited Amanda, a quiet little one with Down syndrome, was puzzled that her suggestion had not been acted upon. In hoping to point out that Amanda was making progress, Virginia had asked Amanda's mother to write down some things that Amanda did during the week so that they could go over the list in the next visit. When nothing was listed, Virginia asked if this was not something the mother wanted to do. "No," the mother replied, "it makes me too sad to see that she is so slow." This mother was still in a state of grief that Virginia had not considered.

Preparing Families for Change

Recognizing that change often enhances family stress, IDEA of 2004 (PL 108-446) requires formal transition plans to assist families in coping with the transition from Part C early intervention services to Part B preschool services. Typically, services move from natural environments such as the child's home or child care setting to preschool classrooms. Services change from a therapeutic model to an educational model in which services are delivered in small groups rather than individually. Focus is on educational needs as well as on helping children learn how to interact with other children and adults. Members of the team who help families develop the outcomes in IFSPs are usually different from those who will collaborate with the family in developing their child's IEP. Children spend more time per week in preschool programs than they might have spent in infant programs. Riding the school bus will be new to children who have been served at home. All of these changes are exciting but they also bring about stress, and home visitors are in a unique position to provide guidance. Some families may be experiencing earlier stages of the grieving process all over again. They are also losing their home visitor, the professional in whom they have developed trust. Happily, some children will have progressed so well that they no longer are eligible for specialized supports and services. Whatever the situation, changes are inevitable and the home visitor is in the best position to provide the support needed for families to navigate these changes with the least amount of stress.

To more clearly understand families' reactions to the changes required at times of transition, it is useful to consider the work of Bridges (2003). He conceptualized transitions according to three zones: ending, neutral, and beginning. Each zone requires different supportive strategies, briefly outlined in Table 2.3.

With enhanced understanding and skills to implement strategies specifically designed to ease early transitions, home visitors can help families celebrate change and be better prepared to cope with future challenges that are inevitable. Table 2.4 can assist families in knowing what to expect during the transition process.

RECOGNIZING AND FACILITATING THE DESIRED OUTCOMES OF FAMILIES

The home visitor is responsible for helping the family identify what it hopes will be accomplished by becoming involved in early intervention services. The IFSP requires that families and practitioners collaborate in the process of identifying family outcomes or what benefits families expect to achieve as a result of services. Bailey et al.

Table 2.3. Three zones of transition

Zone	Supportive strategies
Ending zone: Something is ending: home visiting, relationships with therapists	Listen. Help identify who is losing what. Expect strong reactions. Offer information. Provide links to other families and resources.
Neutral zone: Families feel that they are nowhere. They might feel anxious because they don't know what is ahead and how they will be affected.	Help families recognize new opportunities and possibilities. Encourage them to generalize skills. Help families visualize how services will be different and what they want—a more or less restrictive environment?
Beginning zone: While families may be excited about new opportunities, families may still be reminded of what they have lost and may still fear the unknown.	Help families clarify the purpose of the transition—too old for services, safer environment. Plan site visits; point out similarities and differences.

Table 2.4. The transition process

The following topics will be discussed:

       Your child's strengths and needs

       Your concerns

       Special education program options (including location)

       Goals and timelines for the beginning of the new program

       The need for any further evaluation

       Who will be on the new team and what will be their responsibilities

       Your special education legal rights

You might also want to discuss:

       How preschool services are different from early intervention services

       Issues such as adult–child ratio, length of day, and year

       Potential for family involvement

       Development of a new IEP for special education services

       Who will assist you in visiting the proposed programs

       Who will be your future contact

       Other families you might talk to who have experienced this transition

       How to prepare your child and the rest of your family for this transition

       Options if your child no longer needs special education services

(2006) stressed the importance of sharing information with parents about their child's condition (a service) to help them realize the benefit of advocating for and getting services that respond to their child's and family's needs (outcome).

The approach that links services with desired outcomes for families as well as their children recognizes the fact that children grow and develop within the context of their family. Therefore, the boundaries between family and child services are often blurred. When children learn to sleep through the night, there is no question that the entire family benefits. We wouldn't be including this chapter in this book if we didn't fully realize that providing support to families, as they face the challenges incumbent in raising a child with special needs, may be more important than providing services directly to children. Programs increasingly understand that documented fulfillment of family outcomes is, indeed, a reflection of program effectiveness.

The Early Childhood Outcomes (ECO) Center funded by the Office of Special Education Programs proposed the following five family outcomes as essential to the promotion of effective early intervention services:

Outcome 1: Families understand their child's strengths, abilities and special needs.

Outcome 2: Families know their rights and advocate effectively for their children.

Outcome 3: Families help their children develop and learn.

Outcome 4: Families have support systems.

Outcome 5: Families access desired community services, programs, and activities. (Bailey et al., 2006, p. 227)

The home visitor is expected to be culturally sensitive in using the perceptive communication skills discussed throughout this book in an informal, conversational approach to helping families identify their strengths, concerns, and priorities. Once families have developed trust and are comfortable in sharing family information that can result in personal outcomes, home visitors are better prepared to offer the resources their families need to ultimately accomplish the outcomes listed above. There appears to be no correlation between the cultural background of home visitors and parental satisfaction (Banks, Santos, & Roof, 2003). Therefore, it is probably not necessary for agencies to be concerned if they cannot provide a cultural match between parents and providers. If services are not available in a family's preferred language, however, and a qualified translator or interpreter cannot be found, then it is obvious that the family's needs may not be met. We have included a section in Chapter 8 that assists service providers in working with interpreters because this is an often neglected, but critical, area of skill development.

Focusing on Strengths, Achievements, and Desires

Home visitors who focus on family strengths and achievements help to build the family confidence necessary for them to adequately advocate for themselves and their child. By avoiding an emphasis on problems or deficits and zeroing in on solution-focused questions, the adaptive potential of families is being supported. Asking parents what seems to have been the most successful approach to getting Matt to stay in his bed is much more positive than asking the parents what problems they have had in getting him to go to bed.

Identifying Strategies that Will Help Families Achieve Desired Outcomes

There is evidence that the extent to which families will participate in early intervention is directly related to the extent to which intervention strategies fit within the family's existing routines, cultural values, and beliefs and patterns of family life (Winton & Winton, 2005).

Family routines and rituals have increasingly become an important consideration, given the shift from intervention that focuses on the child to services that meet the needs of the family as a whole. Evidence even suggests that family routines and rituals are actually associated with the quality of the marital relationship (Spagnola & Fiese, 2007).

When children have developmental disabilities, however, families are often faced with the challenge of altering their time, energy, and resources to best meet the immediate needs of the child (Guralnick, 2004) and may sacrifice other family needs to do this. When interventions are embedded in family routines, families are less likely to view the interventions as just one more demand that has been added to their day. Given the importance of creating early intervention practices that are contextually relevant, Chapter 4 offers guidance in how to encourage and facilitate intervention through family routines.

SUMMARY

Given that a primary role of the home visitor is to support families in their efforts to nurture their children in the most optimum ways possible, it is essential that home visitors understand how day-to-day stresses affect parent–child interactions and family functioning. Viewing families as a whole and realizing that they are more knowledgeable about their child than anyone else allows home visitors to more readily establish a truly supportive relationship. Valuing the diversity of family structures, beliefs about child-rearing practices, and establishment of family priorities helps develop the trust so necessary to success as a home visitor. Empowering families through the ability to connect emotionally, facilitation of effective communication skills, and being available to offer resources and guidance, home visitors will promote the best family development possible.

3

Building Home Visitor–
Family Relationships

"They won't care what you know
until they know that you care."

–Unknown

Research tells us that a strong predictor of the outcomes of early
intervention is the quality of the relationship between the primary
service provider and the family (McWilliam, 2005). In fact, the relationship between home visitor and family members is crucial for intervention for the child to be effective. Findings from several studies have
indicated that families are typically satisfied with the early intervention services they receive (Spiker, Malik, & Hebbeler, 2007; Summers,
Hoffmann, Marquis, Turnbull, & Poston, 2005). At the end of early
intervention, most parents felt that it had made a significant impact on
their child and their family as a whole. Moreover, they had become
confident in their ability to help their child develop and learn: They
knew how to advocate for services, and they had support networks
(Spiker et al., 2007).

Overall, these studies concluded that although family satisfaction is fairly good and some family-centered practices are being implemented, certain components of service delivery continue to be less
than best practice; that is, they remain professionally centered, with
limited coordination among professionals, and families are not always
the primary decision makers in the early intervention services they
receive. As home visitors, we want our relationship with a child's family to not only meet their needs but also be warm, accepting, respectful, and empathetic.

The parent–home visitor relationship is a dynamic process that varies both in nature and in effect as a result of the personal characteristics of the parents and the home visitor as well as the dynamics of the larger environment. The personality, values, and attitudes of parents and home visitors affect the relationship between the two. Furthermore, the parent–home visitor relationship is influenced by characteristics of the larger social systems, such as the parents' neighborhood and the race, ethnicity, schooling, and social class of the parents and home visitor. All of these factors are working as the parent and home visitor co-create their relationship (Klass, 2007).

CURRENT KNOWLEDGE

A number of researchers have identified a variety of family-centered practices considered to be ideal (Crais, Roy, & Free, 2006; McWilliam, Snyder, Harbin, Porter, & Munn, 2000). These include identifying the family's most important concerns, asking the family what the child does well, making positive comments about the child, explaining all assessment results, asking whether the behaviors observed are typical of the child, summarizing the assessment results, and identifying next steps for the family and professional.

Identifying the Family's Most Important Concerns

During the first visit, the home visitor encourages the mother or caregiver to tell his or her story—several times if necessary. Westby, Burda, & Mehta (2003) described this as *ethnographic interviewing*. That is, the caregiver has the opportunity to select the important information to share. It is best to think of it as a series of friendly conversations in which the home visitor introduces open-ended questions to assist the parents in sharing their experiences. As mentioned previously, asking questions too quickly can turn an interview into a formal interrogation. Usually the story is eagerly told, but often questions are necessary (e.g., "What is it like to live with Mary?"). This is a descriptive question that is broad and general and allows the parents to describe their experiences, their daily activities, and the people in their lives. What it is like to live with a child, no matter what child, opens a dialogue (or monologue) about what is really going on in the household. Another way of getting the history on a first visit is to ask about a typical day. "Tell me about a typical day with Mary," or if the presenting problem involves a routine, you might say, "Tell me about a typical mealtime (or bedtime)." This also gives the home visitor information about routines or lack of routines. Some parents will say that no day is typical; they are all different and unpredictable. You might then ask about yesterday (a weekday) and then about a weekend day. Later, it is appropriate to ask more structured questions such as, "What kinds of things has the doctor told you about [the child's] tantrums?" When faced with a litany of problems, it is important to ask what the child does well—perhaps asking the parent to think of this for the first time. The home visitor can use the child's strengths as something to build on.

Active listening skills are called for here: clarifying, repeating salient points, rephrasing, or just being still and maintaining eye contact (if that is comfortable culturally). The home visitor who is building rapport spends more time listening than talking. By the same token, she is aware of the body language of the storyteller.

It is important to take a few notes, such as who is the child's physician, what medications is the child taking, who else is working with the family, who is living in the home, as well as vital statistics such as date of birth, birth weight, and so forth. It is not, however, the time to take copious notes. If a formal assessment instrument is used, it is preferable that it come later. This first visit is a get-acquainted visit, and the relationship building should not be hurried. (In some instances, the first visit is the only visit by the specialist. If so, building a relationship is not the primary reason for the visit and expediency may become necessary.)

On subsequent visits, some *appropriate* questions are

- "How have things been going?" This gives the family an opportunity to tell what is most important at this time and to set the agenda for the visit.
- "Do you need any information to help with that?"
- "Should we try to solve this?"

- "Would you like me to show you?"
- "Do you have anything new you want to ask me about?"
- "Is there a specific time of day that does not go well for you?"
- "Have you had any appointments in the last week? Any coming up?"
- "Do you have enough or too much to do with your child?"

Some *appropriate* strategies are

- Keeping silent
- Offering developmental guidance
- Listening empathetically
- Repeating and clarifying what has been said

Some *inappropriate* comments are

- "It's really a blessing in disguise."
- "Well, it could have been worse."
- "I feel your pain."
- "You'll get back to normal soon."
- "Everything happens for a reason."
- "It's always darkest before the dawn."
- "The good Lord never gives us more than we can handle."
- "Some day we'll look back at this and laugh."

Judy, a student in an early intervention program, accompanied Phyllis, an experienced home visitor, on a first visit to the home of Anthony, who had been newly diagnosed with cerebral palsy. Phyllis introduced Judy to Anthony's mother, and then she introduced herself to Anthony's grandmother and sister, age 6, who were also in the room. Anthony sat on his mother's lap during the hour visit. Judy became more and more impatient as Phyllis did nothing to interact with Anthony at all. Instead, she said, "Tell me about Anthony." "How do you comfort him when he cries?" "You mentioned that it takes a long time to feed him. Tell me more about that." Judy left the home thinking that although the visit was not completely wasted, she and Phyllis could have done more with the child. It took Judy many visits before she really understood that the mother needed to tell her story and the home visitor needed to really hear it before anything of real substance could be accomplished. By fully listening, Phyllis learned a great deal about the dynamics of the family, about the mother's interactions with Anthony, and about the mother's parenting style. Laying out priorities would come later. Anthony's mother didn't ask any questions; instead, she was intent on telling her story. Phyllis was also laying the groundwork for a relationship with the grandmother and the sister. In many cultures, the grandparents are the true heads of the family. Whatever is decided later will need to be accepted by the grandmother or it will not be implemented.

Say Something Positive About the Child

The most important time to do this is during the first face-to-face visit with the child. Every child deserves praise, such as for having beautiful long eyelashes or a winning smile. Throughout the first visit, do not miss opportunities to reinforce positive comments.

Explain All Assessment Results

Assessment (e.g., the IFSP process) is one area in which parents have traditionally played less of a role (Crais et al., 2006). Early interventionists tend to think that parents lack the knowledge and expertise to adequately assess their child—that tests can only be administered in a standardized manner—and so the early interventionists are hesitant to give up their role of primary decision maker (Bruder, 2000). Research has documented, however, that parents can be reliable informants providing accurate descriptions of their children's abilities and basic development (Crais, Douglas, & Campbell, 2004). Asking parents to participate and give their opinions in the assessment process is an excellent opportunity to help them pinpoint the child's strengths and needs—for example, asking parents to help identify assessment strategies to use in assessing their child, including asking if the behaviors are typical of the child. When they are part of the process, parents are likely to follow through on recommendations. After the initial interview, the assessment provides a unique opportunity to set the stage for collaboration for family-driven services versus professionally driven ones (Crais et al., 2006). The family should have an opportunity to read the assessment report and any recommendations, so they can make comments, before the report is submitted to anyone else. This is another opportunity for collaboration. In a team, all perspectives should be represented in reports.

OTHER HOME VISITOR BEHAVIORS THAT BUILD RELATIONSHIPS

As Pawl and St. John observed, "How you are is as important as what you do" (1998, p. 1). When we are invited into people's homes and personal space, we must observe common courtesies with special attention to the following.

Be Reliable

This should not have to be said, but being reliable also means being a stable person in a chaotic world, and you may be the only person who is stable in the world of your family. Be on time—call if you will be late. Follow through on what you say you will do; bring the article or object promised. Make the call you said you would make and make the contact you said you would make. All of this builds trust in a relationship.

Act Like You Are a Guest in the Home

The home visitor is a guest who is friendly but not too friendly. If refreshments are offered, accept graciously, at least occasionally. Sometimes a caregiver spends her days isolated from others and may view her visitor as her one social contact of the day or week. If the television is on, the home visitor can talk in such a soft voice that she can not be heard unless the television is turned off. Effective home visitors take cues from parents; for example, they should ask the parents' permission before touching or picking up the child, and they should refrain from entering other rooms of the home unless invited (Klass, 2007). The home visitor should always ask if it is all right to use objects in the home (e.g., a child's toys, kitchen items).

Respect Cultural Practices within the Home

Slip-on shoes are always safe. If shoes are outside the door, indicating that they are not worn inside, slips-ons can be removed easily. The home visitor greets everyone in the home who is visible, even if they do not speak the same language. Providing culturally appropriate service means not only respecting and fitting within the home's culture but also coming to grips with the fact that the family in many ways will need to adapt to the prevailing culture within the United States. Providing information to the family includes helping them to understand other institutions within the community and how their family can interface with those institutions—for example, the importance Americans put on being on time for an appointment with someone who can be helpful to their child. Nowhere is this need more important than in preparing for an IFSP or IEP meeting. Members of the team must strive to be culturally sensitive, but so also must the family, and it is best that this information is imparted by someone who is trusted rather than by a stranger at the meeting. Perhaps the cultural practice most misunderstood by families not from the United States is that infant programs and school districts are required to provide appropriate service but not *every* service that the family might desire for their child.

Another way for the home visitor to be a conduit between parents and institutions is in the parents' encounters with professional jargon. When terms that parents do not understand are bandied about, the parents may or may not ask for clarification, depending on their personal assertiveness. If they do not, they may very quickly be out of the loop, even though they may speak English and the meeting is conducted in English.

People relate most readily to people who are similar to themselves. This is especially true in language use. If you don't speak the parents' language, arrange for a translator (see Chapter 6). The ideal situation is to have a home visitor with the same ethnic background, language, and socioeconomic background. This book assumes that assignments are made without such matching.

Abandon Your Agenda

Families are dynamic. The family that the home visitor left last week may not be the same family she encounters this week. Family members get sick, the employed become unemployed, parents are estranged, relatives die, siblings need attention, and routines change to meet changing needs. The visit to the school or the park or the grocery store that was so carefully rehearsed may not have taken place. Relatives come to visit and the household must adjust. When the home visitor walks in the door and asks, "What's new?," she must be prepared for anything and for the priorities of the visit to change.

> *Glenda, the home visitor, had planned her visit to Melanie. First she would help Marta, Melanie's mother, to increase Melanie's "tummy time" to 5 minutes with the help of a visual toy for Melanie to watch while she was on her tummy. Then she and Marta would assist Melanie while she built a block tower. But when she arrived at the home, Melanie was asleep and Marta was very upset. The formula from the Special Supplemental Nutrition Program for Women, Infants, and Children (WIC) had arrived and it was not the formula that was ordered. Marta did not speak English well enough to call the WIC office and explain what had happened. The immediate priority became obtaining the correct formula. Glenda spent her time in the home on the phone with the WIC office. When she left, she had assurance that the correct formula would be exchanged for the incorrect one. Marta was relieved; her child would have what she needed to eat. What could be more important than that?*

Observe Yourself

Effective home visitors are able to work on two levels at the same time. On one level, they are completely engaged in interactions with the parent and child, and at the same time, they observe the interactions during the visit and are aware of their own reactions and feelings. When home visitors can relate to the family and at the same time be aware of their own feelings and make decisions based on those feelings, they are more likely to be effective. The following case illustrates working on two levels at the same time:

> *Wilma, a speech-language pathologist, worked for more than a year with Josh, who was being raised by his grandmother Nancy. Josh was a passive child who was delayed in all areas. A primary concern was Josh's inability to communicate his wants verbally or by gesture. On this day, Nancy's daughter Andrea (not Josh's mother) and her 2-year-old daughter were visiting the home. Josh had just learned to walk, and during the session he climbed onto the sofa and walked from one end to the other. Nancy swooped him up to remove him from the sofa. Josh then uttered his first word: "No!" whereupon Nancy slapped his bottom and said, "Don't say no to me." Wilma, delighted that Josh had expressed himself verbally, was appalled that Nancy had punished his behavior. She was aware of her feelings: She wanted to change Nancy's perspective, while honoring Nancy's primary role with her grandson and not damaging the relationship she had built with the grandmother. She said, "Nancy, he said a word." Nancy said, "I know, but he can't say no to adults." Wilma turned to Andrea and asked if her daughter ever said no to her. Andrea said, "Oh, yes, but I just ignore it." Wilma then said to Nancy," I know obedience is important to you, but could you just take him down but ignore the no?" Nancy said she could do that, but Wilma made a note to revisit this subject on her next visit. She would need to help Nancy discriminate and reward an appropriate no and ignore what she judged to be an inappropriate no.*

FIRST IMPRESSIONS

In Chapter 1, we established that our philosophy of home visiting is that of collaboration; we are not experts who must be listened to and our advice taken without question. It is therefore imperative that this collaborative philosophy be apparent from the first contact with the family. We have stressed also that home visiting should be family driven, not agency driven. If the focus of the program is to support the parent–child relationship, it should be shown early in the home visitor–family relationship. A problem-solving approach should be established as early as possible, with the focus on what is going well in the family instead of what is going wrong.

The first contact is likely to be by phone after a child has been identified either as one to be assessed or as one who is eligible for services by a home visitor. Such an encounter can get off to a bad start, such as in the next example. No one who is a home visitor or who is a service provider knowingly or deliberately plans to create distrust, and yet some things clearly can and do undermine trust. Note the violations of the previously mentioned philosophical principles.

"Mrs. Rodriquez? This is Joan Eliot. I'm an Infant Educator, and I was given your file by the assessment team at the Washburn Center."

"Yes, they told me someone would call."

"Okay, we need to set up times when I can come out to your home and work with Melissa. I have Tuesday at 3:00 open in my schedule now. Is that okay?"

"Well, Melissa is usually napping then. Just what is it you are going to do?"

"Well, as they told you, Melissa is delayed in her development and she needs some special help. I can come out and establish some goals for her to work on."

"What kind of goals were you thinking of? We just found out from our doctor that Melissa has some problems and my husband and I think she's pretty normal."

"Did you get a copy of the assessment report? There are some goals written in it that the team thought she should work on."

"What team is that?"

"The assessment team that saw her two weeks ago. Did you get a copy of the report?"

"Yes, but I don't think they really got a true picture of Melissa. She doesn't act the way they said she did when she's here with us."

"Okay, we can talk about that. But we can start working on her goals. Do you think Melissa will be awake by 4:00 on Tuesday? That's about the latest I can get there."

"Okay, but I would like my husband to be here when you come. I'll see if he can get off work then."

"That would be nice. I'll see you at 4:00 next Tuesday."

In this first contact, Joan was clearly driven by her agency's agenda—to see Melissa at a time convenient for Joan and to begin working on the goals established by the assessment team. It may seem unlikely to Mrs. Rodriguez that the family's needs will be considered. If family goals were also on the agenda, it could be quite a surprise to Mr. and Mrs. Rodriguez. The following encounter illustrates these points. Notice how this home visitor sets a collaborative attitude from the beginning.

"Mrs. Porter? This is Lillian Garcia. I'm an Infant Educator with the Washburn Center. Did someone tell you that I would call?"

"Yes, they did."

"I was looking at the report from the assessment team. It looks like Kevin has a lot of strengths and things he does well."

"Yes, he does. My husband and I don't think that report really fits Kevin. He doesn't act like that around us."

"One of the reasons I will be visiting you in your home is to see Kevin in familiar surroundings and to get to know both of you there. I'd like to find a time that I could come out and meet you and we could decide how I might help your family."

"Well, my husband and I just found out from our doctor that something is wrong with Kevin. We just told that doctor that he had trouble sleeping and then all this happened."

"We should certainly talk about the sleeping problem and anything else that you see that your family and Kevin need help with."

"Could you come when my husband is here?"

"I would certainly like that. Right now my latest appointment is at 4:00 or I can come early in the morning, say 7:30 or 8:00."

"Eight o'clock would work for him. He doesn't leave until about 9:00."

Note that Lillian did not volunteer to make her visit at night or on Saturday to accommodate Kevin's father. Collaboration means some negotiation without either party being inconvenienced more than necessary. Lillian was willing to visit Kevin at a time when the visit suited both schedules.

First Visit

The first face-to-face visit by the home visitor sets the stage for the all-important relationship with the caregivers. This first visit is devoted to getting acquainted with the family, hearing their story, and learning their priorities. It may or may not include some assessment of the child or of the family interaction. If the visit is occurring because of an already existing IFSP, the goals for the child and family have been decided on. It remains for this home visitor to decide with the family how those goals are to be prioritized (there also may be new family priorities that were not known or were not so important when the IFSP was written). There may also be new information from medical or other professionals that needs to be taken into consideration. We will start with the home visitor ringing the doorbell. She may be carrying a toy bag, although that runs the risk of having the child or a sibling insist on exploring everything in the bag immediately. Better to have only a file containing the information already gathered about this child and family and a pencil. Note taking will be kept to a minimum as it interferes with listening, but taking notes sometimes is important.

Greeting

The home visitor greets whoever answers the door by presenting a card with her name and the agency's name, phone number, and e-mail on it. Families may have many professional visitors in the months after a child's diagnosis, and the home visitor's name can be lost among them. She will also take off her shoes if there are other shoes by the door or ask if she should take them off if there are no other shoes there. She will greet the child and siblings equally and find something positive to comment on about the child (e.g., "What beautiful curly hair," "Look at those big brown eyes"). If there are other adults in the home, she will greet them also, giving them cards and noting their names. This is particularly important in homes in which the culture honors grandparents and they are visiting or live there.

Hand Cleansing

Before sitting down, the home visitor asks where it would be convenient for her to wash her hands, or she obviously uses a hand sanitizer that she carries with her. Hand cleansing is an essential part of every visit. The home visitor may have come from another home and another child, and many children are fragile and particularly susceptible to germs.

Getting Down to Business

Sitting down with the caregiver, usually the mother, the home visitor relates that she has read the preliminary information (previous assessment or IFSP) and would like to hear how things are going for the child and family. This is the time to encourage the parents to tell their story. The home visitor can ask, "What is it like to live with Melissa?" This may bring up new issues, such as sleeping or eating or having tantrums. The home visitor looks for solutions with the family: "What have you tried that worked?" "Have you gotten any help with that?" "Why do you think that is happening?" "Would you like some help with that?" "Would you like us to work on that?" Now is a time to ask if they are satisfied with their medical professionals. Sometimes parents are dissatisfied but afraid to change primary care physicians or specialists because they don't know of a better one. The home visitor should have a list of practitioners whom other families have found satisfying in working with children with special needs. The home visitor also should ask the parents if they are informed about the local Parent Resource Center if there is one or online associations that are specific to a child's disability such as Down syndrome support, apraxia support, or autism support. Go over the IFSP goals, if they exist, and ask if they are still what the family wants to address. What is the most important? If there is still time, it is helpful to go over a typical day from the time the child wakes up in the morning to bedtime and waking periods during the night. That includes all food eaten and how it is eaten. Many families do not have a family dinner; children are fed first and do not observe parents eating.

Summarize and Prioritize

Agree now on a time for the next visit and if that time will be a permanent time or if the family wants to decide from week to week. Go over the priorities and goals and ask if that covers all of the family's concerns. Assure the caregivers that you will work on these issues together so ensuing appointments should be at a time when they are present. Perhaps a visit will need to happen during a mealtime or when a sibling is absent. Ask the caregiver to call if the child, sibling, or caregiver is sick so that the visit can be rescheduled. Go over resources that you will bring next time or that you will call about. Ask if the family has other questions for you now. Tell the parents that you can be reached by telephone (office if you don't want to give your home or cell number) or by e-mail.

During the first visit at 8:00 in the morning, Joan visited Melissa and both of her parents. They had had a bad night. Melissa had wakened several times and it was obvious that the family was on edge. Melissa was eating cereal in her high chair, Mr. Rodriguez was dressed for work, and Mrs. Rodriguez was in her robe. Joan said how well Melissa was eating her breakfast and holding her spoon. They sat at the kitchen table. The story from the mother would have to wait for a later time as the father had very specific questions about when Melissa would walk and talk. Joan brought a chart without ages (see Appendix) with her and together they found where Melissa fit on the chart. The chart was left with the parents for future reference and to show other family members. Joan also promised to bring information on sleeping patterns and to check with the service coordinator about promised formula that had not been delivered. Joan noted that Melissa was having a hard time sitting up in her high chair and made a note to herself to suggest a rolled-up towel behind her back next time. This time she just wanted to establish herself as working with them on shared goals. The most important goal for this family was to help Melissa sleep through the night. Joan asked about Melissa's typical day. There was some discrepancy between the parents about the bedtime routine, how often Melissa woke at night, and how many times each of them got up with her. Joan took careful notes on the typical day and included it in her initial report, which she gave to the parents later. The typical day forms a baseline on which to measure progress. After she made an appointment for the next visit (Mr. Rodriguez did not find it necessary to attend now that he had met Joan), Joan filled out her summary sheet (see Appendix), left a copy with the parents, and left.

ESSENTIAL FAMILY SERVICES

Given the state of our present knowledge, it would be reasonable to begin work with the family by providing essential family services—information needs, resource needs, and needs for emotional and social support—and then design and implement an early intervention plan to meet family needs (Guralnick, 2005). Such a plan must be consistent with the family's goals, values, priorities, and routines.

In general, service goals can be organized into three categories: information and services needs, resource supports, and social supports.

Information and Services

Children with special needs create a requirement for information and services on the part of families. The family needs information concerning details about the child's diagnosis and long-term prognosis; developmental guidance regarding day-to-day interactions, such as managing sleep, feeding, and behavior; understanding the child's cues in order to respond correctly; and the most effective intervention programs, child care arrangements, and individual professionals. The task of gathering information relevant to their child's health and development and then integrating that information is complex but vital in order to maximize all three family patterns of interaction.

Online Information

Given society's increasing reliance on the Internet, it may be the primary source of information for both home visitors and parents. It is not unusual now for parents to meet home visitors with information and opinions that they have gotten from the Internet. Professionals are no longer gatekeepers to information; increasingly, the Internet is providing a means of equalizing the balance of knowledge-based power between parents and professionals. Home visitors can use this new medium in their collaboration with parents, at the same time keeping in mind its benefits and limitations in meeting parents' needs (Zaidman-Zait & Jamieson, 2007).

Parents and home visitors alike need to be aware, however, of the benefits and dangers of this type of information dissemination. On one hand, the Internet provides parents with easy access to thousands of pages of information on an as-needed basis, and it provides parents the opportunity to establish communication with professionals in privacy and anonymity. It can also serve as a source of emotional support by facilitating interaction with other parents who have had the same experiences (Zaidman-Zait & Jamieson, 2007). For example, parents may learn about relatively rare conditions and clinical trials that doctors might not have mentioned or been aware of, or they may learn about specific behavioral modification strategies that are effective with children of a certain age who have a particular disorder. On the other hand, the Internet also presents major problems, including little or no monitoring of the quality, reliability, and currency of the information. In addition, so much information is available that a family may experience information overload (Martland, 2001).

Parents are highly receptive to information from sources they trust when they perceive it to be relevant to their needs, but parents cannot use what they cannot understand, so be sure the information you provide is easily understood. The home visitor can help the family sift through this information for accuracy and reliability by referring them to, for example, Healthfinder, a federal web site developed by the U.S. Department of Health and Human Services (http://www.healthfinder.gov), which functions as a resource for finding the best government and nonprofit health and human services information on the Internet. A similar example is the Health on the Net Foundation Code of Conduct for medical and health web sites (http://www.hon.ch). The HONcode does not intend to rate the quality of the information provided by a web site; rather, it defines a set of rules, including holding web site developers to basic ethical standards in the presentation of information, and helps to ensure that readers are aware of the source and purpose of the data they are reading. Still another resource is the Tufts University Child & Family Web Guide (http://www.cfw.tufts.edu), which lists web sites that disseminate information on child development, including information on specific disabilities.

Resource Supports

Second, a child with special needs often creates additional *resource needs*, particularly financial needs. Even with public programs that provide early intervention, out-of-pocket expenses may be considerable. Resources are needed to help families accommodate to changes required at work and during leisure activities as well as to coordinate the schedules of the professionals and family. Unless these resources are available, the family interaction patterns can be stressed.

Emotional and Social Supports

Finally, there may be a need for emotional and social support for families in carrying out their parenting role. Families need to maintain a sense of control because they are the ones responsible for their child and maintaining balance in their lives and the lives of their other children. When one feels out of control, family patterns of interaction are likely to be compromised.

Another expectation of the home visitor is to provide linkage to parent support groups. It is amazing how much comfort families derive from being with other families who have had similar experiences with their own child with special needs. Federal and state funding has been provided throughout the country for the establishment of Family Resource Centers. These centers provide information, workshops on a wide range of topics, and support groups for siblings as well as caregivers of people with all types of disabilities. The Appendix provides resources to assist home visitors in helping families to contact their local family resource center.

In his presentation "Home Visiting," McWilliam (2005) outlined our promise to families as early intervention home visitors as
follows:

1. Information and service needs
    - We will inform you.
    - We will teach you how to teach and do other things with your
      child.
    - We will tell you about your child's disability.
    - We will tell you about resources.
    - We will teach you about child development.
2. Resource supports
    - We will give you access to materials you will need.
    - We will get the equipment, including assistive technology,
      you need to help your child's development.
    - We will make sure you have access to financial resources to
      which you are entitled.
3. Social supports
    - We will support you emotionally.
    - We will be positive with and about you.
    - We will be responsive to you.
    - We will pay attention to your whole family, especially the pri-
      mary caregiver.
    - We will be friendly to you.
    - We will be sensitive to you.

In the following vignette, note how the home visitor served the
family by addressing the information needs, resource needs, and emotional needs of the family while bringing intervention to the children.

*Muriel was a home visitor assigned to a set of triplets (Maggie, Brian,
and Chuckie), ages 2½, each of whom had a range of developmental
problems. They lived with their parents, Ann and George, and their
half-sister Louise, age 12. George also had a 15-year-old son who
spent summers with the family. George was a firefighter and Ann*

worked 2 days each week outside the home. When she worked, either George or a paid sitter cared for the children.

Muriel could identify the following needs for Ann and George's family.

1. With triplets, there was little time to think of quality time when one of them needed to be rescued most of the time, thus putting Ann and George in a constant crisis mode. Especially stressful was the relationship Ann had with her daughter Louise from a previous marriage. Louise at 12 was pressed into service to watch one or more of the children. Usually she accepted these duties, but at times she obviously resented this parenting role. Added to the chaos of having three children under age 3 were the developmental problems of each child. Maggie, the largest and most advanced in development, resented the attention her brothers had from their parents. Brian climbed over the fence in the back yard at every opportunity and ran toward the street. He was sweet and docile but he had no fear or memory of warnings and rules. Chuckie, the smallest and most delayed triplet, exhibited characteristics of pervasive developmental disorder. He had frequent meltdowns, particularly when thwarted, and he required much attention. Family routines revolved around day-to-day survival. The parents felt that their lives were out of control.

2. Taking the triplets out of the home presented logistics difficulties. When Muriel asked about the children's favorite places to go, Ann answered that they loved the park, but when she took them there alone she felt that they were not safe because she could not handle three children at once.

3. Keeping these children safe was of primary importance to the family and required most of the child care time. The emotional component loomed large because Ann and George realized the stresses they were under. They also worried about the burden they put on Louise but were unable to mitigate it because they needed her extra pair of hands.

DEVELOPING A PLAN OF
INTERVENTION FOR THE FAMILY

Although the family's needs seemed obvious to Muriel, the needs that Ann and George identified were primary. In their collaborative plan for intervention with Muriel, Ann and George focused on their needs for information and resources and accepted Muriel's emotional and social support for their family.

Ann and George asked for information about how to handle Chuckie's meltdowns, which were stressful for the whole family. Muriel recommended a developmental pediatrician who could give a more specific diagnosis for Chuckie. Ann and George did not ask for help keeping Brian safe in the yard nor did they seek help with Maggie's withdrawal from her brothers. Muriel suggested that Ann and George send Maggie to preschool with typical children when she was 3 because Maggie was ready to have more enriching experiences. Preschool posed a financial strain for the family but they decided it was worth the sacrifice. Muriel mentioned the fence that Brian loved to climb and wondered if it could be made higher. George, who was planning some activities away from home with his visiting son, agreed that repairing the fence would be a good project for them to work on together.

At the IFSP meeting, Muriel recommended respite care so that George and Ann could have some relief from the stress of constant care. She recommended a home-based social worker to help Ann with her relationship with her daughter Louise.

From the beginning, Ann made it plain that she considered Muriel's sessions as opportunities for her to have free time for herself. When Muriel suggested a session in which they all went to the park, Ann became enthusiastic about taking them. Both adults were busy every minute supervising the sand play, swinging, and sliding. Other children in the park were curious about the triplets and were incorporated as role models for all of the activities. Language activities just happened, as did turn taking and gross motor and fine motor activities. Ann took a video of the experience, and the whole family viewed it with George later, which served as an opportunity for language activities in describing what was happening and for building each child's self-esteem when they were the focus of the video.

Muriel modified her approach by playing with the children in their well-equipped back yard in good weather. Muriel could only have the children in the yard if Ann participated in the play because Brian ran to the fence to climb over it if he was unsupervised. Muriel had well-formulated individual goals for the children from their IFSPs, but she did not impose work on specific goals for Ann. Instead, Muriel modeled language and motor activities and pointed out to Ann how well a child was performing during play. Goals and achievements were shared during the next IFSP, and Ann was a participant in setting new goals for the next 6 months. An unplanned consequence was that Maggie, who previously had as little to do with her brothers as she could, began to play with them. At first, Maggie would not participate in Ring Around the Rosie instigated by Muriel if she had to hold a brother's hand. Gradually, however, she joined the circle because it looked like just too much fun to be left out.

Could this family have made such gains without Muriel? Up until Muriel's home visits, Ann spent her outside time with the triplets protecting them from each other and intercepting Brian before he climbed over the fence. She had no opportunity to observe the children in any developmental way or to think how she might enhance that development. Muriel identified stressors that were giving the parents a sense of loss of control and mitigated several of them. She gave them information (developmental guidance) as they observed their children and resources (pediatrician for a diagnosis, social worker for Ann's relationship with Louise, preschool for Maggie), and she built their confidence when playing with the children. She helped with the safety issue by suggesting that the fence be made higher, which George agreed to do with his older son.

Building Rapport

So far, we have addressed the tasks of the home visitor to relieve stress by providing information and resources and giving social support.

Next, we address the personal characteristics and behaviors of the home visitor and his or her role in building rapport with a family.

Personal Characteristics of the Home Visitor

In the previous vignette, Muriel's task was to provide services to help alleviate the family's stresses while providing individual intervention for each of the children. Is it enough to assess needs and develop intervention? Of course it is not. What did Muriel herself have to do with the success within this family? She had rapport with the family; if she hadn't, they would not have followed her suggestions.

If the reader did not consider that he or she had the personality to be an early interventionist, he or she would probably not be reading this book. When asked why one wants to become a professional in this field, most people would answer that they love children and that they want to help others. Many people outside the profession believe that home visitors must have a lot of patience that they themselves could not muster and that they couldn't possibly deal with the problems that home visitors encounter.

"They won't care what we know until they know that we care" is an axiom that we would do well to keep in mind. Believing that a home visitor has a caring personality is necessary but not sufficient. The family has to know that we care through our behavior. Think of the early home-visiting pioneers in Chapter 1. The families that they served had no doubt that the home visitors truly cared about them.

The apprehension that a family may feel upon learning that a home visitor is coming cannot be overestimated. As one mother said: "When the speech pathologist said she was coming out, I scrubbed everything—even the slide 'til it shone. I was so scared." There may be confusion about what an early interventionist does, particularly when the message to the family has been that they will work together on family problems. The desire to make a good first impression—to be seen as good and caring parents—can be overwhelming. In some cases, parents may not have sought out the home visitor program and may not really understand why the home visitor is there; consequently, they may not feel safe (Klass, 2007). Is this person a guest? Should she be offered refreshments as you would a guest in your home? Should we be in the living room or the playroom? Should I pick up all of the toys? The first face-to-face meeting will set the stage for the relationship building that is so important to success.

Connecting with Siblings

When we think of family relationships we often think of our relationship with the parents and other caregivers, but the siblings of a child with special needs are part of the family and have needs that mirror those of the parents—just from a different perspective. Often, we are confronted with what to do about a sibling who stays with the parent as part of the visit and who wants to interact and play with materials brought for the target child. It isn't appropriate to discuss the child with special needs or the parents' emotions when the sibling is listening. How much attention should the home visitor give to the sibling?

For children who are feeling left out and who have difficulty dealing with the emotional aspect of having a brother or sister with special needs, a resource for the parents is the Family Resource Center mentioned previously. Groups for siblings of children with special needs are led by people with experience on the group dynamics of children and adolescents who are faced with this as a challenge

in the family. Emotional issues for the sibling can be discussed in that setting with other siblings and professionals who are trained to deal with issues that cannot be addressed during the home visits.

For the situation in which a sibling must be present if a parent is present, the home visitor should try to enlist the help of the sibling. Siblings make good models for whatever the home visitor wants to show: listening to a story, rolling a ball, "feeding" the doll, rolling over, and so forth. Every home visitor has encountered the sibling who is determined to sabotage the session and vies for the mother's attention. Here we must remember that *family focused* means that all children in the family, in fact, each person in the family, is as important as any of the others. This child is communicating a need and it must be met, however distracting it may be for the visit. This sibling is the focus of sibling groups mentioned previously. If the behavior persists, it might be best to schedule the home visit when the sibling is otherwise occupied. There are always exceptions: the younger sibling who must be held, or falls down, or lets the dog in (pets are another matter), or is hungry at that moment. The home visitor who takes the time to deal with the sibling's need demonstrates to the parents that he or she cares for and is there for the whole family. Taking the time to ask about school work or to see a picture the sibling drew or providing materials for the sibling to create something during the visit that can be admired when the visit is over is time well spent.

SUMMARY

This chapter addresses the service that the family receives by an early intervention home visitor. A strong predictor of the outcome of early intervention is the quality of the relationship of a primary service provider with the family. Research has identified the family-centered practices considered to be ideal: identifying the family's most important concerns, saying something positive about the child, explaining all assessment procedures, asking whether the behaviors are typical of the child, summarizing all assessment results, and identifying the next steps for the family and the professional. The tasks of the home visitor in service to the family are primarily to provide information and services, resource supports, and social supports. Important for building rapport and relationships with the family are the personal characteristics of the home visitor and the behaviors that show caring. A spirit of collaboration should be established in the first contacts with the family. Siblings may feel left out of the home visit and should be incorporated into the session.

4

Structuring Home Visitation

"Start where you are. Use what you have.
Do what you can."

–Arthur Ashe

In Chapter 1, we addressed the framework of home visitations. Now, we implement it in order to structure our visits in keeping with sound philosophical principles. As home visitors, we strive to fulfill the following tasks:

- We must provide information about typical development and about disabilities.
- We must provide resources for families.
- We must teach families how to teach and enjoy their child.
- We must respect and work within the family's culture.
- We must nurture relationships within the family.
- We must support the families emotionally.
- We must empower parents to be and feel competent, and we must provide service that is functional and evidence-based whenever possible.

Approaches that provide information and guidance about development, offer specific information about an individual child's disability, provide resources, and empower caregivers are most effective.

In Chapters 2 and 3, foundations for understanding and developing a productive relationship with families were established. First, phone contacts were discussed as were guidelines for the first visit. In that crucial first visit, the home visitor is advised to listen as the family tells the story of life with the child, goes through a typical day in the household, and establishes some priorities for the course of future visits and intervention. Building trust is not only an important first step, but it also is equally important throughout the intervention process.

So far, we have addressed *services that the family receives*. Now we will address the other part of home-based services: *intervention that the child receives*. As Shonkoff and Phillips wrote:

> Programs that combine child-focused educational activities with explicit attention to parent–child interaction patterns and relationship building appear to have the greatest impacts. In contrast, services that are based on generic family support, often without a clear delineation of intervention strategies matched directly to measurable objectives, appear to be less effective. (2000, p. 11)

After reassuring the family that you care, it is important to tell them what you know—to engage in strategies with the family and child that will move them toward the goals that have been mutually agreed on. For the new home visitor, this can be the scary part. For the experienced professional who has worked with children without considering service to the family, this is the comfortable and familiar part. The latter group, however, will need more skills in the home than "dumping the clinic on the living room floor" (McWilliam, 2005). The focus of this chapter is what *happens* during a home visit in early intervention. What does the home visitor actually *do*?

APPROACHES TO INTERVENTION

The particular characteristics of the child, including the nature and severity of the disability and the child's health status and temperament, will point to the kinds of interventions that are most appropriate. The needs of a child who is medically fragile and technology dependent or a child who has a severe behavioral disorder will differ from those of a child who, although severely delayed, is in relatively good health and has an easygoing temperament. Other factors related to the disability might be the number of professionals and agencies necessary to meet a child's complex needs or the degree of responsiveness and attachment demonstrated by the child for the parent or caregiver.

Similarly, family characteristics, including priorities and values, family structure, resources, cultural background, and attitudes toward intervention and disability, will help determine the specifics of the home visiting approach. Some mothers might prefer home visits that focus a great deal on learning about the disability, accessing research and web sites related to the disability (see Chapter 3), and gaining as much information as possible about different intervention services. Other mothers with limited social and financial resources may need a more relationship-based approach that focuses on providing her with emotional and material supports, as well as on strengthening her relationship with her infant (Klein & Chen, 2006).

Home Visitor Direct Approach

The home visitor who has a professional background in a specialty area may focus primarily on the child. This direct approach includes drill, drill-play, and home visitor-modeled formats (explained later in this chapter) that may involve stimulus–response–reward. A high level of structure is provided with clear targets and reinforcement schedules. Drawbacks to this approach center around the child's inability to use the target skills outside of the session (Harris, 2002). That is, children cannot transfer skills learned in home visit time to non-home visit time. Specialists need not be limited to direct approaches, however. Their roles can be broadened to include consultative services with other specialists, generalists, and caregivers.

Home Visitor Indirect Approach

This approach is also referred to as *naturalistic* or *child-centered* intervention. The focus is on helping the caregiver carry out activities during the time with the child. The home visitor follows the child's focus of attention and reinforces the child's actions that occur as a result of the child's interest in the play environment. It most closely follows the way typically developing children learn. Naturalistic techniques may be employed by generalists and caregivers in any setting in the home or community. This approach has the advantage of, perhaps, being applied more hours than the one-hour visit by the specialist. As McWilliam (2005) stated, it isn't the contact hours, it's the intervention the child receives that creates changes. The home visitor gives developmental guidance and suggests resources while helping the caregiver to problem solve. She acts as a sounding board for the caregiver. That does not mean that the home visitor does not do some modeling, but it is more along the lines of, "Would you like to try that?" "Would you like me to help you (show you) with that?"

There are well-founded differences in the appropriateness of each of the above approaches that are grounded in the child's disability. Highly structured approaches are most often used with children on the autism spectrum (see Chapter 6) and with apraxia, where drill involving repetition of a motor act and hands-on help works well. Indirect and combination approaches work best with children who have language delays, who lack childhood experiences for natural learning, and who do not respond well to direction.

Combination of Home Visitor–Directed and Child-Centered Approach

Strategies in this category involve some combination of direct and indirect approaches adapted to a particular environment, child, or behavioral goal. Following the child's lead continues to be a core component. The child's environment is structured around activities of high interest and motivation (Harris, 2002). As any caregiver knows, not all learning activities are interesting to children. Activities that are interesting almost guarantee that children will benefit from the learning opportunities. The home visitor might do symbolic play with the child, encourage joint attention in book sharing, introduce stair climbing, stretch muscles, or set up ways to practice pointing and pincer grasp. The caregiver is encouraged to carefully observe and try out the modeled strategy. With each strategy, the home visitor explains why it is being used. For example, when the home visitor is looking at a book with a child, she tells the caregiver the importance of shared attention for improved concentration, for receptive language, and for relationship building—all skills needed for future learning and language development. The home visitor should, however, be prepared for a caregiver to be uncomfortable with a modeled strategy and consequently not adopt it.

When the focus of the intervention is on adult–child interaction, readers should refer to the models of interaction intervention thoroughly discussed in Chapter 5. These include adult–adult and triadic models. We have discussed these models separately, but home visitors may combine them with the indirect and combination approaches reviewed above, depending on the needs of the family.

TEAMWORK AND ROLE RELEASE

Teamwork has been discussed earlier in the context of families being included as equal members of the intervention team. A great variety can be found in the key persons making home visits. Families can experience stress and frustration related to the many providers and the need for coordination of services. For example, they may receive conflicting recommendations for activities and interventions for their child, or they may not understand the roles of the various service providers. Therefore, the family is best served when these services work together and collaborate (Klein & Chen, 2006). McWilliam (2005) called the "Got a need, get a service" mentality outmoded because a primary caregiver or home visitor can incorporate the expertise of many disciplines into their interventions.

It is essential that occupational/sensory integration therapists, physical therapists, and cognitive and learning specialists combine their resources to examine not only the function of their individual specialty, but also how the systems of hearing, cognition, sensory integration—to name just a few—work in concert to optimize the integrated skills of a developing child. Not only should professionals in varying disciplines meet around the table at the IFSP meeting, they also should communicate regularly. The importance of co-treating should be valued. Goals and activities for sensory integration, physical therapy, speech, and development of auditory skills can be integrated into single activities. For example, a child's sensory integration needs should be met during a speech session. That is, his back should be fully supported and his feet placed firmly on the floor. Similarly, the goals of occupational therapy can be integrated appropriately into a cognitive activity such as when a child is helped to use a pincer grasp to reach for a puzzle piece or to use both hands to build a block tower.

To that end, a *transdisciplinary* model including *role release* is recommended for planning and implementing intervention. The transdisciplinary approach means that team members work across disciplinary boundaries, i.e., they may release their traditional professional role and assign or allow another member of the team to fulfill that role, including actually training another professional in one's own discipline. Boundaries between specialty disciplines are loose— goals and objectives that seem to fall into a specialty area can be carried out by a generalist or another specialist. When professionals share one another's perspectives and skills to provide a whole child model of delivery, the child is protected from receiving *splinter therapy* when only isolated skills are addressed. It should be the goal of every early intervention program to collaborate and integrate these principles and strategies to address each of a child's special needs. Teams using the transdisciplinary model have reported positive effects on their team members (Kaczmarek, Pennington & Goldstein, 2000). However, some professionals who feel they are giving away their expertise to those without the background to use it may feel threatened by the transdisciplinary model.

ASSESSMENT FOR PROGRAM PLANNING AND MONITORING

Program planning is the natural consequence of an assessment process. Through the assessment process, information obtained from the evaluation of the child will be integrated with the parents' priorities to develop a meaningful plan for future visits. Comprehensive program planning looks at the needs of a child as a member of the family. It responds to those needs and to the family's needs, building on the strengths of both. The child's needs should be expressed in outcomes or objectives that include opportunities for skill acquisition, parent–child interaction guidance interventions, development of presymbolic/symbolic play functions, learning strategy intervention, and provision of environmental and social structures that will make experiences meaningful. The IFSP should also include services and supports that contribute to the well-being of the family as caregivers to the child (Poulson, 2003).

Formal and Informal Assessment

Traditional educational and medical models of service delivery have viewed assessment only as the necessary prerequisite for the obtainment of services needed for children. Typically, such assessment focuses on psychometric data that will certify a child's eligibility for a particular program. Program planning based on such data usually centers on a deficit model and highlights developmental milestone failures that need intervention. The family-centered model, however, incorporates looking at the individual child in the context of how developmental and interactional strengths, vulnerabilities, and disabilities interact to influence the child's capacity to effectively deal with persons, objects, and events of his or her world. The family-centered model sees the assessment process as the first significant step in quality intervention and not merely an entry point for intervention programs (Poulson, 2003). Multiple assessment procedures can be used: record reviews, formal assessment, parent interviews, informal play, and observation of the ways the caregiver and child relate.

Formal assessment calls for the use of systematic observations using standardized procedures. There are several norm-referenced and criterion-referenced assessment tools that will provide a framework for the evaluation of fine motor, gross motor, adaptive behavior, receptive-expressive language, and daily living skills. These tools will

yield information about the attained developmental level for each domain of development. The well-educated home visitor will have studied these assessment tools, and they will not be addressed here.

The unique opportunity for the home visitor is for a more relaxed, informal approach that need not involve the administration of prescribed items but can rely on the observations of the child's responses to his everyday play, feeding, dressing, and social situations. The child can, thus, be observed in spontaneous interactions with toys, objects, and people of his choice. Making time for this aspect of program planning cannot be overemphasized. Several areas of development are usually assessed informally: emotional development, social interaction, presymbolic/symbolic functioning, and select sensorimotor schemas. Several factors, such as those noted in Table 4.1, must be integrated with the behavioral data obtained during the assessment process to develop the clear understanding of the child's skills and special needs that is required in planning a subsequent program (Poulson, 2003).

Observation should capture how the child understands, anticipates, and signals during such daily living activities as parent–child play, bathing, feeding, diapering, dressing, being lifted, and going to bed and how he relates to familiar toys, family members, and household pets. Parents should determine whether the assessment process adequately captures the abilities of their child. Children provide valu-

Table 4.1. Factors to be considered in interpretation of assessment

State of alertness
Social-emotional qualities
Capacity for self-regulation
Prematurity
Neonatal history
Impact of specific disabling conditions on the acquisition of skills
Nutrition and physical health status of the child
Medical history
Family history of separations, stresses, and changes
Experiential opportunity to interact with objects, people, and events
Cultural beliefs and values of the family
Exposure to two languages or language other than that of the examiner
Medications given to the child during or before the assessment process

able information about their temperament, regulatory capacity, and style of interaction by the manner in which they engage in the assessment process: social signaling behaviors such as eye contact, prolonged regard, mutual gazing, gaze aversion, smiling, turning to voice, vocalizing, joint attention, object pointing, and raising arms to be held. These factors often play as salient a role in program planning as does the developmental data.

Such a comprehensive assessment process may not be accomplished in one home visit. Rather, assessment is an ongoing process that is incorporated into the fabric of future home visits. Caregivers have a continuing opportunity to provide input as progress is assessed for the next IFSP. Constant monitoring of progress allows home visitors the opportunity to revise intervention according to the nature of the child's progress.

STRUCTURE OF THE HOME VISIT

Visits can be weekly, monthly, as needed, just before an IFSP, or as an occasional component of a program that is primarily center based. This chapter addresses the structure of visits in a traditional home visit program where home visits outnumber center or clinic visits. The intensity of home visits depends on the child, the family, and the goals of the IFSP. Visits are traditionally one hour because one hour

is a unit for billing by the agency. Less traditional half hour sessions may be arranged if they fit a child's attention span best. The format described below assumes that visits are weekly for one hour.

Format of a Home Visit

Home visits in early intervention are known to follow somewhat the same format at the beginning and the end of the visit. There is considerable variation, however, on what happens in the middle, which takes up the majority of the visit. These variations have philosophical underpinnings. A solid personal philosophy together with knowledge of effective strategies are essential. A format for the visit, after the first get-acquainted visits addressed in Chapter 3, may be the following: 1) Arrival and Greeting, 2) What's New?, 3) Today's Activities, 4) Reflect and Plan for the Next Visit, 5) What's Coming Up?, 6) Anything Else?, and 7) Good-bye. The primary elements of a home visit are discussed in Table 4.2. (See the Appendix for the record-keeping form.)

Arrival and Greeting

This part of the visit, including introductions and hand cleansing, has been discussed in Chapter 3. It is advisable to bring along a large,

Table 4.2. Elements of a home visit

Arrival and Greeting
Exchange greetings with all family members and visitors. Cleanse hands.

What's New?
Review events of the week. Record progress or concerns.

Today's Activities
Direct and indirect intervention may include listening, suggestions, assessment, modeling, review, new activities, and so forth. Record.

Reflect and Plan for Next Visit
With caregiver, note if activity was comfortable, if it should be tried again, how it could be modified, how it could be included in daily routines, and if the purpose of the activity is understood. What would the caregiver want to do next time? Are there resources the home visitor should bring next time? Record. This is the next lesson plan.

What's Coming Up?
In the next week, are there changes in routine, visitors, outings, or visits by other professionals? Physician visits? (A list of questions can be formulated to ask other professionals.) Record.

Anything Else?
Allow time here for anything the caregiver has not brought up.
Record keeping and good-bye
Leave the top sheet of the Visit Record with the caregiver. Gather belongings and leave.

washable blanket that can be used as a defined space on the floor for the home visitor, the child, and the mother to sit on if it appears that there is no clean space on the floor. The parent may ask if the home visitor would like water or a beverage. It may be important to the parent to offer something to a guest in the home, and the home visitor may actually offend by not accepting. Sitting for a few minutes with a beverage is not wasted time because it establishes a segue into the next part of the visit.

What's New?

The record-keeping form in the Appendix has a space for recording the answers to this question about what has happened since the last visit. Of particular importance are doctor visits, outings, unusual visits from others, illnesses, and changes in behavior. This may be the time that the home visitor hears that last week's suggestions were acted on, or the parent may say that things were so chaotic this week that nothing was tried. It also may be that the parent does not think of something until much later in the visit or at the end, at which time it should be recorded. At this point, the home visitor can ask about a decrease in any behavior that is the focus of intervention, such as vomiting episodes or crying in the night. By asking specific questions followed by, "Anything else?" the home visitor avoids cutting off the flow of information.

Today's Activities

What happens at this juncture may vary depending on the home visitor's approach to intervention (direct, indirect, or combined) and on the home visitor's professional background. This is where the personal philosophy discussed in Chapter 1 becomes important. A quick review: *Experience changes the brain,* thus it would follow that we must provide experiences wherein a child wants to do something, learns how to do it, and repeats the successful action. *We allow a child to learn in his or her individual way* and we provide developmental guidance. *Development is optimal when built on nurturing and emotional relationships. The parents know their child best. Culture influences every aspect of development.* Given these philosophical principles, it seems that what happens next in the visit should follow a naturalistic, non-contrived course, built on individual child development. It is assumed that parents are emotionally invested in the course of development and will partner with the interventionist in planning and evaluating the course of intervention. Specific strategies are addressed later in this chapter.

Where to Begin

Because the IFSP has specific outcomes that have been agreed on, it would seem reasonable to begin with the first outcome and proceed with the program plan. The next step up in development, however, is not the place to begin the focus of the sessions. Instead, *start from where the child is;* that is, find the developmental stage the child has mastered and enjoys and reinforce that. Beginning at the next stage can lead to frustration for the home visitor and the parent. Success and trust are the goals in early visits.

> *Marilyn, a home visitor, assessed Matthew for cognitive and communication skills. Matthew was very delayed; he made only fleeting eye contact, avoided interaction, did not point or look at books, used no signs, did not turn to his name, and did not have a sense of turn-taking. His mother Joyce's main concern was communication. Marilyn was stumped about where to begin with Matthew. He seemed to have no skills to scaffold. His IFSP goals, "respond to verbal and gestural commands" and "wave bye-bye," seemed far beyond him. Joyce said he did enjoy Pat-a-cake, which he did by clapping his hands a few times. She showed Marilyn that when she wore a Burger King Crown while feeding him, Matthew looked at her. That was where Marilyn would start. She and Joyce engaged him in Pat-a-Cake, working to engage him in longer clapping. She suggested that Joyce put a sticker on her nose to draw his attention to her face and reward him for looking at her. When Marilyn returned to the home the following week, Matthew had progressed with longer attention spans in both activities. Marilyn asked Joyce to show what she had achieved and commented on her success. Her next step was to add rhythm to the game together with rolling and stirring motions. She explained to Joyce that conversation consists of turns and interactions and together they were working toward communication.*

Toy Bag or Not?

There is a difference of opinion concerning the home visitor's bringing a bag of toys versus using only materials already in the home. In the former, the home visitor should be prepared for the child or sibling to immediately clamor for the toy bag. Very little can be accomplished until all of its contents are examined, which is a definite disadvantage. McWilliam (2005) argued for using materials already found in the home because they then could be used in appropriate ways between visits. In the rare home where there are no toys, or where the toys are not developmentally appropriate, household items can be used as toys. Brandt (2001) has cataloged household

items that can be used by children at various developmental stages (see the Appendix). For each item there is a sensory play strategy, more advanced play schemes, and language concepts that the toy can help to develop, all written from the child's perspective.

Reflect and Plan for the Next Visit: Recommendations

Whatever today's activities may be, the home visitor should move to the next step of the visit—Reflect and Plan for the Next Visit—well before the current visit ends. Allow at least 10 minutes for reflection and planning. The home visitor will need to make notes about the visit at this point and can ask questions such as, "Do you want to try that during the week?" "Are you comfortable with that?" or, in the case of increasing a skill such as staying on the tummy without crying, "How long do you think he stayed? . . . Good! That is an improvement of a minute from last week." Progress is noted, but not just by the home visitor. The parent is also evaluator and recorder.

This is the time to plan what will happen during the time between visits. If a consultation is called for, record that on the Home Visit Recording Form with things the home visitor will do or bring to the next visit. Make a note of objects or reading materials that are left with the caregiver. One copy of this recording form will be left with the parent and one taken with the home visitor. A task of the home visitor is to assist the parent in assembling a notebook in which to file all the session records. Such a notebook is also valuable for keeping important information concerning the child's interventions: assessment reports, medical records, cards from service providers, etc. The session record can be reviewed at the next visit and is a welcome reminder to a home visitor who has many cases to remember. What is written on the record under "Recommendations for Next Visit" may serve as the "lesson plan" for that visit, keeping in mind that it may change depending on many dynamics of the child and the family.

What's Coming Up?

If the home visitor does not ask about what's coming up, visits to other professionals, physicians, and recreational activities can be missed. There may be questions the home visitor would like the parent to ask the physician, or recreational activities may be planned that present opportunities to practice functional activities. Visits from friends and relatives may occur that change the dynamics of the family and their routines.

Anything Else?

Experienced home visitors know that often the subject that the parent wants to discuss will not come up until the home visitor is ready to leave. The subject may be important, but when it is left until the end of the visit there may not be enough time to address it adequately. If the issue can wait, the home visitor can say, "That is really important and I want to talk about it. Can we put that down as the first thing to talk about the next time?" If it is a crisis situation, the home visitor must deal with it the best way he or she can and the visit will have to run overtime. Of course, the subject should have come up with "What's New?" but sometimes, for whatever reason, the parent did not feel comfortable mentioning it until the last minute. If a parent has a pattern of this behavior, the home visitor will do well to end the session and get to this subject earlier, when adequate time can be given to the subject.

Record Keeping and Good-Bye

If possible, the record-keeping form should be three sheets of different color carbonless paper. What is written on the top sheet (e.g., white) goes through to the home visitor's copy (e.g., yellow) and to the agency's copy (e.g., green). The home visitor tears off the top sheet of the record-keeping form and gives it to the parent, gathers up anything she brought with her, and leaves. This is usually a time to practice the functional skill of having the child say good-bye, whether by gesture or verbally.

STRATEGIES FOR INTERVENTION

In the following sections, we will look at various strategies in current use for early intervention. Not all are research based, but all are effective in at least some situations.

Unique Role of Modeling

Because literally all strategies in the next section involve modeling to some degree, it is appropriate to discuss modeling as a technique here. According to Keilty,

> For true modeling to occur, the interventionist is actively demonstrating the strategies with a full explanation of what she or he is doing and thinking about while engaged in a two-way conversation with the caregiver. After modeling occurs, caregivers need the opportunity to practice and receive feedback. (2008, p. 36)

The eight steps of modeling (McWilliam, 2005) are listed in Table 4.3. It is important to emphasize that a child must be given adequate time to respond to a model. If the child does not respond, the demonstration should be simplified or separated into parts.

Strategies in Current Use

There are many strategies from which to choose. We can think of strategies in a *continuum of naturalness*. Eisenberg (2004) outlined five strategies from drill to free play (see Table 4.4) on this continuum. To illustrate each of these, we will use Jack, whose target behavior is making eye contact, and the intervener will be the home visitor. The caregiver, coached by the home visitor, also can easily carry out these strategies.

Drill

Drill consists of an antecedent stimulus, the child's response, and a consequent reinforcement. The antecedent stimulus may include instruction or modeling. Only the target response is accepted, and a response by the child is required. The motivation for the child comes from the consequent reinforcer, which may be praise, a token, or play activity (e.g., taking a turn). The reinforcer is unrelated to the target. Prompting may be given and feedback is provided about the accuracy of the response.

Table 4.3. The eight steps of modeling

Talk to the parent about your suggestion.
If the parent does not appear to understand, ask if the parent would like to be shown.
Tell the parent what you are going to do.
Do it.
Tell the parent what you did, and point out the results.
Ask the parent if he or she would like to try it.
If the answer is yes, watch the parent trying it. If the answer is no, leave it alone.
If yes, praise the parent and give a limited amount of corrective feedback.

Source: McWilliam (2005).

Table 4.4. Intervention strategies

Drill
Drill play
Structured play
Quasi-naturalistic play
Free play
Routine-based intervention
Family-guided activity-based approaches

Source: Eisenberg (2004).

The home visitor moves her face into Jack's line of vision while he is looking at a toy. She moves the toy to her face and says, "Jack, look at me." When Jack looks, the home visitor gives a verbal reward, "Yay! You looked at me!" or a token reinforcer such as food. In this case, she gave Jack the toy he was looking at.

Drill Play

Drill play uses play as both a motivational event prior to the child's response and a consequent reinforcer. In all other aspects, drill play is like drill above.

Jack and the home visitor are playing a game that Jack enjoys: They are taking turns shaking a tambourine. The home visitor moves the tambourine close to her face and says, "Look, Jack!" When Jack looks, she gives him the tambourine to take a turn. After his turn, the home visitor takes the tambourine and says, "My turn," and repeats the game.

Structured Play

Structured play is a further modification of drill therapy, in which play is used only for motivation to encourage the child to make attempts at the desired response. The child gets to participate in the play regardless of his correct or incorrect responses. A second attempt after an unsuccessful attempt is only provided if the child is receptive.

Jack and the home visitor are playing with a stuffed bear and putting it to bed. The home visitor holds the bear up to her face and says, "Look, Jack. Bear wants to go to sleep now." Jack reaches for the bear and makes eye contact with the home visitor. The home visitor gives Jack the bear and he puts the bear into the crib. After playing that the bear has gotten up and eaten, the home visitor repeats the procedure. This time Jack does not make eye contact but gets the bear anyway.

Quasi-Naturalistic Play

In this approach, the environment is set up to encourage the child to produce the desired behavior. Included in this model is incidental teaching, in which prompts to assist the child in producing the target are given only after the child has initiated an interaction. Embedded routines with the caregiver supplying the incidental teaching are examples. The home visitor and the caregiver decide what the targets are and go through the already existing routines of the day that provide a reason for the target to take place. Quasi-naturalistic play has many elements of routine-based intervention, which is discussed later.

Jack's mother reported that Jack loved to watch certain tapes. He initiated an interaction in which he went to the TV, pointed to the tape he wanted, and then stood facing the TV waiting for her. It was her idea to wait to put the tape in until Jack looked at her. After pointing at the TV and whining, his signal for putting a tape in the VCR, and getting no response from his mother, Jack looked at her to see what she was doing and she immediately put the tape in. She also said, "Good, Jack. You looked at me."

Free Play

In free play, the child talks or acts in response to what is happening, but the specific opportunities for responding are not determined by the adult. This is *child-centered play*. The adult follows the child's lead and provides natural consequences without giving any feedback about accuracy. As in quasi-naturalistic play, the environment may be set up to elicit target behaviors, but no prompts are given if the child does not produce the desired target.

> *Jack and his mother are looking at a picture book. As Jack points to pictures, his mother names them. She pauses between his pointing and her response to give Jack a chance to look at her before she names the picture. She will name the picture, whether or not Jack looks at her.*

Routine-Based Intervention

In addition to the five strategies from Eisenberg (2004), we have added two strategies to Table 4.4 that are currently in favor in early intervention. One practice that is being validated by research is embedding intervention goals in everyday activities (Bernheimer & Weisner, 2007). This practice evolved from the traditionally more structured method of instructing the parent on how to *do therapy* in the ensuing week. In essence, several minutes per day were assigned to parent–child practice, with the home visitor evaluating and checking for progress in the next visit. How much better it is to show the parent how to give a child experiences embedded in existing daily routines that would further the mutually agreed-on goals. Such an approach seems vastly more family friendly than assignments that take up another portion of the parents' already overloaded schedule. This approach has been widely advocated in the absence of empirical data to the contrary. In fact, through extensive family stories during longitudinal research, Bernheimer and Weisner (2007) found that interventions were not likely to have an impact if they were not slotted into daily family routines.

Routines include mealtime, bath time, caring for pets, dressing and undressing, walking outside, playing at the park, shopping for food, bedtime stories, play groups and play dates. For example, in the bath time routine, naming body parts, the concepts of hot and cold with water, and in and out of the tub are natural language-learning opportunities if the parent voices them while bathing the child. Bath time also provides an opportunity for range of motion exercises.

Family-Guided Activity-Based Approaches

Family-guided activity-based approaches enhance teaching and learning by embedding intervention outcomes into *child-initiated* play, daily routines, and activities identified by the family as frequent, meaningful, and comfortable (Family-Guided Approaches to Collaborative Early-Intervention Training and Services [FACETS], 2007). Being family guided is an ongoing process that facilitates the family–home visitor partnership. Families are provided with information and given choices from the initial point of contact. The family-guided approach promotes family decision making by providing opportunities for families to make meaningful choices, *including the choice to not be involved* at a point in time.

The family-guided approach differs from other models in that it provides families with flexible options for involvement plus the support and resources to make informed decisions about their participation. (In Chapter 3, the intervention with the family with triplets is an example of the Family-Guided Activity-Based Model.) No option is excluded from consideration. Emphasis is placed on supporting parent choices for identification and involvement in activities, routines, and play to assist their infant or toddler to acquire functional skills—the skills the child will need in his or her daily life. The complete Family-Guided Activity-Based Approach may be found at http://www.parsons.Lsi.ku.edu/facets or by searching on the Internet for Facets Kansas University. Following are lists of what FACETS is and is not about.

FACETS is

- Responding to family concerns and priorities with a flexible program in the family's natural environment (e.g., Grandma's home for child care)
- Involving the family in teaching functional skills during daily routines using their own objects and toys
- Considering all possibilities within family routines and activities as contexts for intervention
- Using existing family routines and providing opportunities for functional activities (e.g., when Daddy comes home, bedtime)

- Respecting the family's choice of routines (e.g., feeding the horses) for intervention and providing supports and suggestions for modifications
- Considering informal support systems (e.g., grandparents, neighbors)

FACETS is not

- Designing activities or assigning routines to target outcomes or arranging a routine to embed outcomes
- Prescribing certain routines (e.g., snack) as the perfect time to target certain skills (e.g., fine motor abilities)

EFFICACY OF STRATEGIES

Policy and practice that reflect the knowledge base gained from evidence-based practice are most certainly in the best interest of children and families involved in early intervention programs everywhere. We can be reasonably sure that early intervention has a positive effect on both target children and their families, but to date we do not have much empirical evidence about what are the most salient components in our work with families. Furthermore, early intervention programs contain numerous components, and it is difficult to identify which of those components or clusters of components are associated with good outcomes. We follow what we have been told in courses and workshops or we buy from a publisher a ready-made program that is purported to have good results. Few of our methods can meet the standards set in the health professions where a practice or method is tested with a well-designed double-blind study. We can, however, put the above strategies to the test of efficacy advocated by Fenichel (2001): soundness, acceptability, quality of implementation, and functionality.

Soundness

When looking at all the strategies discussed previously and the evidence for their success, we find that all have evidence for their soundness and all are effective when applied to the appropriate situation, child, and family. A number of researchers (Fey, 1986; Law, 1997; Shriberg & Kwaitkowski, 1982) have looked at the efficacy of the different models for improving communication skills. Eisenberg (2004) has summarized these researchers' findings as follows: the drill therapies provide opportunities for a large number of attempts at specific language targets, and there is evidence that these therapies are effective in getting the child to produce new language forms. These new forms, however, may not generalize into spontaneous language when the therapy session is over. More naturalistic approaches have been shown to generalize better into spontaneous use. (The more structured intervention approaches—including drill play and structured play—may provide the extra support that some children with significant language impairment need.) In general, the most naturally occurring and most functional and routine-based strategies yield the best results for most children.

Acceptability

Now we apply the test of acceptability. Acceptance by the intended recipients is crucial. If it doesn't make sense, it won't be replicated. As McWilliam (2005) said, "Parents need to own the goals." How readily accepted by the caregivers are the various strategies? For example, does it really matter whether or not we embed intervention goals in routines?

Of the small body of research designed to give us acceptability data, Dunst, Bruder, Trivette, and Hamby (2006) summarized two studies in which parents were asked how they felt about embedding intervention goals in family routines as opposed to using spontaneous activities in family routines that resulted in teachable moments. Results suggest that parents prefer to think of creating ways to reach the desired behaviors in normal family routines, instead of having structure imposed on them. Parents have their own ideas about how they and their children should participate in family life. If they feel that the home visitor is meddling by telling them how to behave in their routines, their reactions can be negative. The following are examples of home visitor-structured and home visitor-guided, but spontaneous, routines.

Emily's parents and her home visitor have prioritized her intervention goals as 1) Emily will progress from cruising to independent walking and 2) Emily will use one word to label pictures in a book.

Home Visitor Structured

1) Emily's mother was advised to embed taking independent steps in the routine of Emily going from the playroom to her high chair at mealtime. Emily's mother was to put Emily in a cruise position holding on to a table in the playroom, announce that it was time to eat, and stand near Emily with her arms out to encourage Emily to take the few steps to the highchair. 2) At bedtime, Emily's mother was to use the routine of the bedtime story. She was asked to look at Goodnight Moon *with Emily. She was to name the objects in the story as Emily pointed to them. Then, she would wait to see if Emily attempted to name the objects after her model.*

Both of the above are strategies that use routines to further intervention goals and they would probably give desired results. The contrast with the following where the mother knew the goal and used a spontaneous routine is small, but significant.

Home Visitor Guided (Spontaneous)

1) Emily's mother is well aware of the goal that is a precursor to walking. When Emily attempted a step from the coffee table to the TV, her mother clapped and praised her. Emily laughed and tried it again for more praise. 2) Emily's mother sometimes looked at books with Emily before her nap time, bedtime, or various times during the day. Emily could always choose her own book. Emily's mother knew the best way to elicit the desired behavior from Emily. When Emily climbed on her lap at the doctor's office, they looked at a magazine together, and when her mother pointed to a picture, Emily said "baby." In both examples, Emily's mother was rewarded with the desired behavior from Emily and she repeated her stimulus and reward behavior regardless of the setting. When the home visitor asked, "What's new?" at her next visit, these successes were recorded and praised by the home visitor.

Quality of Implementation

Our third test is quality of implementation. The quality of the intervention that is actually delivered and received by target children and families is of fundamental importance (Fenichel, 2001). The ultimate impact of any intervention is dependent on both provider (home visitor) expertise and the quality and continuity of the personal relationship established between the service provider and the family being served. As we have seen from the examples above, how and in what manner natural learning environment practices are operationalized are important in terms of the benefits to the child and the feelings of well-being of the caregiver.

Intervention for the child depends on what occurs between visits (McWilliam, 2005). That is, children learn skills and make developmental gains as a result of repeated interactions with their environment, dispersed over time—not in massed trials once or twice a week. Thus, recommended practices are those that focus on supporting regular caregivers—that is, the people who spend enough time with the child to make a difference—to carry out effective interventions. It would seem that for the early interventionist home visitor who is a generalist, quality of implementation includes prioritizing goals and moving toward them, problem solving and developmental guidance, and some modeling. Hands-on work with the child will be limited more specifically to demonstration, assessment, and showing that the visitor cares for the child; seldom will it be to teach the child directly.

There are parents, however, who want structured *homework,* and there are children who are passive and unmotivated to take risks and must be led by a hands-on approach. There are parents who are overwhelmed and want the home visitor to "fix it" without their involvement. These attitudes are not conducive to the best quality of implementation but they must be dealt with and the ideal strategy must be approximated, keeping in mind that the most naturalistic and functional strategy is probably the most efficacious.

This in no way diminishes the role of each of the individual disciplines; professionals from the various disciplines have expertise that is very much needed by regular caregivers. Specialists will need to understand that quality of implementation means that intervention suggestions need to be customized to the individual caregiver who might not carry out the interventions the way the specialist would if the specialist lived with the child (Rapport, McWilliam & Smith, 2004).

Functionality

Our final test is of functionality. When we examine the strategies above, we can see that *drill* would be the least natural and functional and *family-guided activity-based* the most natural and functional of those mentioned. Drill is used to teach a child a skill that is planned as functional, but it is not functional in the teaching. The new skill is learned in isolation and is not connected to a function the child needs at the time. It may be, however, the easiest and often the only approach that is practical for a particular child and family. We won't throw out drill, but we will try for naturalistic approaches and to quickly tie drill to natural consequences whenever possible.

A comprehensive study of best practices in early intervention was undertaken by Rapport et al. (2004), who sought information from literature reviews, scientific experts, stakeholder focus groups, and field validation of the practices. The most salient of the points uncovered in this research are these: Interventionists (home visitors) select child and family priorities for intervention based on *child and family functioning* (not services) and use activities within the range of current functioning (i.e., individually appropriate activities). For example, oral-motor activities might be prescribed to improve a child's oral-motor tone. This is considered a *service* because it does not address *why* the child needs to have better oral-motor tone. In contrast, a *function* focus would be to teach a child to chew so that he can eat more solid food. A service focus does not readily identify the functional outcome, whereas a function focus, by definition, does. Another important point of a function focus is that interventions tend to be appropriate for regular routines and able to be carried out by regular caregivers (versus specialists only). They also are naturally delivered at a higher rate (multiple times per day) than service-focused interventions, which are directly linked to intervention provided by a specialist (e.g., once a week).

CONCLUSIONS FROM TESTS OF EFFICACY

Thus, the best strategies from the research will be
- Naturalistic
- Spontaneous in family routines
- Accepted by caregivers
- Well implemented
- Functional

Kaili, who is visually impaired, is staying at her grandmother Tutu's house. She needs a diaper change. Kaili sits on the floor banging a kitchen whisk on a stainless steel bowl and then on the floor and back again to a plastic bowl. Occasionally she stops to lick the cold strands of the whisk with her tongue. She is banging so loudly that she doesn't hear the approaching footsteps of Tutu, who suddenly whisks Kaili into the air onto her shoulder (Kaili didn't drop the whisk.) Tutu carries Kaili into the bedroom and, without a word, plops her back onto the bed. With quick efficiency, the pants are pulled down, the diaper pulled off, the bottom wiped (yikes, that is cold!), a new diaper taped on, the pants pulled up, a quick kiss to the forehead, and then back on the floor again—this time facing the opposite direction.

Kaili's daily routine of diaper changing is a natural opportunity to develop language, motor, self-help, and cognitive skills. The home visitor could have helped Kaili's Tutu identify one of Kaili's daily routines to work on language or transitions or self-help. Tutu could have let Kaili know it was time for a diaper change by touching the new diaper to her leg or handing it to her. She could have carried Kaili or she could have pulled Kaili in a blanket or laundry basket to the bedroom to give her a connection with movement other than through the air. Tutu could have prompted Kaili through words and touch to raise her legs to help with taking off her pants. In this way, Kaili learns from an everyday routine. She learns sequence (what happens next), and from beginning to end she learns to associate actions and the name of real objects and events with experiences. The home visitor can help Tutu think about the things that are used during a diaper change and put them together for Kaili to explore and Tutu to name. The container could hold wipes, washcloth, diaper, powder, and whatever else would be appropriate. When Kaili is old enough, she can get the container when requested and hand the items to Tutu.

The container idea can be extended to any area of the house and used for any routine. Regular daily routines and schedules provide a variety of concrete experiences to encourage communication skills.

PARENTS AS INTERVENTIONISTS

Providing the most effective nonstructured play intervention requires much parent education and is hard work for both the home visitor and caregivers. It is often given up as too difficult. Family-guided and routines-based interventions are rewarding to child and caregivers and should be used when appropriate and discarded when not appropriate. Goldstein, Walker, and Fey (2005) summarized the advantages of using parents as interventionists:

1. They provide a way to maximize the chance that intervention takes place consistently, frequently, and in functional contexts.
2. The quality of intervention is greater with parents embedding intervention, increasing the chance of intervention of sufficient intensity.
3. Caregivers taught to facilitate development of their children feel more competent and confident. They comment on developing higher expectations for their children.

As these authors pointed out, however, implementation of naturalistic strategies may require time, energy, expertise, and the type of relationship with the child that are beyond the means of many parents. Furthermore, taking that much responsibility for the intervention is beyond the desire and ability of some parents. The ability of caregivers to attend to the individualized needs of young children is influenced by both their internal resources (e.g., emotional health, social competence, intelligence, educational attainment, personal family history) and the external circumstances of their lives (e.g., family environment, social networks, employment status, economic security, experience with discrimination). The cumulative burden of multiple risk factors and sources of stress compromises the capacity of a caregiver to promote sound health and development (Fenichel, 2001). Many children with special needs are in foster care and single-parent families. Homes of children with special needs face more stresses and social risk factors than homes of children with typical development, as the NEILS (Scarborough et al., 2006) report shows. In short, as in the FACETS approach discussed previously, parents should be able to opt out of the intervention process if they consider that they are not in a position to take part at some time or entirely. Home visitors must respond to the level of participation that a caregiver is willing to give and design the treatment plan accordingly.

SUMMARY

The structure of a home visit relies on philosophical underpinnings. The approach a home visitor uses depends on the discipline and training of the home visitor; that is, is the home visitor a generalist or specialist? Generalists and specialists can have overlapping roles in a transdisciplinary teamwork approach.

The structure of the home visit also relies on careful program planning that, in turn, relies on formal and informal assessments. Traditional home visits can be divided into a seven-part format: Arrival and Greeting, What's New?, Today's Activities, Reflect and

Plan for Next Visit, What's Coming Up?, Anything Else?, and Good-Bye. The section on Today's Activities involves strategy, has the most variability, and is individualized for the child and family. Strategies can be conceptualized as on a continuum from least natu-ralistic (drill) to most naturalistic (routines). Evidence-based prac-tice calls for four tests of a strategy: soundness, acceptability, quality of implementation, and functionality. We conclude that strategies that are naturalistic, spontaneous in family routines, accepted by caregivers, well implemented, and functional are best. These strate-gies, however, may not be best for some families. The task of the home visitor is to choose which strategies are appropriate for each child and family.

5

Facilitating
Adult–Child Interaction

*"Any time you are in the home and the child smiles,
and the parent smiles, you are doing your work."*

–Victor J. Bernstein (2007)

Recall that in Chapter 1 the fourth core principle on which we shape our philosophy is that "Nurturing and dependable human relationships are the building blocks of healthy development. Relationships depend on emotion, and the role of emotion in learning can not be overestimated." It follows from the first core principle that "Human development is shaped by a dynamic and continuous interaction between biology and experience" (Shonkoff & Phillips, 2000). Thus, relationships, and in particular the relationship of the primary caregiver with the child, are the heart of the matter. Furthermore, that relationship is built on repeated positive (or negative) experiences.

THE CAREGIVER–INFANT RELATIONSHIP

Intervention must be based on the assumption that early mental and motor development and progression of that development are based on the quality of the interactions between infants and caregivers. The caregiver–infant relationship is the single most salient primary factor in the child's developmental course. Early infant developmental progression takes place in the caregiving environment. The central environment for a young recovering infant is the family. Home visiting programs allow providers increased opportunity to be a part of the family's experience and to form a trusting and meaningful alliance between parent and professional. Through this alliance, the parent and professional can develop a shared view of the child as a family member and community participant, dependent on nurturing relationships for success. Home visitors may play unique roles in supporting infant–caregiver attachment. Because attachment is so important, this chapter is devoted to a thorough discussion of the home visitor's role in nurturing this relationship.

Our philosophy is that both attachment and interaction are within the purview of the home visitor. Many home visitors and employing agencies have attachment and interaction intervention as part of their program goals. If so, the focus on the caregiver–child relationship should be stated on the handout materials given to caregivers at the intake visit. If the focus is not explicitly revealed during the intake visit, the caregiver may be surprised (and possibly annoyed) when the home visitor begins to address those areas during the home visits. The home visitor's responsibility is to discuss the importance of this focus and obtain consensus from the family that attachment/interaction goals will be targeted.

Relationship Terminology

We want to make a distinction among some of the terms used to discuss relationships. *Bonding* refers to the feelings of a mother toward her newborn baby. *Attachment* grows from bonding and is reciprocated by the infant. *Interaction* is what passes between caregiver and child. It occurs through the use of *communicative signals*. Both caregiver and child have a part to play in that interaction and each may have disturbances in the signaling that interferes with the interaction. In this chapter, we discuss attachment and intervention related to it separately from interaction signaling and intervention related to it.

Evidence-Based Practice

Research generally shows that the quality of a child's social-emotional environment (e.g., caregiver nurturing, responsiveness, encouragement, stimulation) is more predictive of long-term child status than are hazardous birth events, including prematurity (Casey, Barrett, Bradley, & Spiker, 1993). That is not to say that the result of prematurity cannot be devastating. When the birth conditions have not been extremely hazardous, however, good parenting and nurturing can overcome many problems. On the other hand, studies have documented that medically high-risk infants, premature infants, and infants with physical disabilities are at greater risk for relationship difficulties. They are also more likely to be injured through incidents of abuse (Gutterman, 1997; Minde, 1993). Factors such as caregiver depression or poverty also add additional risk (Heffron, 2000). Extensive developmental research has found relationships between particular characteristics of caregiver–child interaction and a broad range of social, emotional, communicative, and cognitive characteristics and outcomes in children. It is now considered best practice in prevention and early intervention to support the caregiver–child relationship in order to support the child's development (Barnard, Morisset, & Spiker, 1993; Bernstein, 2002; Bromwich, 1997).

When caregiver–child interaction is explicitly recognized as a component of the early intervention process, interventionists tend to be highly aware of the interactions between caregivers and children (McCollum, Ree, & Chen, 2000). Casey et al. (1993) also found that informal clinical observation was as reliable a tool for assessing mother–infant interaction as were more sophisticated methods (e.g., videotaping, standardized measures). This is good news because clinical observation is most often all that is available to the home visitor for assessing the interactions between mother and infant or child.

INFANT MENTAL HEALTH

Currently, many different kinds of programs designed for the birth-to-three population, including early intervention for children with special needs, are integrating concepts and approaches drawn from the broad field of infant mental health research and practice (Heffron, 2000). This is occurring because expanding evidence indicates that relationship-based approaches support lasting outcomes

(Mahoney, Boyce, Fewell, Spiker, & Weeden, 1998). The term *relationship-based preventive intervention* describes preventive intervention that consciously integrates an emphasis on caregiver–child relationships and on the intervener–family relationship as a framework for delivery of many kinds of services including those from early intervention home visitors.

Heffron (2000) made a case for shared roles for developmental specialists and infant mental health specialists. Developmental specialists include all those for whom this book is meant: early childhood special educators, early interventionists, physical therapists, occupational therapists, speech-language pathologists, nurses, and so forth, who have expertise in infant development. Infant mental health specialists include psychologists, psychiatrists, counselors, and so forth, who have expertise in infant mental health. Both groups use relationship-based intervention promotion and preventive intervention. Their shared domain includes these questions:

- What do this caregiver and this baby bring to the relationship?
- How can I help the mother enjoy the infant?
- How can I help this infant elicit what he or she needs from the mother?
- How can I help this parent see and encourage this baby's development?
- How can I use my relationship with this infant and mother to address relationship risks arising from infant characteristics such as medical conditions, developmental disabilities, temperament extremes, and/or family characteristics such as isolation, chemical dependence, and family violence?

In addition, the home visitor developmental specialist has unique expertise to bring to the mother–infant relationship by asking these questions:

- What can my disciplinary expertise contribute to this infant–mother relationship?
- What does this infant bring to this relationship that impedes a positive infant–mother relationship?

- What interventions can mitigate the challenges this baby brings to the relationship?

> In order to develop normally, a child requires progressively more complex joint activity with one or more adults who have an irrational emotional relationship with the child. Somebody's got to be crazy about that kid. That's number one; first, last and always. (Bronfenbrenner, 1979, p. 159)

ATTACHMENT

Attachment has been defined as a strong bond with special people that leads us to feel pleasure and joy when we interact with them and to be comforted by their nearness during times of stress (Vacca, 2001). It follows the bonding that takes place at birth. Strong early attachments between an infant and the parents or other caregivers underpin all aspects of development (Graham, White, Clarke, & Adams, 2001; Pilkington, 2006).

Attachment parenting is a style of parenting that addresses an infant or child's need for trust, empathy, and affection in order to create a secure, peaceful, and enduring relationship. This style requires a consistent, loving, and responsive caregiver, ideally a parent, especially during the critical first 3–5 years of life.

Reciprocity is another important element of attachment. The actions, emotional states, and characteristics of the parent or caregiver affect the infant. Equally, the signals, emotional states, and characteristics of the infant affect the parent (Pilkington, 2006). Home visitors must become astute at observing and understanding the reciprocity that occurs between caregivers and children.

The need for physical protection, safety, and regulation is present in all of us. The provision of these elements is important in the development of secure attachment between a caregiver and an infant. These ingredients, or "irreducible needs" (Brazelton & Greenspan, 2000), are the right of every child. They are crucial in forming a firm foundation for future development. Home visitors have timely opportunities to influence the provision of the ingredients for the well-being of children (Pilkington, 2006).

The following list of needs was developed at the Attachment Parenting Symposium at Harvard Medical School (Scoby, 2000).

- Attunement: Being in tune with baby and developing loving connections allows parents to respond in developmentally appropriate ways, thereby meeting their emotional needs.
- Touch and holding: Close physical contact occurs through skin-to-skin holding, touch or massage, baby carrying, or wearing soft baby carriers.
- Physical needs that must be met: These needs include good nutrition, physical care, warmth, safety, and breastfeeding (or if bottle-feeding, the use of breastfeeding-like behaviors such as holding during feedings, eye contact, and so forth).
- Continuity of care/predictability in environment: Having a consistent, responsive, caring primary caregiver helps facilitate bonding and attachment.
- Comfort: Comfort includes responding empathically to the baby and soothing the baby when he or she is upset.

- Adoration: It is important for the baby to know unconditional love and to feel adored and accepted; this provides a secure emotional base.

- Protection: Protection involves providing the baby with a safe physical environment both within and without the home and a safe emotional environment in which emotions can be expressed and trust can be developed.

- Sensory stimulation: The growing brain needs input; much of this need can be met naturally through the motion, sight, and sound of being kept physically close and carried by the mother.

- Positive daily interactions. Parents should provide positive verbal and physical responses and communicate with and respond to the child.

- Opportunities for exploration and mastery: Babies need flexibility in their home environments and to be provided opportunities to be able to safely explore and have some control in order to develop skills and confidence.

- Limits and boundaries: Limits and boundaries should be taught in accordance with the child's developmental level to develop and enhance safety, social skills, and respect and empathy for others as they get older.

- Modeling: Parents mirror positive behavior back to the child; because children learn from parents' and others' behavior and want to be like their parents, parents must be examples of the type of behavior and demonstrate values that they want their child to acquire.

Types of Attachment

Siegel (1999) built on the work of Ainsworth, Blehar, Waters, and Wall (1978) to describe different types of attachment with different parents. Ainsworth's classic study called the *Strange Situation* described children's reactions when their mothers left a room that was unfamiliar and then returned to the child. The children's reactions were classified as indicating secure attachment, avoidant attachment, or ambivalent attachment.

According to Siegel (1999), parents who are emotionally available and are able to read and respond to their babies' cues and mental states generally have children who are *securely attached*. The children orient to and seek reassurance from the parent and desire proximity to the parent but also have internalized a sense of security that enables them to explore in unfamiliar situations. About 55% of children experience this type of attachment.

Another 20% of babies have what is called *avoidant attachments* to their mothers. These babies do not show fear or distress when the mother leaves and seem to ignore their mother's return. They do not seek the nearness of the parent and, rather, focus on toys or other aspects of the environment. The mothers of these babies are unavailable emotionally to the children, do not perceive or respond to the child's needs, and even seem to reject the child (Pilkington, 2006).

A third classification called *ambivalent attachment* describes a mother who is inconsistently available, tuned in, or responsive and who imposes on the baby her own state of mind, and a baby who is anxious, difficult to soothe, and overly preoccupied with the parent in the Strange Situation. Approximately 5% of children show this type of attachment to their mothers.

Finally, about 20% of infants show a *disorganized/disoriented attachment* to their mothers. Infants who experience abuse and neglect or disoriented interactions in the first year are most likely to demonstrate this type of attachment. In the Strange Situation, when the mother returns, the baby appears disorganized and disoriented, avoids eye contact, and may turn in circles or even "freeze" in a trance.

Interference with Attachment—Parents

All parents love their children and want what is best for them, but circumstances that produce stress (e.g., trauma, poverty, substance abuse, teen parenting) can interfere with relationships. Add to these the stress of having a child with a special needs diagnosis and all that that entails, and the stress levels escalate. As Trout and Foley explained:

Many sick and handicapped infants and toddlers live in a world where parents are disappointed, angry, confused and lonely. Perhaps even more striking, however, is the fact that parents of such children often do not know why they feel this way, and some are not aware that they feel this way at all. They may have a vague sense that some basic pleasure in infant–parent interaction is missing; that "It just doesn't feel the same to pick up this baby" as it felt when they picked up their earlier, healthy newborns; that there is a sense of emptiness when the infant cannot look at them, will not nuzzle, arches stiffly, or screams when touched. Successful and supportive interactions between infant and caregiver occur when both parent and infant are maximally available, emotionally and physically, and when a pattern of contingent, attuned responsiveness is developed that helps them to "fit" together. Handicapped infants may not be available in these ways, and the fit does not come easily. From the parents' point of view, it may be simply that it is not pleasant to go to Johnny's crib, that it is immensely frustrating to try to put on his snowsuit, to feed him, or to carry out the home assignment delivered by that well-meaning specialist from the early intervention program. (1989, p. 59)

Interference with Attachment—Infants

Infants shape interaction by communicating through their behavioral cues, which caregivers, in turn, interpret. Infants who have had a rocky start in life are more likely to give aberrant cues that are difficult for caregivers to understand (VandenBerg, Browne Perez, & Newstetter, 2003). Those infants are

- Born prematurely: Those infants who spend weeks and months in the intensive care nursery may have some behavioral or developmental difficulty including behavioral disorganization.
- Born with special needs—congenital syndromes or medical complications: For example, infants with heart problems may be very lethargic and may have lengthy stays in the hospital.
- Born at term but not behaviorally well organized: This includes problems with self-regulation and self-calming. He or she may

have difficulty with behaviors and tolerance of environmental stimuli.

- Born to high-risk families and environments: Infants raised in families with difficulties in their everyday lives or who have health issues or social problems may be at risk for developmental difficulties.

INTERVENTION FOR CAREGIVER–INFANT ATTACHMENT DURING FEEDING

The home visitor may start intervention with simple education or anticipatory guidance. Guidance can include informing the parent of new information, interpreting the behavior differently for the parent, positively commenting on a behavior of the parent or infant, modeling, experimenting with a new way, and ending with a positive comment about the relationship. For example, for a child who is premature and having a difficult time with feeding, the home visitor can provide the following:

- Informing: The home visitor talks about how an infant who was born prematurely has been putting all of his or her energy into recovering, growing, and breathing. Feeding demands a great deal of energy all at once.
- Interpreting: Discuss the need for rest during such demanding activity as feeding. The infant's behavior seems to be saying, "I need a break."
- Positive commenting on the infant's uniqueness: Help the parent realize the infant's unique ability to let the parent know when he or she is tired and that he or she can signal his or her needs.
- Modeling: Model restructuring the feeding to be less stimulating. Together, list the signals of fatigue and need for a break. Model slowing the feeding down and letting the baby set the pace.
- Experimenting: Try different feeding positions, or try creating a quiet place in which the infant could be fed with slow pacing.

- Positive feedback: Comment on the baby's ability to let a caregiver know what he or she needs and the parent's sensitivity to the infant's cues as the parent begins to acknowledge them.

THE INFANT MENTAL HEALTH MODEL FOR ATTACHMENT INTERVENTION

The infant mental health model focuses on such activities as reading the infant's emotional cues, encouraging caregivers to match the infant's affect, assisting the caregiver in responding quickly and appropriately to the infant's cues, and reinforcing and commenting positively on the interactive relationship between the infant and the caregiver (McDonough, 2004). The interventionist typically provides this input to the caregiver *as it is occurring*, within the immediate context of interactions with the infant (Klein & Chen, 2006). Following are guidelines using infant mental health principles (Pilkington, 2006):

- Accentuate the positive. Comment on the parent's positive behavior that strengthens the caregiver–child relationship (e.g., "Look at the way your baby smiles when you look into her eyes.")
- Nurture your caregiver–provider relationship. The quality of the relationship between the parent or caregiver and the service provider has often proved to be a key aspect of promoting infant–caregiver attachment. That relationship can serve as a secure base for parents who are beginning to apply more mutuality and caring in relationships with their child and with others. Take time during visits to ask how things are going for the caregiver. Demonstrate your caring and respect in your interaction with and treatment of each caregiver as a person and as a partner in the development of the child.
- Use "speaking through the child" to help caregivers understand the child's needs and reactions and realize the importance of responding to the child (e.g., "It feels so good when you wrap me up snugly like that").

- Promote reading the child's cues and signals and responding appropriately in order to meet the child's needs consistently (e.g., "Your baby turned away when you brought the toy near. Do you think he doesn't like the toy and would prefer another or perhaps is sleepy and just doesn't want to play right now?").

- Encourage age-appropriate and developmentally appropriate strategies to facilitate nurturance and comfort (e.g., soothing and rocking; skin-to-skin contact; using calm, soft verbal communication; giving loving touch; eye contact; singing; playing and enjoying the child; showing warm and positive regard of the infant; using gentle words and facial and body expressions).

- Reframe to show the parent a different perspective of the child's behavior so as to respond more appropriately (e.g., "Is your child bad, or is she trying to tell you that she is jealous of the new baby and doesn't have the language to express her feelings?").

- Consider individual family/cultural expectations and incorporate them into intervention. For example, some families or cultures place value on children being quiet and unobtrusive, whereas others encourage much conversational interaction and enthusiastic play. Seek to match these differing values when suggesting attachment strategies.

- Because reciprocity is a vital part of the social-emotional relationship, model desired interactive behavior and then encourage the caregiver by coaching the interaction. An example is a reciprocal play exchange such as stroking a stuffed bear, then offering the bear to the baby to stroke, then waiting for the baby to offer the bear back.

REFERRALS FOR HELP

If a home visitor does not come from a social work or psychology background, providing intervention for a parent who does not attach to his or her baby, who is depressed, anxious, extremely stressed, or overwhelmed, is beyond the training of a home visitor. Furthermore, the welfare of the infant requires that an intervention occur so that the infant will not be harmed physically or psychologically. A tip sheet for guidelines for referral, Red Flags, is included in the Appendix. If the parent shows signs of a severe disorder, the home visitor should discuss referral resources with his or her supervisor and get help as quickly as possible.

SUCCESSFUL INTERACTIONS

There is a wide range of individual differences in normal interaction among dyads. However, successful parent–child interactions have several common characteristics:

1. High degree of synchrony, in which the individual behavior streams of the two partners in the dyad (parent and child) are mutually interdependent

2. State of mutual engagement in which each partner is both available to, and responsive to, the other. When one partner is an infant, important characteristics of the adult partner include emotional availability, sensitivity to the infant's emotional cues, and contingent responding to emotions and emerging cognitions expressed through vocalization, gaze, and actions

Building on the concepts of high synchrony and mutual engagement, interventionists, particularly those who fostered language development, devised intervention approaches that called for modeling "attention regulation." In this approach, joint attention, a developmental skill in which a child learns to attend to the same object or event as an adult, is necessary for learning language (Vigil and Hwa-Froelich, 2004). Tomasello (2003) defined two interactional styles: attention directing and attention following. In attention following, the adult attends to the child and then makes a comment on the object or event of interest to the child. In attention directing, the adult directs a child's attention to the object or event to which the adult wants the child to attend. Tomasello (2003) and Saxon (1997) agreed that children acquire more words and maintain joint attention for longer periods when the caregiver engages in an attention-following style. Interventionists considered attention following to be the optimal interactional style, and they taught parents to follow the child's lead as a language-facilitation technique, such as "It Takes Two to Talk" (Manolson, 1992).

It should be noted that any kind of joint attention activities for children and caregivers should be encouraged when there have been none, without causing caregivers to worry that they are doing it the right or wrong way.

INTERVENTION IN A CULTURAL CONTEXT

Parents may do what they do because of cultural beliefs. Differing cultural traditions will influence the parenting behaviors that parents from different cultural backgrounds define as appropriate, including those behaviors seen during parent–child interaction.

The above research on attention regulation was based on middle-class North American and European populations (Vigil, 2002). In studies with other ethnic groups, caregivers did not engage in an attention-following style and used a more direct style. Following a child's lead likely falls into the cultural value of fostering independence. In contrast, caregivers with an interdependent value system may use a directive style to ensure that children follow and obey caregiver goals (Vigil & Hwa-Froelich, 2004).

For instance, a language-based intervention that emphasizes following the baby's lead might feel quite familiar and acceptable to the white American mother, whereas to a Korean mother it might feel as if the home visitor were questioning her ability to show devotion to her baby. When parents engage in behavior that a particular home visit approach would describe as needing intervention or when they violate the assumptions of an intervention approach by sitting back and leaving the interaction to the interventionist, the first question that the home visitor should be asking is, "Why?" What does this interaction look like through the eyes of this parent and this child? Home visitors must develop the ability to learn from individual parents and families the cultural frames that they bring to their interactions with their children (McCollum et al., 2000).

Kathleen was at her wit's end in her work with Raza, an Egyptian mother and her husband Mosul, a Pakistani. Their two little girls, ages 13 months and 2 years, reflected the conflicts in the home over child rearing. Raza told Kathleen that her grandparents who raised her had spoiled her, and she did not want to do that with her children. Mosul, on the other hand, was strict one minute and gave in to their crying for something the next. Most frustrating for Kathleen was her attempt to get Raza to play with the girls. She modeled getting on the floor and interacting with them and their toys. Toys were kept on a high shelf and not available to the children because Raza said they would fight over them. So the girls jumped on the furniture or watched TV. Both girls had severely delayed language skills, and the 2-year-old showed her frustration by having tantrums. When Kathleen invited Raza to get on the floor with them to play, she was met with a stare; Raza did not move from the couch. Kathleen thought that Raza was close to a breaking point and consulted her supervisor, Maryanne. Maryanne said that in some cultures parents think that play is something that children do without parent involvement. She cited research that Vietnamese and Mexican parents did not see play as important (Vigil & Hwa-Froelich, 2004). She suggested that Kathleen ask Raza some questions about how she was raised and what she most enjoyed in her childhood. She could talk with Raza about what was important to her in raising her children.

Raza said she could have anything she wanted as a child but no one played with her. Clearly she did not see play interaction with her children as part of her role; she did see her role as an instructor for her children, but she was frustrated by her husband's lack of structure, which she saw as important for her instruction. Kathleen could not impose her culture's interaction patterns where they were rejected. She would instead work on ways that Raza could interact in a more structured and directive way than "just playing" when she was alone with the girls. She would also begin an alternative communication system for the oldest child to express her needs, and she would work with Raza to interpret her children's cues.

Successful Caregiver–Infant Interaction Signals

As we have seen, the dynamic interactions between infant and care-giver that are so vital to the development of attachment begin at birth and perhaps before birth (with the mother reacting to movement patterns from the fetus). Only recently we have discovered that the infant has an equal part to play in this interaction; previously, the entire burden for the interaction was thought to rest with the care-giver. The manifestations of these interactions are in overt signals (communications) such as gestures, eye gaze, pointing, vocaliza-tions, reaching, and showing from the baby, and responsiveness on the part of the caregiver. The interaction depends on the compe-tence of both members of the dyad. A body of research on these early communication signals is documented in healthy babies and recep-tive, responsive caregivers. A general outline of the growth in those communications follows with implications for intervention when growth in either infant or caregiver is compromised by disability or unpredictable interactive style.

Infant Communication Signals

In early stages, infants give cues that tell caregivers when they are ready for interactions and caregivers learn to read them. If caregivers try to interact when the infant is not receptive, the caregiver may read this as a rejection. The home visitor can help caregivers to read these infant cues as illustrated in Table 5.1.

Infants' preverbal communication development at the earliest level is based on the interplay of eye gaze, gesture, and attention. Further successful communication with caregivers is characterized by reciprocity, consistency, and predictability, which systematically build on one another and result in intentional communication (Reinhartson, 2000).

Stages

In the beginning, infants produce signals that are interpreted by the caregiver as if they were intentional: reflexive signals such as crying to indicate hunger, displeasure, or discomfort. Caregivers respond to

Table 5.1. An infant's signals for engagement and disengagement

Engagement cues	Disengagement cues
Your infant wants to communicate with you when she or he	Your infant wants a rest from brain activity when she or he
Stops moving	Turns head away
Gazes intently at your face	Cries, becomes fussy
Has smooth arm/leg movements	Burps, hiccoughs, passes gas
Reaches out to you	Has droopy eyelids
Turns head or eyes to you	Arches back
Stretches fingers/toes to you	Falls asleep
Slows or stops sucking activity	Squirms or kicks
Smiles	Has pale or red skin
Coos	Turns away eyes
Begins babbling/talking	Exhibits fast breathing
Has eyes wide open	Yawns
Exhibits a brightened face	Wrinkles forehead
Raises head	Has dull-looking eyes
	Frowns
	Places hand to mouth

From Hotelling, B.A. (2004). Newborn capabilities: Parent teaching is a necessity. *Journal of Perinatal Education, 13*(4), 43–49; adapted by permission.

them. Next, the infant produces preintentional signals, such as excited arm movements or a smile in recognition. As caregivers begin to recognize these behaviors and begin to respond in contingent, consistent, and predictable ways, the infant begins to use these signals as intentional means of communicating. This begins about the age of 8–9 months (Reinhartson, 2000).

These intentions include behavioral regulation (controlling another person's behavior), social interaction (child's ability to draw attention to him- or herself) and joint attention (child's ability to share a pleasurable experience with someone else). At about the same time, identifiable gestures emerge, such as reaching for a desired object or raising arms to be picked up. The next stage is identifiable words, which emerge at about 13 months.

Eye Gaze

From 1–2 months, babies scan faces and fixate on eyes. This mutual gaze between infant and caregivers, which often is accompanied by smiling, is rewarding and has an important effect on emotional bonding and attachment. Feelings of comfort emerge as an infant's caregivers provide contingent and predictable responses.

At approximately 3 months of age, eye gaze is intriguing to the infant and usually is held by a range of facial expressions made by the caregiver. Infants discover that their caregivers' faces are responsive and convey meaning. Responsive caregivers use animated facial expressions such as big smiles or head nodding to acknowledge the infants' behavior and to hold their attention for ongoing interaction.

At approximately 4–6 months, an infant learns to look toward the focus of the mother's attention and then to direct her to the object of the infant's attention. This use of eye gaze is critical to the process of infant–caregiver reciprocity.

Joint Attention

Toward the end of the second month, infants are better able to control their visual attention by moving their gaze toward and away from interesting sights while producing emotional expressions that are interpretable. By about 5–6 months, infants begin to hold and play with objects as the focus of attention. Then, at about 8–10 months, infants can actually begin to follow a caregiver's general direction of gaze. At about 9–11 months, infants can direct attention to caregivers and objects using gestures such as giving and showing, followed by pointing.

Gestures

Gestures communicate meaning and are consistently interpreted by other people. Gestural behavior of caregivers is the key element in the development of communication in the infant. Caregivers click their fingers, point, touch, pat the infant's head or back, and hold or rub the infant. Caregivers must also time their gestures in response to the infant's cues so that the infant's attention will be maintained. As infants develop their gestures, they often wait for the caregiver to respond. The ability of the caregiver to respond accurately to gestures such as these is critical to the development of communicative interaction. When eye gaze accompanies a gesture, it means that the infant is becoming intentional. By 1 year of age, the child's wide array of gestures that began as unintentional eventually become intentional. These may include reaching, waving, or motioning to get help or gain the attention of the caregiver (Reinhartson, 2000).

Reciprocity

In reciprocity, both infant and caregiver have the opportunity to communicate and have the obligation to respond. Reciprocity requires trusting one's partner, which arises from predictability of the other's action. It is important that the caregiver's responses be consistent. The infant also needs to know that the caregiver's responses are predictable. Up until 6–7 months, infants' signals are often random and unintentional. By about 7 months, however, they may no longer be happy with a general or nonspecific adult response. It is then that infants learn to use signals that produce specific effects.

Francis was videotaping Jobella and her 3-month-old daughter Tiffany, who had Down syndrome, in their home. When the session ended, Francis left the tape running while she and Jobella, who was holding Tiffany in the crook of her arm, talked about Tiffany's upcoming appointment with the pediatrician. Jobella's head was turned toward Francis, and as they talked, they noticed Tiffany becoming more and more fussy. Jobella turned her face to Tiffany who instantly quieted and began to coo. Jobella waited for her turn and repeated Tiffany's cooing sound. Tiffany smiled and engaged her mother in a "dance" of reciprocal vocalizations that was caught on videotape. When they replayed the tape, it was apparent that Tiffany had communicated her desire to have her mother look at her and interact with her. Jobella was a natural responder. Her voice was high-pitched and quiet in volume, and she took her turn when Tiffany paused in her vocalizations. Tiffany and Jobella were learning to be reciprocal with Tiffany leading the way. Francis documented the signals: "Tiffany thrashed her arms and legs for attention. She quieted with eye gaze and vocalized for reciprocal interactions."

INTERACTIONAL PATTERNS OF CHILDREN WITH DISABILITIES

In many studies, characteristics of interaction that differ from those described above have been interpreted as deficits, and a prominent goal of early intervention has been to change the characteristics of these interactions to match those ideal characteristics described in the developmental literature. However, there is danger in this approach. In the case of infants with disabilities, interactive differences in caregivers may represent adaptations necessary to support the child's engagement with the partner or with a play object. Interventions that set out to change these characteristics without first understanding why the differences occur could be counterproductive.

Very few studies have addressed the implications of interactional patterns of infants with severe physical impairments. Children

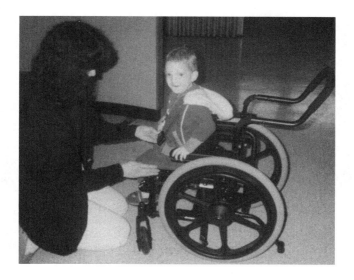

with disabilities influence caregiver reactions not only because care-givers may have difficulty reading the child's signals but also because of the emotional impact the disability may have on the parents. The all-important reciprocity may be jeopardized by the caregiver's feel-ings of loss, resulting in possible withdrawal or rejection of the child, which disrupts the normal pattern of communication opportunities. Some classic studies have compared interactional patterns of moth-ers and their children with cerebral palsy to mothers of children with either developmental delays or typical development. The mothers of children with cerebral palsy were more physically directive com-pared with mothers in the other two groups (Bailey & Slee, 1984; Brookes-Gunn & Lewis, 1984). Children with cerebral palsy often miss their turn in the interactional process, are generally less respon-sive and more compliant, and are more dependent.

For a child with visual impairments, gestures and visual gaze have little value. Smiling behavior is also typically delayed. These chil-dren may compensate with hand and body movements that can be misinterpreted as stereotypical. When a child with visual impairment is perfectly still, it can indicate attentiveness or interest in the adult.

Wilcox, Kouri, and Caswell (1990) speculated that in severe motor impairments, abnormal muscle tone, lack of muscle coordination, and inability to maintain normal posture may affect both a child's verbal and nonverbal interaction patterns. If children have motor impairments, caregivers may not interpret the child's cues as easily. These children may not be able to produce consistently readable signs and may not be predictable in their responses. Caregivers may take their turn without waiting for the infant.

APPROACHES TO INTERVENTION FOR CAREGIVER–INFANT INTERACTION SIGNALS

Although there are few studies of interactional patterns of children with disabilities and their caregivers, a few implications can be drawn. First, home visitors and caregivers must be sensitive to not only the physical and sensory characteristics of the child but also the emotional needs of the family and the developing patterns of caregiver–child interaction.

It is important to remember that the form of the signal (how it is produced) is not as important as the function of the signal (what the signal means). If any signal is produced, it should be interpreted as accurately as possible and given meaning. If a signal is produced and no one responds or it is responded to inconsistently, then the signal will eventually diminish. The child may then lose interest in trying or use only those signals he or she knows will produce a response and thus limit his or her signals. It is essential, therefore, that home visitors spend time with caregivers observing how the child interacts within natural settings and with those people familiar to the child (Wilcox et al., 1990). Motor movements or eye gaze may be atypical and, in the beginning, unintentional. Home visitors and caregivers must be aware of the environment in which signals are produced and the meaning with which they could be associated. As caregivers and home visitors assign meaning to these signals, they have the potential to become purposeful. For example, an infant sees his or her bottle and purses his or her lips into a kissing posture. The caregiver says, "Bottle? You want your bottle?" while handing the baby the bottle. Each time the lip pursing occurs, the caregiver responds the same way by handing the baby the bottle. If each time the lip pursing occurs, the caregiver responds the same way, the baby begins to associate the signal and the bottle. In other words, the behavior or lip pursing brings about a predictable result, changing what began as an unintentional signal to an intentional one. Thus, it should be interpreted as a communicative signal if it meets the following criteria (Reinhartson, 2000):

- It is intentional—used to communicate something to someone
- It is consistent—produced in the same manner each time
- It is predictable—the caregiver knows what the child wants

If it is decided upon as a true communication signal, it should be documented so that all caregivers can respond in the same manner each time it is produced. This means that we have helped the child to move from preintentional communication to intentional communication and thus given him or her one more way to function within the family.

> *Bobbi visited Noel and her son Phillip for the first time. A babysitter had shaken Phillip, who had been a typically developing baby and was now cortically blind and severely motor impaired at 18 months. As Bobbi asked about life with Phillip, she asked Noel how Phillip communicated with her.*
>
> *"Oh, he doesn't communicate at all," she said.*
>
> *"Does he give you any signals of what he wants?"*
>
> *"No, nothing."*
>
> *"I notice that he sits so he is touching you at all times. What do you think he is telling you by doing that?"*
>
> *"I don't know, but he gets fussy if I am not beside him."*
>
> *"Do you think it could be that you are the most important person in the world to him and that he doesn't want you to be away from him?"*
>
> *"I never thought so, but I guess that's right."*
>
> *Bobbi documented seeking body touching as Phillip's signal for wanting security.*
>
> *"It seems that he is very clearly saying that. He may be communicating some other messages through his body language that are important to watch for. We can talk about that some more."*

Models for Interaction Intervention

Klein and Chen (2006) provided illustrations of two dyadic interaction models.

Adult–Adult Dyadic Interactions

In an adult–adult dyadic interaction, the home visitor interacts primarily with the caregiver. Recently, the development of relationship-based intervention models has focused primarily on the relationship between the home visitor and the caregiver (Bernstein, Campbell, & Akers, 2001). In these models, the activities of intervention home visits often include a great deal of talking and listening. The home visitor encourages the caregiver to discuss problems, reflect on the infant or family's accomplishments and challenges, and, as the trusting relationship develops, express feelings and emotions. The theory of this model suggests that the establishment of a relationship between the caregiver and the adult will empower the caregiver and thereby enhance the caregiver–infant relationship. This approach has been suggested as an appropriate model for working with high-risk mothers where attachment is of concern.

An example of adult–adult interaction is a routines-based assessment with the caregiver (McWilliam, 2003). The home visitor interviews the caregiver to identify typical daily activities and to determine those daily activities in which special problems arise with the infant, as well as to select natural opportunities to teach or generalize infant skills. Familiarity and predictability (due to repetition) make routines an ideal way to foster early interactions and lay the foundation for later conversations. Routines may be anything that parents and children do together often (e.g., daily routines of the household, people games, caregiver's own routines). Table 5.2 lists some of the common problems parents create within daily routines.

The home visitor may enact change by helping the caregiver to

- Start the same way each time. Give the routine a simple name.
- Plan the child's turn. (During diapering, it is easy to play the game of Peek-a-boo. Once the adult has covered his or her face

Table 5.2. Parents' role in routines: Common problems

Does not give the child a chance to interact; goes too fast or just entertains
Uses different words/actions each time
Stops when child wants to continue
Does not know what to expect from the child
Changes the routine too soon

From Weitzman, E. (2005). *Routines: Powerful ways to promote interaction and language learning.* Paper presented at the American Speech-Language-Hearing Association convention, San Diego; adapted by permission.

with the diaper and said "Peek-a-boo," he or she should wait for the infant to indicate with sound or action, including change in facial expression, that he or she wants the game repeated.)

- Repeat the same sounds, actions, and words each time. Think of the routine as a series of steps and follow them in the same order each time.

- Keep the end the same so the child will know what to expect next.

When adult–adult dyadic interactions become the primary activity of the home visit, there may be decreased opportunity for direct impact on the infant. The immediate problem is how to engage the infant (and often siblings) during these conversations. In addition, a predominantly adult–adult approach may be insufficient when an infant has complex needs that are best met using very specific kinds of techniques, responses, and interactions. Helping caregivers become familiar and comfortable with such techniques is time consuming. It also places significant demands on the knowledge and expertise of the home visitor.

Triadic Interactions

A triadic interaction, in which the home visitor attends to both the infant *and* the caregiver, holds the best promise of enacting change. A three-way interaction is established, preferably involving a routine. Sometimes these activities are extended to include other family members or other interventionists. Triadic interactions often require significant skill on the part of the home visitor because they require dividing one's attention between the caregiver and the infant. Some home visitors who use this approach may choose to be accompanied by an assistant, particularly when siblings are involved. Triadic interactions might also be viewed as a "collaborative consultation" approach. The home visitor establishes an interactive partnership with the caregiver as each contributes respective knowledge and skills in supporting the child's learning and development. Together they seek to solve challenges and celebrate the child's accomplishments.

An example of triadic activities is supporting/teaching effective caregiver–infant interactions that have been the focus of this chapter. In these activities, the home visitor may model interactions with the infant for the caregiver, observe the caregiver and infant during play or daily routines and provide feedback, or videotape the caregiver or other family members interacting with the infant (Klein, Chen, & Haney, 2000).

> *Christy visited Rachel and her son George, 14 months, who has Down syndrome. Rachel's main concern was George's communication skills. She worried that he would not be able to carry on a conversation with her. Christy asked Rachel to play with George as she usually does and asked if she would give her permission to be videotaped for their personal use only. Rachel agreed and held George on her lap while she introduced toys to George in rapid succession and she made non-speech sounds with them: a slinky toy (ba-ba-ba) (always a favorite, she said), a rattle, and a tambourine. When they replayed the tape, it was obvious to Rachel that George had turned away from all of the offered toys. It was also obvious that George had no opportunity to take a turn as Rachel's rapid-fire presentation did not allow it. Christy suggested that George sit on the floor facing Rachel and that she imitate whatever he did. George picked up the tambourine and shook it. Rachel held out her hands and George gave it to her. She shook it and gave it back to him. He laughed and repeated the action, looking into her face. The game lasted for several minutes. Then Christy gave Rachel a jar of bubbles. When Rachel blew them, George made a sound and a hand gesture that Rachel immediately imitated.*

Rachel thanked Christy for teaching her how to imitate and play with her son and helping them both to have fun.

SUMMARY

Because the caregiver–infant interactive relationship is crucial to the optimal development of the infant, many early intervention programs have been built on helping caregivers learn to use responsive social and communicative interaction patterns. This chapter is devoted to the home visitor's nurturing the attachment relationship between an infant and caregiver. When there are interferences with the capacity to form attachments in either the caregiver or the infant, the home visitor has the task of intervention for building attachment. Models from infant mental health are best used for that intervention. The focus includes reading the infant's cues, encouraging caregivers to match the infant's affect, assisting the caregiver in responding quickly and appropriately to the infant's cues, and reinforcing and commenting positively on the caregiver's abilities. Culture plays a role in the caregiver's responses and in his or her reinforcement. If attachment is a focus of the home visitor's intervention program, it is recommended that the caregivers are told at the outset that the home visitor can be helpful with attachment.

An additional task is to help the infant and mother to produce signals and read each other's signals that are necessary for their reciprocal interaction. Both infant and caregiver have roles to play, but the caregiver is more capable of change. Typical signals for interaction by the infant are eye gaze, gestures, pointing, vocalizations, reaching, and showing. Home visitors have the task of helping the caregiver to read the infant's signals, although they may be aberrant, and to respond to them. There are several models for intervention in signals for interaction. As with other interventions, embedding opportunities for interaction in daily routines or games are the most efficacious ways for the family to employ interaction. The home visitor is advised to work in a triadic model of intervention with caregiver and child.

6

Guidelines for Intervention for Children with Various Disorders

with contributions from Carole Osselaer

"Anything that interferes with the child's ability to interact with the environment in a normal manner is a potential source of, or contributing factor to, the presence of developmental delay."

—Rossetti (2001)

In Chapter 4, we discussed the format of a home visit and strategies to reach the goals for family-guided intervention in the home. Those strategies are on a continuum from most directive to least directive as a result of the interaction of a child, family, and home visitor. The specialist is usually most directive and hands-on with the child during some part of the visit. The specialist can choose from many techniques and strategies resulting from his or her background and education. Consultants are most often asked, "Have you ever seen a child with _____?" "What do I do with a case of _____?" "Is this behavior part of the presenting problem, or is it unusual for this child to behave this way?" This chapter focuses on very general strategies for the generalist home visitor who visits children with the most common disabilities. It is meant to be a starting point. The generalist should not hesitate to ask for help and collaboration from a specialist or consultant (e.g., supervisor, physician, public health nurse, nutritionist) in a variety of areas.

PRIMARY AND SECONDARY DISORDERS

Home visitors are service providers essentially because a young child has a disorder that can be classified as primary, with limitations directly related to the pathology associated with the disorder, such as low muscle tone in Down syndrome or increased muscle tone in cerebral palsy (Bartlett & Palmisano, 2002). Secondary impairments develop over time. An example is limited range of motion or weakness in hand muscles that are the result of non-use of the involved hand when the primary disorder limits its use. Ultimately, reaching or grasping for toys may be affected by either the primary or secondary impairment. A child with a primary disorder of autism or apraxia of speech may have the secondary disorder of social isolation that results from failure to communicate.

A secondary disorder may also result from environmental causes, defined as a result of a primary disorder interacting with daily functioning. For example, children with visual problems, hearing loss, or cognitive disorders may not take part in the caregiver–child interaction and nurturing that is so important for stimulation of the child and relationship building for the parent–child dyad. Thus, the home visitor is charged with treatment of primary (the presenting problem) and preventing or treating secondary disorders.

Home visitors who expect that the primary concerns of parents center on cognitive and motor delays of their children will soon find that parents will often prioritize adjustments of daily living to be their first concern. Indeed, when we think of functional goals, functioning within the family's lifestyle may mean addressing a child's behavior—behavior that is out of the typical range for even 2-year-olds or behavior that looks to be at risk for escalation. Such behaviors that concern parents include poor eating and sleeping, inappropriate behavior with peers, and tantrums. It is often the case that until these behaviors are addressed, parents cannot turn their attention to the developmental deficits that made the child eligible for service. These behaviors are often referred to as challenging behaviors.

In this chapter, we address the concerns most cited by parents and caregivers. Some are primary problems and some are secondary, but they are the causes of stress in family and child functioning. The home visitor who listens to those concerns and addresses them in the beginning of the intervention will gain the confidence of the concerned caregiver. We begin with so-called functional or challenging behavioral issues and then move to other common disorders.

CHALLENGING BEHAVIORS

Behaviors that we call challenging, meaning that they do not fit the norms of infant and child behaviors, are often termed *maladaptive.* On the contrary, research supports the notion that these behaviors can be quite adaptive for the child, effectively providing them with desired consequences (Wickerson-Kane & Goldstein, 1999). Challenging feeding, sleeping, and tantruming behaviors can be learned as a means of escaping the requests being made by caregivers. The intervention, therefore, is to substitute developmentally appropriate behaviors for the maladaptive behaviors. It is hoped that these new, functional behaviors will make it possible for the child to communicate his or her needs in developmentally appropriate ways (see pp. 163–165).

FEEDING DISORDERS

The thought of a mother feeding her infant by breast or bottle makes us smile because it is a happy occasion. The proximity of their faces close to each other allows for first interactions and communications—a mother's cooing sounds and a baby's pleasure in the feelings of satiation. Thus, feeding is an emotional experience for mothers and babies from birth. Perhaps no other process has such emotional underpinnings for both mother and baby. Mother has the satisfaction of knowing that she is providing for her child—a measure of her love. Baby is receiving food and love but also is giving feedback that the mother is making him or her satisfied and happy. A child's difficulty with eating for any variety of reasons triggers strong emotional responses in caregivers and immediate modifications in the behavioral interactions around feeding.

Feeding is a complex behavior with multiple interwoven processes with roots in the sensory system. These include the sense of appetite and satiation; internal satisfaction or pleasure from eating derived from internal biochemical and sensory feedback; volitional acts of taking in food and chewing; oral motor skills; oral sensations of touch, taste, and temperature; swallowing reflexes; emotional associations; and interactive behavioral patterns—all of which take place in the physical and social context of eating and within a developmental and experiential history for a particular child (Cullinane & Ausderau, 2001). Given the complexity of the feeding process, is it any wonder that so many special needs children also have feeding problems?

It is estimated that 25% of all infants and children have some complication with feeding, and up to 80% of children with developmental disabilities have some complication with feeding (Tarbell, 2003). In other words, we can expect that most of the children seen by home visitors will have some issues with feeding. Most at risk are premature infants born before 34 weeks' gestation. The ability to suck, swallow, and breathe at the same time, requisite for nipple feeding, is not developed until that time in the fetus. Many other health conditions also impair eating. In our experience, feeding problems most frequently begin when an infant has a physiological problem that makes feeding difficult or actually painful. The pain could be from the discomfort of having a nasogastric tube inserted through the nose into the esophagus, an inability to breathe while feeding, reflux, or swallowing discomfort. The infant or child may cope with these discomforts with avoidance behaviors that escalate into full-blown feeding disorders. It is most helpful to think about children who won't eat as having poor learning experiences with food.

Feeding within the Cultural Context

Children who have not learned to eat are found in every culture. The way that caregivers view the refusal to eat can vary by culture. Children who do not eat may be force-fed more readily in some cultures, usually at the urging of grandparents. Some caregivers will tell their home visitor that they were force-fed as children and they continue to do it with their own children. If eating is ever to be considered as pleasurable and satisfying, feeding children by force is not conducive to helping children associate pleasure with eating. Home visitors who encounter force-feeding have a challenging job to convince caregivers that inflicting pain for refusal to eat is counterproductive. The home visitor's task, therefore, is to show a better way.

Need for a Feeding Specialist

Feeding disorders are serious, and the home visitor who is a generalist should not hesitate to ask for help from a feeding specialist, usually a speech-language pathologist or an occupational therapist who has had special training in feeding disorders. When should a feeding specialist be consulted? In Table 6.1, Toomey (2002) lists red flags that, if present, indicate that a feeding specialist should be consulted.

How the Home Visitor Can Help

It is essential that the home visitor who does not specialize in feeding disorders does not attempt to feed a child. Neither should she bring any food into the home. However, the home visitor can begin some strategies that will create a good environment for learning to eat. The overall goal of all treatment with children who will not eat is to create a situation that positively reinforces normal, healthy eating patterns. The five main categories of strategies are discussed below (Toomey, 2002). Often, these are all that are necessary to get a child on the right path to eating.

Structure

Having a routine to meal times and eating in the same room, at the same table, with the same utensils are all things that capitalize on the need for repetition in learning. The routine itself can get the child ready to eat. Alert to the routine by hand washing. Check that the child is sitting in a supported position with feet not dangling. He or she should be sitting upright, not leaning back, so that the hands can come to the mouth and are not needed for balance.

The person who is feeding the child sits in front of him or her and smiles when introducing foods. Particularly important is for the caregiver to avoid showing fear if the child appears to be choking or

Table 6.1.   Red flags indicating the need for a feeding specialist

Parental history of an eating disorder, with the child not meeting weight goals
Ongoing poor weight gain (percentiles falling) or weight loss
Ongoing choking, gagging, or coughing during meals
Ongoing problems with vomiting
More than one incident of nasal reflux
History of traumatic choking incident
History of eating and breathing coordination problems, with ongoing respiratory issues
Inability to make transition to baby food purées by 10 months of age
Inability to accept any table food solids by 12 months of age
Inability to make transition from breast/bottle to a cup by 16 months of age
Aversion or avoidance of all foods in specific texture or food group
Food range of fewer than 20 foods, especially if foods are being dropped over time with no new foods replacing those lost
Infant cries and/or arches at most meals
Family is fighting about food and feeding (meals are battles)
Parent repeatedly reports that the child is difficult for everyone to feed

From Toomey, K.A. (2002). *Feeding strategies for older infants and toddlers. Pediatric Basics, 100*, 2–13; adapted by permission.

gagging. (It is dangerous if the child stops breathing but gagging is not cause for alarm.) The child looks for emotion on the caregiver's face, and seeing alarm will alarm the child. Children with a hypersensitive gag reflex can be helped by chewing on a chewy toy of some kind—something nonedible in the mouth that is not dangerous, to move the gag reflex from the front to the back of the mouth.

Social Modeling

Children learn to eat through observation of others. Family meals are critical to providing children with multiple opportunities to learn about eating. If parents do not object, ask them to overemphasize chewing with their mouths open to model chewing with their back teeth. This is not a time for manners. That will come later. Parents should be positive about what they are eating and convey that this is a happy time for the family.

Positive Reinforcement

Do not let mealtimes be struggle times. Meals should be pleasant and enjoyable. Use verbal praise, smile, touch, clapping, and even a cheer; all are positive reinforcers.

Make Foods Manageable

Children should be given food that they can manage to eat in small, easily chewable bites or in long, thin strips that the child can easily hold. A child will not eat what she knows she can't handle, and this is very frustrating for her. A rule of thumb is to include a total of three foods on the plate at one time and one tablespoon per each year of a child's age of each of those foods. New foods need to be presented repeatedly with positive reinforcement.

Have Children Use Their Cognitive Skills

Teach children about the physical properties of foods so they will know how to make foods work in their mouths. Describe the food as cold, smooth, squishy, or hard so that children know they need to use their strong back teeth. After eating, emphasize that your "tummy feels so much better and is telling you it's happy because it ate some food."

Children with Gastroesophageal Reflux Disorder

Gastroesophageal reflux disorder (GERD) is very common in premature infants and often persists into the first years of life. GERD occurs when an infant's muscular sphincter allows acidic, gastric fluids to reflux, or flow backward into the esophagus and sometimes reach as high as the mouth or nose. Children who experience reflux can be irritable and fussy and spit up or vomit as the acid causes a burning sensation. Adults call this sensation heartburn. The condition can be normal and temporary for the vast majority of babies. Some children with severe reflux will refuse to eat because of esophagitis but be content to eat small amounts when the esophagus heals. Others will perceive a small amount of reflux as dangerous and painful and refuse to eat at all. The home visitor must be vigilant for signs of respiratory distress and even pneumonia in children with reflux because these conditions can signal *silent reflux* and aspiration where the refluxed food has come up as high as the oral pharynx and been aspirated into the lungs, sometimes without coughing or other symptoms. This is a serious medical condition. A specialist who may recommend medical intervention should see the child. Simple coping mechanisms for preventing reflux include

- Do not overload when feeding. Parents concerned about increasing their child's weight may try to feed that last bit in the bottle, only to have the whole feeding come back up. Avoid long periods without eating, scheduling feeding every 2 hours, gradually extending the time. Don't allow "grazing" so that the child will be hungry (Toomey, 1999).
- Keep the child upright and quiet (no rough play or stomach compression) for at least 20 minutes after feeding. Elevate the head of a bed or changing table by raising the feet of furniture, not the mattress.

- Parental reaction to the spitting up or vomiting can change a natural process into a behavior problem if the parents react with obvious distress. When an episode happens, just smile, say something soothing, and clean up the child.
- Parents should consult their pediatrician for severe reflux because some medications are effective.

Children on Gastrostomy Tubes

It is very important to state that if a child is fed by gastrostomy tube (g-tube), a team of specialists, including a physician, should be in charge of weaning the child from the tube and into oral feeding. The physician determines the child's readiness to eat (e.g., orally, consume only water or thickened liquids, only taste the food, nothing per oral [npo]). The home visitor can assist the process by facilitating the cycle of eating and satiation that tube-fed children often miss and which causes problems later when the child does not associate the cycle of hunger-eating-satiation. When an infant is fed by tube, a pacifier or bottle filled with formula or breast milk, if it is allowed, should be in the child's mouth so that sucking and feeling full become associated. Later, the tube-fed child can sit at the table with the family with the tube apparatus behind him or her. The child can continue to suck on a pacifier, have tastes, or eat what is offered as the formula runs through the tube, once again associating the growing fullness with mouth activity and eating. If a tube-fed child has not had these experiences, feeling full and the process of eating are not associated and must be painstakingly learned in the weaning process.

Linda visited the home of Ramesh and his parents Sangita and Raj. Ramesh, age 2, had always been a picky eater who ate better when he was distracted, first by the television and then by the antics of whoever was feeding him. He required songs and poems and physical antics before he would open his mouth for food. Sangita and Raj were worn out, and the behavior was ever escalating so that meals took well over half an hour. Sangita's parents were visiting from India. Ramesh would not allow his grandparents to feed him. He would eat only for his mother or father. Both parents worked and longed to have respite from the mealtimes. Linda solicited information from all family members, including the grandparents, and made some recommendations with all present. Put Ramesh at the table with the adults for family dinner, not in his highchair where he anticipated conflict. He is not to be the center of attention. Put food on his plate that he can eat, and if he wants something from someone else's plate, give it to him. Give him a spoon. Make the mealtime pleasant. For the other two meals, put him at the table with one other adult who is also eating and with no distractions. Linda also recommended that Ramesh learn to drink from a straw and left some handouts about teaching straw drinking. The recommendations were given in a conference mode with all of the family adults, and Ramesh's grandmother suggested that their family meal would be better at noon when all of the adults would more likely be present than at night. The family then began to plan for the seating and what would be served. It was a family decision-making event.

Linda revisited the home 1 month later. Sangita was no longer worried about Ramesh's eating. He was eating with the family, and he was eating well. His family was very pleased with his progress. The grandmother said, "Linda, we took your recommendations and did them but there were two things that we didn't do. We don't eat with utensils—we eat with our hands—so giving Ramesh a spoon and fork were not what we do. Also, we don't drink from straws. Ramesh would never see any of us do that, so we decided not to do it."

Linda had an epiphany: Why didn't I think of that? This family was honest and true to their culture, and Linda had made assumptions that were not valid. They took what made sense to them and discarded what did not—and the results were successful.

SLEEPING DISORDERS

Just as the home visitor encounters difficulties with eating when in the home for some other special need, problems with sleep become apparent as the home visitor inquires about family routines. Sleep problems occur with typical children, but with special needs children they can become exacerbated by other developmental complications. For example, the child who does not eat well or who has reflux can fall into the habit of falling asleep while held by a parent after a feeding and refuse to change this habit. When children have comforting ways to fall asleep, they are understandably loath to give them up. In our experience, the bedtime routine is far from routine. Children may be allowed to fall asleep anywhere as they become exhausted and are then carried to bed. They may fall asleep being held by a parent or in the parents' bed. They may waken in the night and must be fed and rocked back to sleep when they are more than 1 year of age. All such habits begin because the parents are comforting and the child has not learned to self-comfort.

Sleep Routines within the Cultural Context

Home visitors who are culturally competent will be aware of cultural differences in sleeping behavior. The family bed is well established in many cultures with all members sleeping together. The bedtime routine described next is from American mainstream culture, in which parents have an expectation that children will not share their bed. If the cultural expectation is otherwise, the home visitor must take that into account and not impose any cultural pattern on those who do not embrace it.

How the Home Visitor Can Help

The home visitor can help most by giving the parents permission to establish a bedtime routine and not feel guilty about disrupting a child who is now able to fall asleep on his or her own. Remember Frances and José in Chapter 2 and their feelings of guilt when they required Peter to stay in his own bed? They thought of Peter as being too fragile to be in a routine that suited the family. It was difficult, but they changed Peter's bedtime behavior.

Establishing a Bedtime Routine

This is a 30-minute period of winding down before bed. If bedtime is 8:30, the routine starts at 8:00. The series of activities should be the same every night and lead up to sleep: a bath, followed by getting dressed for sleep; then some quiet, calm time such as reading from a favorite book (the television is off). Children who have a snack after dinner should have finished it and should not be fed just before bed as it can interfere with sleep. If the child awakens in the night, stay by the bed and pat the child on the back or give the child his or her thumb or a pacifier (if dealing with an infant), but do not pick up the child. Say soothing things such as, "Mama's here, you're ok. You can go to sleep now." At first, stay until the child falls asleep, fade to patting and reassuring, and then leave the room. This routine can be very effective but also very difficult to accomplish, especially if the parents have differing views on bedtime.

Sandra and Philip were parents of two girls, both of whom were premature. Sara was now nearly 3, and Karen was 13 months. Both girls were underweight and difficult to feed, which was very frustrating for Sandra. Sandra stayed at home with the children, and Philip came home fairly late. Sara took a nap by falling asleep on the living room couch when she was tired. The family ate together. But after dinner, the girls played with their father and the television was on. By about 10:00 p.m., Sara showed signs of being tired. Philip put her on his lap and gave her a bottle of fortified formula while watching TV. She fell asleep, and he took her to bed. Sandra complained to her home visitor that she was so frazzled at the end of the day that she wanted the girls to be in bed, but her husband would not change his routine with Sara. Although Sara was long past the time to take a bottle, her weight gain and poor eating were of primary concern to the family. Clearly, this routine was satisfying to both father and daughter but very unsatisfying to the mother.

Circumstances prevented Heather, the home visitor, from speaking directly to Philip, although this would have been the best course. She suggested that Sara might be ready to give up her nap, as it was often very late in the afternoon, and she could be ready for bed earlier.

Philip could then take her into her room and hold her with the bottle where it was quiet. Gradually, the amount of formula in the bottle can be reduced (with the calories substituted at other times) and then a cup of a little milk can be given. Sara could be put in bed while still awake after this routine. Sandra said she would try to have her husband do it, but neither she nor Heather were hopeful of change unless Philip was convinced—which was unlikely. Heather needed help. She made a referral to the team social worker to visit this home because the undercurrents of conflict were preventing changes in this family.

SPEECH AND LANGUAGE DISORDERS

This section is not intended for specialists in speech and language disorders who already have the expertise necessary to assess and plan a program for a child with speech and language delays or disorders. It is written for the generalist home visitor who encounters a child with what appears to be a speech and language delay or disorder. When should the speech-language pathologist be called in? According to a panel of experts called together to form guidelines for evidence-based practice in various disorders (Noyes-Grosser, Holland, Lyons, Holland, Romanczyk, & Gillis, 2005), when a child 18–36 months old has a speech/language problem, but the developmental assessment indicates no general developmental delay or other developmental problems, initiation of speech/language therapy is recommended for severe speech/language delay if

- At 18 months, no single words
- At 24 months, a vocabulary of fewer than 30 words
- At 36 months, no two-word combinations

For the decision to initiate speech/language therapy for children 18–36 months old who have a milder delay in expressive language only and no other apparent developmental problems (normal language comprehension, no hearing loss, and typically developing in all other ways), it is important that the speech pathologist be asked to use his or her clinical judgment.

How the Home Visitor Can Help

The generalist home visitor can use some techniques for initiating communication that are applicable to any child with communication or cognitive delays. These techniques are used prior to a child's first words—precursors to language development—and also fall into the category of social-emotional development. It is fairly easy to carry out these suggestions and to encourage parents to follow them.

Imitation

For the child who does not imitate yet, the strategy is to imitate the child. The earliest imitation naturally occurs when the parent and child carry on the first conversation or "dance" with the parent imitating the child's babbling, which stimulates more babbling. If the child is not babbling, the adult can imitate a motor act that the child has done in an exaggerated manner: touching his or her own face, sticking out his or her tongue, using his or her hands, and calling attention to the imitation. The child will usually repeat the act to see the adult imitate. This can be extended to Pat-a-cake and Peek-a-boo, then other fingerplays. If the child makes an utterance at any time, it is imitated immediately with the hope of starting a conversation of sounds without words. Nonspeech sounds that most children will imitate in play are sounds of cars, planes, and animals, which can be used with a gesture.

Taking Turns

Parents are used to taking turns with their baby, but usually the parent takes the turn with the baby unaware of the give and take. In this strategy, the home visitor carries out an activity (e.g., slapping a drum or top of an inverted pan, then handing it to the child to take a turn and imitate). The child may imitate the action, and the home visitor holds out his or her hand to receive back the drum. If the child does not willingly give back the drum, the home visitor gently takes it, makes a drumbeat, and hands it back until the child gets into the routine. Other articles can be a xylophone (play three notes and hand it over), a play workbench with a hammer, and so forth. Explain to the parent that conversation is taking turns. You are also building attention span and interaction.

Shared Regard

In this activity, both child and adult are sharing their attention to a common object, such as a book. The desired action from the child is for him or her to look at the book, look at the adult, and then look at the book again. The home visitor points to an object on the page but does not name it until the child looks at the home visitor. This activity has many variations, but the child is actively engaged with the adult, not just looking at a book with the adult looking on. Again, this activity is a communication act that does not require speech but is a precursor to speech conversation.

Play Games

Pat-a-cake and Peek-a-boo are more than just fun and games. Being highly repetitive with simple roles for both child and parent, these games help infants learn such things as the rules of give and take in conversations. "I'm gonna get you" is a game in which the parent looms toward the infant or child and says something such as "Ah, boom," which makes the child laugh. "Walking fingers" or "Creepy-crawlies" are games in which the parent's fingers crawl up the body of the child to make the child laugh. "So big" is a game in which the parent extends the child's arms overhead and says, "How big is _____? So big," providing a combination of visual, auditory, and tactile stimulation.

MOTOR DISORDERS

Motor disorders result from primary neurological conditions, usually diagnosed as cerebral palsy or conditions of low muscle tone. Interventions for the primary condition and prevention of secondary disorders are the specialty of occupational therapists and physical therapists. The home visitor has a significant part to play in carrying out the recommendations of those specialists in creative ways and in involving parents in routines-based activities.

Evidence-based practice has established that motor therapy carried out in the clinic once per week or less is not effective in changing motor patterns (Mahoney, Robinson, & Perales, 2004). The authors speculated that the failure of the therapies to make a difference had most to do with working directly with children as opposed to working collaboratively with parents. Furthermore, the authors stated, "The most notable feature of contemporary motor intervention research is the lack of it" (p. 296). Making the intervention activity based in already existing routines and play shows the most promise (Valvano & Rapport, 2006). Thus, the charge for the home visitor fits neatly into our philosophy as stated in Chapter 4: The best strategies are naturalistic, spontaneous in family routines, accepted by caregivers, well implemented, and functional.

How the Home Visitor Can Help

The contribution of the home visitor in collaboration with a motor disorders specialist cannot be overestimated in dealing with motor disorders. Early intervention is believed to be important in reducing the progression of impairments and preventing secondary impairments that have long-term effect on functional activities. Functional activities are important for participation in daily routines (e.g., eating, bathing, playing, being otherwise involved in the routines of family life; Valvano & Rapport, 2006). The challenge for the home visitor is to structure practice and sensorimotor experiences that support the target behaviors and increase participation. Well-chosen toys are critical to engage young children in meaningful activity. An interesting task should encourage exploration, repetition, and problem solving, which are critical for learning. The following example illustrates the creativity called for by the home visitor after the assessment and intervention plan have been designed by a physical therapist.

Madison, age 2 years, had a rare chromosomal disorder with neurological impairments that involved severe intellectual and developmental disabilities and low muscle tone. She was unmotivated to explore or reach out for toys. Her visual perception was questionable. She did enjoy interaction with her brothers and parents, and she smiled and laughed when they played with her. Madison's parents wanted her to sit without support so she could sit on the living room floor and also sit in the bathtub. Her individualized family service plan (IFSP) had the goal, written by the physical therapist, that Madison would sit for a period of up to 5 minutes. When placed in a sitting position without support, Madison collapsed. Then, a family friend gave her a toy: When it was switched on, the panel lit up with bright lights and sounds, similar to the panel on a pinball machine. Madison loved it. She loved to kick the switch with her foot and would sit with a straight back while the lights and sounds displayed. Madison practiced sitting several times per day because of this toy. Her home visitor thought of moving the toy into the bathtime routine. Madison sat up in the tub and watched while her parents caused the panel to display.

On a subsequent visit, the physical therapist noted that Madison had to "lock" her arms close to her sides to maintain sitting. She was developing a secondary disorder involving under-use of her arms and shoulders. The recommendation was to motivate Madison to reach while sitting. The home visitor suggested that they adapt the toy by putting it on a block so that the switch was at arm level for Madison. Using her foot was now too difficult to turn on the switch, but Madison's mother modeled turning it on with her hand and moved Madison's hand to do so. The home visitor also suggested to Madison's mother that she use a game for Madison to reach out to touch her eyes, nose, and hair. Madison needed more support to keep her balance while sitting and reaching, but she smiled and participated, so her father learned to support her during this activity. Support was faded as she gained more strength. She could participate in this activity with her parents and her brothers at least once per day. Family interaction was strengthened along with Madison's motor skills.

Guidelines for motor skill development are outlined in Table 6.2. Regardless of which team member, specialist or generalist, serves as the primary service provider, the goal remains the same—functional independence within typical daily routines. Natural movement is not the goal. A task can be achieved through many different means, and coordination patterns are individual based on a child's movement patterns. However, an abnormal pattern (e.g., locking, head thrust forward as compensation) should never be encouraged. Activity-based motor interventions are designed with this goal in mind.

Table 6.2.   Guidelines for motor skill development

Use toys to promote play, exploration, and problem solving in order to reach functional goals established collaboratively with the motor specialist.

When presenting toys, focus on activities in the environment and tasks that increase the child's access to the goal activity.

Plan to have the practice distributed throughout the day.

Physically guide the child in ways that the toy can be used. Provide motivating cues to continue with the task.

When the variations on a task are provided, give the child time to process them and provide feedback on the child's success.

Provide guidance with generalizing a skill to a new environment (such as sitting in the bathtub and in the high chair).

From Valvano, J., & Rapport, M.J. (2006). Activity-focused motor interventions for infants and young children with neurological conditions. *Infants & Young Children, 19*(4), 292–307; adapted by permission.

COMMON ESTABLISHED DISORDERS

The term *established disorders* in this context refers to those disorders in which a diagnosis has been made that makes a child eligible for home visitor services. In the previous examples of feeding, sleeping, behaviors, speech and language, and motor issues, a definitive diagnosis was not necessarily made. The following sections focus on developmental delay (genetic and idiopathic), Down syndrome, autism spectrum disorders (ASD), fetal alcohol syndrome, and children who are medically fragile. In these cases, the disorder itself drives the intervention from the home visitor.

Developmental Delay

Developmental delay is, in essence, an umbrella term for several types of disability. It is often used when the source of a child's delay is not clear. For example, a speech delay can result from a number of causes. Some states limit this term to those children who do not qualify for one of the other disability categories. The criteria for developmental delay vary across states with the most common criterion used as 2.0 standard deviations below the mean in one developmental area or 1.5 standard deviations below the mean in two developmental areas. In most states that use a percentage-of-delay criterion, the criterion is a 25% or 30% delay in one or two developmental areas. Some states also permit informed team consensus, professional judgment, or informed clinical opinion, in lieu of test scores, to ascertain eligibility (Division for Early Childhood, 2001).

Cultural Differences in Developmental Delay

As we have said throughout this book, families must be an integral part of all aspects of assessment and intervention with the children seen by the home visitor. It is incumbent upon the home visitor to be culturally competent—that is, to understand the cultural background of the family and take it into consideration in all program planning. When team members and home visitors collaborate with families in which a child or an adult parent has a developmental delay, several cultures are likely to emerge, including the home visitor's personal background, discipline, and organizational culture and the family's culture. For example, the presence of a developmental delay in some cultures can be perceived as a gift or spiritual sign, whereas in other cultures it can be seen as a curse or punishment for a wrongdoing by a parent or family member. These varying perspectives on the concept of disability will influence the role and expectations of families and community members in service provision (Prelock, 2006).

> Meredith, a physical therapist, was invited to speak to a group of parents of children with Down syndrome. The meeting was held in a church's religious education room. She prepared her talk to include ways that parents can provide motor practice for their children to strengthen the hypotonia (low muscle tone) that is part of the Down syndrome phenotype. In her audience of about 15 parents, she noticed looks of hostility in some and polite smiling and nodding in others. After the talk, a mother approached her:
> "I enjoyed your talk tonight, particularly the part where you said that our biggest job as parents is to provide a loving home and enjoy our children instead of being teachers all the time. You know, we feel that

*God has given these children to us because we have been specially cho-
sen to care for them. God doesn't give you more than you can handle."*

*Meredith believed that Down syndrome was an accident of
nature, but this was no place to voice that belief. She nodded, neither
agreeing nor disagreeing, as the mother continued about her religious
beliefs. Even though the cultures were different, her job was to work
with parents to provide the best information and help she could give
them. That information would not include how Down syndrome
occurred unless someone specifically asked for it.*

Down Syndrome

It is beyond the scope of this book to address the genetics involved
in Down syndrome. Over the past few decades, research has begun to
converge on a specific behavioral phenotype, or a distinct profile of
behavioral outcomes associated with Down syndrome (Fidler,
2005). Early developmental findings suggest that in both infancy and
later development, mixtures of strengths and weaknesses can be
found within all areas of functioning. Although children with Down
syndrome are as varied as other children, they typically display
strengths in visual-spatial skills, short-term memory, and nonverbal
communication. Typical areas of deficit center on language, with
expressive language lagging behind receptive language. Vocal imitation is impaired but motor imitation, especially with the hands, is a
relative strength (gestures). Children with Down syndrome enjoy
interaction with people rather than objects. Motivation for exploration and perseverance is low compared to same-age peers. Finding
ways to keep a child with Down syndrome engaged in a play session
can be challenging because they will avoid opportunities to learn new
skills and avoid repeating new skills learned previously. These children ask for help perhaps more often than they need to because the
struggle to "do it myself" is not a priority. Assessment becomes difficult because these children are inconsistent in responding. This
inconsistency may be caused by rapid shifts in attention and lack of
motivation (Miller & Rosin, 1998). Most children with Down syndrome face serious motor challenges: extreme motor delays and

abnormal movement patterns. Hypotonia and hyperflexibility are common. These atypical motor outcomes seem to become more evident toward the end of the first year of life (Fidler, 2005).

Early Intervention in Down Syndrome

Parents and some early interventionists may assume that the purpose of early intervention is to *accelerate* the pace of development, but most experienced interventionists will see their role somewhat differently. Their most important role is to *support* development by teaching specific strategies that can be learned as neuromaturation proceeds. Home visitors will want to monitor developmental milestones outside their area of expertise and work to prevent maladaptive patterns and secondary disabilities from emerging and interfering with skill acquisition. They will educate parents in a home program and facilitate referral if serious medical or neurodevelopmental problems occur (Capone, 2004). For example, children with Down syndrome are prone to middle-ear infections that can produce temporary conductive hearing loss that can also become a chronic problem. More than 75% of young children with Down syndrome are found to have at least a mild hearing problem at some time in childhood. Many have visual acuity deficits with myopia being the most common (Miller & Rosin, 1998). It is the home visitor's responsibility to provide information, perhaps outside his or her area of expertise, about the treatment and prevention of otitis media and to provide information about visual testing and follow-up treatment.

Down syndrome has perhaps more empirical evidence for interventions than any other disorder, but there is still a strong need for interventions that are rooted in good science. Parents can be barraged with claims for alternative and unconventional therapies, such as high-dosage vitamins and minerals that have not been tested and proven to be effective. These high-dosage vitamins and supplements may be associated with unpleasant side effects as well. However, a significant number of parents would still recommend them to other parents on the basis that their child's appearance improved (Bidder, Gray, Newcombe, & Evans, 1989).

In two studies involving children with Down syndrome, the importance of time sensitivity and early implementation in intervention has been demonstrated (Sanz & Balana, 2002; Sanz & Menendez, 1995). It is unnecessary to wait for the inevitable deficits in expressive language to become apparent to begin intervention. Home intervention services should focus on preventing expressive language impairments before they become pronounced. Continuous reinforcement for socialization in infants between 2 and 8 months has been shown to increase vocalization rates (Poulson, 1988). Parents can be taught to use techniques such as back chaining, prompt fading, and social praise as rewards for effort. The implementation of just any intervention is not sufficient for improving developmental outcomes. Teaching strategies should capitalize on strengths and should focus on visual-vocal and visual-motor processing. Strategies that emphasize auditory learning are likely to increase frustration for all concerned. Thus, the teaching of imitation of motor acts, early gestures, picture exchange, and signing utilizes strengths and minimizes frustration. A movement to emphasize early reading with sight vocabularies with children with Down syndrome also shows promise (Fidler, 2005; Miller & Rosin, 1998). Intervention approaches can more readily target areas of deficit by embedding them in tasks that involve areas of strength. To increase practice of motor foundations skills, it may be useful to embed motor tasks in play and other social contexts in routines, being sure to provide a steady flow of motivational feedback. For example, to improve and maintain appropriate posture, a child may work on the skill by sitting at a table engaging in a fine motor task that is of interest (Fidler, 2005). Suggestions for working with children with Down syndrome are found in Table 6.3.

Other Syndromes with Intellectual and Developmental Disabilities

Another genetic disorder that the home visitor is likely to see is Williams syndrome, with a phenotype quite different from characteristics of Down syndrome. Williams syndrome illustrates the importance of utilizing information about the phenotype of various disor-

Table 6.3. Pointers for working with children with Down syndrome

Use strengths to enhance deficits.
Strengths are in visual-motor, motor imitation, and sociability skills.
Use signing, picture exchange, and gestures during reading.
Do not wait for inevitable motor and expressive language deficits to appear.
Use high-motivation activities for working on deficits (e.g., motor).
Encourage self-reliance and less asking for help.
Use steady positive feedback.
Prevent secondary disorder (e.g., hearing loss).
Monitor development.

Source: Fidler (2005).

ders because the strengths and weaknesses of individuals with Williams syndrome are so divergent from those in Down syndrome. Children with Williams syndrome have strengths in language skills, auditory short-term memory, and music. Contrary to Down syndrome, these children display deficits in visual-spatial constructions and difficulty with loud sounds. Strategies for teaching to their strengths include music activities and games to enhance their motor movements and knowledge of where they are in space. Older children with Williams syndrome have many fears and anxieties and need help in making friends; hence, the home visitor can help with preventing or ameliorating the onset of such stresses.

Information about strengths and areas of deficit exists only for a small number of the 750+ known genetic disorders. Many children with a genetic disorder are eligible for early intervention under the umbrella term *developmental disability*. In the case of rare disorders, the home visitor may learn from the parents who have done research on the disorder. Having experience living with their child, parents can be excellent sources for other parents who are new to the diagnosis. Over the years, parent–professional organizations have risen to help families and professionals working with children with many disorders. Groups are most often nationally based, often with state or regional chapters. Umbrella organizations include the Alliance of Genetic Support Groups and the National Organization for Rare Genetic Disorders. The Internet is an excellent source of information about these organizations as well as the National Down Syndrome Society (www.ndss.org), the Williams Syndrome Association (www.williams-syndrome.org; Hodapp, DesJardin, & Ricci, 2005), and the American Association on Intellectual and Developmental Disabilities (www.aaidd.org).

Behavior Problems and Developmental Delay

Children who can communicate their needs and emotions in appropriate ways, form relationships with peers and adults, solve social problems, and control their emotions are more successful in school and in life. When children have delays or disruptions in communication, social development, or adaptive behavior, they may engage in challenging behavior that gets their needs met or that expresses their wants or desires. In this manner, challenging behavior can be viewed as a skill deficit or developmental issue (Division for Early Childhood, 2005).

Children with developmental delays have a much higher incidence of behavior problems than do children who are typically developing. Studies vary in the percentages of behavior problems; however, one study reported that children with developmental delays were three times as likely to be in the clinical range for problem behaviors as early as age 3 years (Baker, Blacher, Crnic, & Edelbrock, 2002). Growing evidence indicates that young children who engage in chronic problem behaviors, especially those who are aggressive in nature, proceed through a predictable course of ever-escalating challenging behaviors (Division for Early Childhood, 2005). Certainly not all children with developmental delays display such behavior, but the increased rate means that home visitors must be aware of the problems and pay attention to them. In fact, children who have milder forms of developmental delay are at greater risk for behavior problems (Crnic, Hoffman, Gaze, & Edelbrock, 2004).

These children pose unique parenting challenges that include intensified behavior management issues. The stress that families experience cannot be overemphasized. Families are often affected by repeated disruption of daily routines, relentless demands on time and energy, escalating conflict within the home, unsolicited advice and criticism from others when challenging behavior occurs, reduced participation in community activities, and increased social isolation (Division for Early Childhood, 2005). The family's stress and fewer positive interactions can have a detrimental effect on the child's challenging behaviors, thus perpetuating them. Family factors alone do not offer a complete explanation for behavior because child characteristics, such as temperament and self-regulatory ability, are also key to understanding these complex problems.

How the Home Visitor Can Help

The home visitor can quickly find him- or herself isolated when asked to deal with intervention for challenging behaviors in a young child. It is important to reach out to other members of the team for help with the various aspects of the problem. Sometimes the behaviors are mentioned at the first visit. In other families, the challenges are not mentioned until trust is established or until the home visitor witnesses a meltdown. Because each child and family are unique, the following are meant only as guidelines for the home visitor:

- **Listen** to what each person who interacts with the child does when the behaviors occur. These are consequent events and they may be quite varied.
- **Help the family to identify the triggers.** Prevent the behavior from occurring if at all possible. This does not mean that the child is never told "no," but when the child is tired or overstimulated, the behavior is more likely to occur.
- **Help the family to identify and communicate feelings.** Because behaviors are most often in response to frustration, and the frustration is most often the result of not being understood, the child and family should be taught alternative ways to communicate (e.g., gestures, pictures, sign).
- **Help the family to note exactly how everyone responds to the child's inappropriate behavior.** Remember the adage: Some attention is better than none. What responses from the child's environment reinforce the behavior to the child in any

way? How can others respond differently so that the child's negative behavior is not reinforced?

- **Help parents to improve their interactions with the child.** Find ways that they can enjoy the child. Build in gradual ways to interact with the environment if they have become isolated (e.g., get an ice cream cone when the shop is not crowded instead of going to a restaurant).
- **Make a behavior plan that is incorporated into the IFSP.** Discuss the plan with all family members and the team of professionals.
- **Refer the family to a family resource center for help with support groups and social support.** They are not the first or only family to face these challenges.

Autism Spectrum Disorders

With the incidence as frequent as 1 in 150 births (Centers for Disease Control and Prevention, 2007), ASD is the nation's fastest growing developmental disorder and a common reason for home visitor services. It is beyond the scope of this chapter to address theories of the causes of ASD or to do an in-depth discussion of treatment methods. Instead, we address salient issues for the home visitor and how the home visitor can serve the family with a child with ASD.

Autism Spectrum Disorders within the Cultural Context

Although autism may be viewed as a universal disorder—one that is present in diverse cultures, races, and economic groups—the course of the disorder may be heavily influenced by culture (Daley, 2002). This includes beliefs about the etiology of the disorder as well as the relative value or stigma associated with it. The same cluster of symptoms in some cultures may reflect negatively on the family, indicating punishment for some transgression on the part of the child's relatives. Dyches, Wilder, Sudweeks, Obiakor, and Algozzine (2004) noted that in African American culture, caregiving for a family member with autism was seen as a responsibility to be shared among siblings and extended family members. One would expect variations in the time frames for identifying autistic-like behaviors among cultures because of differing beliefs about the course of typical development and the importance of certain behaviors. It is important that home visitors identify and explain the symptoms of the disorder within the cultural context of the child's family. For example, a child's lack of eye gaze, few verbalizations, and failure to initiate interactions with adults are often considered to be symptoms of ASD. However, the appropriateness of each of these behaviors varies considerably across cultures. It would be inappropriate to develop a treatment program designed to facilitate behaviors that are not consistent with the family's cultural norms or values (Cromwell, Belgum, & Kohnert, 2005). Thus, it is critical to understand what aspects of socialization are most important to the family of each individual child with autism.

Early Identification

The "wait and see" method, often recommended to concerned parents, can lead to missed opportunities for early intervention during this critical time period. A current study (Landa, Holman, & Garrett-Mayer, 2007) revealed that autism often involves a progression, with the disorder claiming or presenting itself between 14 and 24 months of age. In fact, half of all children with autism can be diagnosed around the first birthday. Furthermore, research indicates that intervention provided before age 3 has a much greater impact than intervention provided after age 5 (Harris & Handleman, 2000, Mundy & Neal, 2001; Woods & Wetherby, 2003). A child may be eligible for home services due to failure to achieve developmental milestones, especially communication interaction. Unfocused concerns can cause great anxiety, whereas determining that a child has ASD can lead families toward concrete information to better understand and interact with their child. Identification also allows for selection of appropriate intervention (Cadigan & Estrem, 2007). An appropriate, thorough evaluation is needed to be certain of a diagnosis at any age and doing an evaluation sooner rather than later is nearly always the best choice. On the other hand, there may be a tendency to jump to the diagnosis of ASD. The home visitor must guard against overidentification as well. Table 6.4 summarizes four red flags that are reasons for concern and referral for diagnosis.

Facilitating a Diagnosis

Even with all of the recent literature on ASD causes and treatment, there is scant help for the early interventionist who suspects that a child has ASD but the family has not gotten a diagnosis, either because they do not recognize a problem or because the pediatrician or family members have adopted a "he'll grow out of it" posture. There are many excellent web sites and sources of information in terms of post-diagnosis, but little has been written about the difficult job of getting a diagnosis. Delayed diagnosis and postponement of subsequent treatment is not serving the family. On the other hand, being uncomfortable with a diagnosis that may have been incorrectly given to a family and saying nothing is also not serving the family.

To the question, "How do I broach the subject of ASD with a family?" we must rely on personal experience. It depends on the stage of awareness of the family when the home visitor recognizes that a diagnosis is needed. Keeping in mind that each agency may have a policy for such situations and that payment for diagnosis varies by agency and state, the following are three possibilities illustrated by Brian and his family.

Table 6.4. Red flags that signal the need to refer

Abnormalities in initiating communication with others

Compromised ability to initiate and respond to opportunities to share experiences with others

Irregularities with playing with toys

Significantly reduced variety of sounds, words, and gestures used to communicate

Sources: Filipek et al. (2000); Greenspan & Wieder (1999).

Brian is not using words at age 2 years. The speech-language pathologist who assessed him noted that his expressive language lagged behind his receptive language scores, but only slightly. Her report included developmental delay or late talking as probable causes. She recommended a generalist home visitor to stimulate language and to help the caregivers in some techniques to speed up Brian's language development together with periodic monitoring from her. Emily is that home visitor.

Responding When Parents Suspect ASD

From the first visit, Brian's mother, Michelle, told Emily that there is more to Brian's problem than late talking. She wondered if Brian could have "autism." She said she couldn't get anyone to pay attention to her: Her husband and mother-in-law thought she worried too much and told her that Brian would grow out of it. Emily listened to her concerns and said, "We now know that autism is what's called a 'spectrum disorder.' A child can have a few symptoms or many symptoms along the spectrum. We also know that with the right early intervention some of those symptoms can be overcome by the time a child enters school. Would you like for me to refer you to someone who is an expert in diagnosing autism? Our agency refers children to a developmental pediatrician, Dr. Curtis. I'll give you her phone number, and I will also send a summary of our concerns about Brian." Note that Emily used the word "autism" only after Michelle did.

Responding to Parents' General Concerns

In this case, Michelle does not ask directly about autism, but she confides to Emily that Brian does not act like her other children did. In particular, he doesn't point to things he wants and he prefers to play alone. She worries about his behavior when he goes to school. Emily said, "It may be that Brian is not getting everything he needs with my once-per-week visits. Do you think that Brian has more needs than are being met now?" Michelle expressed her satisfaction with Emily as a visitor, but said she didn't see enough improvement in his overall behavior. Emily said, "I share your concerns about Brian, and it would help us all to get more information. There is a web site you can look at for some more information. It's First Signs at www.firstsigns.org." In this case Emily did not use the word "autism" because Michelle did not use it. After Michelle visited the web site, she asked Emily if she thought Brian had autism. Emily replied that Brian showed some of the signs that were indicated on the web site. She then brought up the subject of Dr. Curtis and facilitated Brian's visit to her.

Responding When Parents Do Not Suspect ASD

Michelle told Emily that Brian is a little slow in talking but she is sure that he will catch up. "After all," she said, "They say that Einstein didn't talk until he was three." At each of her visits, Emily asks about social progress goals on Brian's IFSP. Whereas it is Emily's task to normalize behavior for some of her other clients whose parents see appropriate behavior as abnormal, she now needs to point out to Michelle that Brian's behavior is of concern. Brian has been to a birthday party in which he went into a corner of the yard and sifted dirt while the other children were playing. Brian had a meltdown in the grocery store, and Michelle attributed it to Brian's being too tired. As these incidents grew in number, Emily said, "Are you concerned about Brian's behavior? It would help me to know how to work with him if I had more information. Additional information might make it easier for you to parent Brian as well. Would you like me to find a specialist to help us better understand Brian's behavior? Perhaps additional assessment would give us valuable insights." Michelle said she would talk with her husband about it and let Emily know. Note here that Emily did not suggest any diagnosis or label for Brian. She asked for further assessment to help everyone work with Brian. The previously mentioned web site can also be helpful in a situation like this.

How the Home Visitor Can Help

Thus, the first task of the home visitor is to be certain that the diagnosis is accurate. Next is to facilitate appropriate treatment. Research suggests which program characteristics are effective for children with ASD (National Research Council, 2001). Although effective programs have philosophical and programmatic differences, they share important common features such as high levels of structure, focus on direct instruction, and substantial hours per week of intervention. However, this evidence-based practice is only as good as the next research study. The home visitor is cautioned that new treatment paradigms are published regularly with varying degrees of evidence. The critical concept here is that there be evidence from rigorous evaluation of a method before it is taken as a proven strategy worthy of recommendation.

Intensive early intervention studies indicate that about half of children with an ASD diagnosis overcome many of the language and social skills deficits that limit their participation with their family, school, and community by the time they enter kindergarten or first grade (Sallows & Graupner, 2005). These rapidly learning children function intellectually within the typical range and are integrated in regular education classrooms. Many continue to display subtle language and social differences but participate meaningfully in school and in their communities. Children with lower IQ test scores, no language, and lack of joint attention or imitation tend to learn less rapidly during early intervention and profit more from a functional curriculum and augmentative communication (Thompson, 2007).

Unproven Remedies

Children with ASD are in particular need of effective practices because they have been especially prone to encounter and suffer unproven and controversial treatments and interventions. A number of these purported ASD intervention methods lack theoretical, clinical, and/or empirical foundation, yet often promise dramatic and all-encompassing improvements and even restoration to normalcy. That is why professionals and parents, who are given opportunities to use methods and treatments that promise dramatic improvements, even if the approach being considered lacks scientific validation, may be willing to take a chance and consider using techniques and strategies that all too frequently have little to offer (Simpson, 2007). The home visitor may serve the family by checking the practice for evidence, but unless it appears to be harmful, the family should try whatever they wish.

Information Sources

The Internet has become a major source of information and misinformation about the treatments for ASD. Also, information from well-meaning friends and family can add to the confusion. Many of these have little or no basis in research. The Autism Society of America (ASA; www.autism-society.org) has a chapter in every state. One parent and professional-friendly resource is Autism/Asperger's Digest (www.futurehorizons-autism.com). Other useful web sites are www.polyxo.com and www.feat.org (Families for Early Autism Treatment). It is crucial to connect the family to support groups in the community or online (Lord & McGee, 2001; Pehlman, 2007).

The home visitor can help the family begin a resource notebook. Often, the professionals who make the diagnosis are not those who carry out the intervention. The compilation of a resource notebook with all of the child's evaluations and recommendations that can travel with the child is an effective tool for sharing information among professionals, for parents' reference, and to record progress.

Beginning Communication Approaches with Children Who Have Autism Spectrum Disorders

The family may say that the child doesn't communicate, but a closer look will show that the child does—although not in the typical way. Tantrums and other atypical behaviors can often have a communicative function. Helping the family to identify these behaviors and why they are used gives them a starting point from which to modify behaviors.

Home visitors, parents, and other caregivers can play a significant role in the emergence of young children's early communicative acts. The evidence-based practice literature describes a number of straightforward actions that appear to enhance beginning communication skills in children who have ASD (Reichle, 2007).

- Attend to child's focus of attention. Adults who interact and name objects that were already the focus of a child's attention increase the child's language repertoire.

- Be responsive to communicative overtures. Responding to the child's communicative attempts (which may be gestures or looking at/touching objects) appears to be very important in creating highly motivating communicative contexts.

- Identify and implement joint activity routines. (See Speech and Language Disorders on pages 151–153 in this chapter). These are games that adults often play with children (e.g., Peek-a-boo, taking turns beating a drum or pounding a play workbench, rolling a ball back and forth). Work toward longer and longer attention to the game. Such joint activities allow for some variation in children's routines and can offer many repetitions.

- Ensure that new communications successfully compete with old. For example, an old behavior might be a scream and point to a desired object, replaced by a new behavior of a sign for PLEASE. Parents can be urged to model the new behavior whenever the child uses the old one and to then respond with reinforcement when the child uses the new behavior.

- Transitions from one activity or place to another may trigger difficult behavior from the child, especially when moving from a preferred activity to a less preferred activity. Using pictures to show the next change or the daily schedule can help the child anticipate what will come next and get ready for it. Using timers and verbal warnings can also help the child get ready and make the transition much smoother. Families can develop and use their own picture schedules as another form of visual support.

Children Affected by Prenatal Exposure to Alcohol

The spectrum of disorders resulting from exposure to alcohol in utero is sometimes called FASD for fetal alcohol spectrum disorders, which replaces the former terms of FAS for fetal alcohol syndrome and FAE for fetal alcohol effect. The latter term differentiated those children who did not display the physical characteristics of face and small stature of FAS but shared the diagnosing disorder of the central nervous system with children with FAS. FASD encompasses all children affected by exposure to alcohol prenatally who display disorders that will be concerning enough to merit service by home visitors. In 1996, the term *alcohol-related neurodevelopmental disorder* (ARND) was introduced, focusing on the central nervous system disorders rather than on the growth deficiency and characteristic face. The brain is the organ in the body most vulnerable to the effects of prenatal alcohol, and the effects on the brain concern caregivers and service providers.

In our experience, the child with FASD who is most likely to be served by a home visitor is an adopted or foster child or is being raised by grandparents. In some cases, the history of alcohol during pregnancy is known, and in the case of adoption, particularly adoption from another country, it is not. If the birth mother is raising the child, she may or may not be in recovery and she may also be in a treatment environment, such as a sober group home. If so, her recovery is considered to be of primary importance; she will need to attend meetings and have a structure of her own. Working with a mother–child dyad in this situation calls for help from a team of specialists, particularly a social worker who can help with these complex issues. We will address some things that a home visitor can do in a home in which the child is not with the birth mother.

Information Sources

The need for information is critical. Following are among the best information and support sources we know:

- Book: *Fetal Alcohol Syndrome: A Guide for Families and Communities* by Ann Streissguth (1997, Brookes Publishing Co.)

- Online information:
  - National Organization on Fetal Alcohol Syndrome (http://www.nofas.org)
  - Family resource (http://www.fetalalcoholsyndrome.org)
  - Support (http://www.acbr.com/fas; click on FASlink)
  - Newsletter (*Iceberg*; http://www.fasiceberg.org)

Diagnosis

If a child has FASD, diagnostic information not only helps people to better understand the syndrome's accompanying challenges but also facilitates appropriate treatment, intervention, and planning. It may be difficult to find a diagnosis, particularly when the child does not have the physical characteristics of the disorder. In fact, the individual features of FASD are subtle enough that many people pass through life undiagnosed (Streissguth, 1997). The home visitor can assist the family if a diagnosis is sought through the pediatrician or a developmental pediatric clinic.

Symptoms

Symptoms of FASD are variable, but the most common are

- Poor habituation in infancy—Difficulty with sleeping, irritability, poor sucking response, going from sleep to hyperalert state, and crying without calm alert state
- Distractability/hyperactivity—Difficulty following directions, temper tantrums, does not learn from mistakes, must be told over and over
- Physical symptoms—Prone to otitis media, vision problems, malocclusion of teeth; may have failure to thrive as weight does not improve with feeding
- Poor social skills—Will go with strangers, good speech but poor understanding

Intervention Concepts

It is difficult to remember that these children are not being obstinate but really cannot behave as others desire and require, so the primary concept is to talk with the parent about what the child's actions are communicating. Thinking needs to shift from *will not* to *can not*. It is not that FASD children cannot also develop aberrant behaviors, but in general they are overwhelmed by the environment and demands made upon them (Sparks, 1993).

How the Home Visitor Can Help

The home visitor can begin intervention with information and developmental guidance about the following:

- Always start with the environment. Don't overload the sensory system; make the environment conducive to helping the child to focus. Structure and predictable routines work best.

- Always provide concrete rather than abstract concepts ("Stop!" instead of "If you do that, _____ will happen").

- Teach the child in very small steps. Practice, reteach, practice, reteach.

- See that the parents have respite. Living with a child with FASD can be as frustrating as living with a child with autism. This disorder is life long, although children can lead productive lives with help and support.

Mona was at her wit's end with Tyler, her adopted son. An example of his behavior was that every night after his bath he threw the towel on the floor, despite Mona's instructions to hang it up. Mona went to a conference for parents of children with FASD and realized that Tyler was not being naughty—he couldn't remember to do what she asked. He was also overwhelmed with loud noises. Mona could not take him to any store where loud music was playing because he held his ears and screamed. Mona and her home visitor, Monica, decided that Mona would intercept Tyler's bath towel before he had a chance to throw it. For the time being, Tyler would not be exposed to loud noises but he could not stay isolated. Mona began to condition Tyler by playing music on the car radio just under his threshold of discomfort. She also got some noisy toys—a drum and "pop goes the weasel" toy—to get him used to predictable noises and to show him a smile when he looked startled. Perhaps most frustrating for Mona was Tyler's behavior on Sunday nights. Every other night he had a predictable routine of dinner and bedtime, but on Sundays the family had a big dinner at noon and just popcorn with TV at dinnertime. Tyler had a meltdown every Sunday night. Monica helped Mona to see that Tyler was communicating that he could not adjust to the change in routine. The family decided to keep their weekday routine on Sundays also, and Tyler's behavior changed accordingly.

MEDICALLY FRAGILE AND MULTIPLE DISORDERS

Today, as more and more premature infants survive with very low birth weight, the probability of having a home visitor to monitor progress and guide parents is high. Prematurity is defined as less than 37 weeks gestation; very low birth weight is 3 pounds, 5 ounces, or below, and extremely low birth weight is 2 pounds, 3 ounces, or below. Developmental problems range from cerebral palsy to brain bleeds to respiratory distress. We will not discuss interventions for the various sequelae (resulting disorders) of prematurity here. The home visitor will come on the scene when the child is stable and has left the hospital. There is now a shift in thinking and concern from survival to development. A public health nurse whose concerns are related to health and adequate weight gain may be assigned to this family. Close collaboration with medical providers is important for the home visitor.

Staying Healthy

Of primary concern is keeping the child from any colds or infections. Anyone planning to visit the home should stay away if there is suspicion of a cold, and universal sanitary precautions have even greater importance than usual. A cold or other infection can set back progress that has been so painstakingly made.

Multiple Problems

Parental concerns above and beyond medical concerns may center on ultimate outcome, state regulation (feeding and sleeping are likely to be erratic), motor problems, and cognitive questions. Home visitors can safely tell parents that children are amazingly resilient, that there is absolutely no way to predict outcome based on problems at birth because the brain can make remarkable recoveries. The home visitor needs to be vigilant and follow up on suspected seizure activity and problems with hearing and vision, keeping in mind that those sensory abilities may not appear until the child has matured.

Janelle complained to her home visitor that Marcus, 6 weeks premature, did not look at her. "He looks at the dog more than me," she said.

"How does that make you feel?" asked the home visitor.
"Kind of rejected, I guess. It's like, can't you even look at me with
all I do for you?"

When the home visitor explained that Marcus could see the dog that was a moving object several feet away, but his sensory system would not allow him to focus on her face, which was close up, until he reached his expected birthday, she understood that she was not rejected.

The following illustration points out the need for collaboration for children who have multiple impairments and the need for emotional support that parents of such children need.

Brittany was delivered at 25 weeks' gestation. Her survival was questionable for several weeks. Claire, her single mother, was devastated to see her daughter in an incubator with numerous tubes for feeding, monitoring, and breathing coming from her body. When she finally came home, she had a gastrostomy tube for feeding and a hiatal hernia. She was diagnosed with a class 4 brain bleed, had a shunt for hydrocephalus, and had questionable vision. Claire was a lawyer who became a fierce advocate for her daughter and getting the services she required: gastrostomy supplies, formula, physical therapy, and a home visitor. As Brittany grew, she learned to eat orally. She had a left-sided motor impairment, which challenged walking, but she learned to scoot. Her speech and language skills were age appropriate, which drew people to her.

Brittany was progressing very well, particularly after her hernia was repaired, when she had a setback. On a visit with her father and his relatives, she had a febrile seizure. The adults around her did not recognize it, and when they finally took her to the hospital she had seized for more than an hour. She now had a diagnosis of epilepsy and was on medication for recurrence, which had side effects of dulling her cognitive abilities somewhat. She now needed to be watched at day care for seizure activity and rushed to the hospital if it occurred.

Brittany had several home visitors who needed to collaborate. Her vision specialist gave her feeding specialist suggestions on presenting food so that Brittany could see it best. Physical therapy was done outside the home, and collaboration was done at the IFSP meetings for role release—how to position Brittany for eating and looking at books and how to challenge her with toys for moving toward them. The feeding specialist, a speech-language pathologist, took on the responsibility for coordination with the neurologist, pediatrician, gastroenterologist, and child care providers. Claire had many challenges with social services in getting the proper gastrostomy supplies, and the home visitor supported her and helped her with navigating the system. When Brittany went to preschool, Claire had other battles because there was not a perfect classroom for a child with as many physical challenges, yet who was cognitively and linguistically as intact as Brittany. Claire held out for an aide to accompany Brittany on the bus ride to school to guard against seizures and she went to Fair Hearing to win her case. Brittany is finally in preschool. Claire knows that she will need to be an advocate for Brittany's services, perhaps until Brittany becomes an independent adult. She keeps in touch with her first home visitors to update them on Brittany's progress and to express her gratitude for their help along the way.

VISUAL DISABILITIES

Visual disabilities, which include low vision, are discussed here not because the generalist home visitor should be an expert in this area but because low vision is often found with other disabilities and must be recognized, and intervention activities must be included in the treatment plan. Most of the children whom a home visitor will see will have low vision only as compared to children who are blind. Babies with early vision loss are at risk for overall developmental delays since early learning is primarily visual. It is not unusual for a home visitor to see children with prescribed eye patches or glasses.

All children with special needs should be screened for visual impairments. Children do not have to be able to talk, read, or identify pictures for a visual impairment to be diagnosed and to have glasses prescribed. It is important to identify and help children who have vision needs as soon as possible as it may be too late to help their vision when they are older. Children with a visual impairment should see a pediatric ophthalmologist, a medical doctor who specializes in diagnosing and treating eye diseases. This may include prescribing eyeglasses, contact lenses, medications, and/or surgery. Many children with multiple disabilities have so many medical and physical needs; vision concerns are often a low priority or are not diagnosed at all. Sometimes parents are so overwhelmed with a child's known disabilities they cannot emotionally think of adding another (visual impairment) concern.

A vision specialist or consultant who is experienced in working with families in the home should be consulted. The vision specialist typically works cooperatively with the family and home teacher. If the child is blind and considered to be solely low incidence, the specialist may work independently with the family.

Working with parents and young children with visual impairments can create some unique challenges for the home visitor. Understanding and supporting a positive parent–child relationship is an important responsibility of the home visitor. Parents who struggle with bonding with their infant who does not make eye contact or use intense eye gaze may need special support and help to be able to interpret the behavior of a visually impaired infant.

Bryon, the home visitor, is making his first home visit to Josh's house, and Josh's mother Anna is having a difficult day. Josh received a recent diagnosis of bilateral nerve hypoplasia. Since Josh's birth, Anna has been having a difficult time. She shared that her husband had read on the Internet that drinking during pregnancy could cause optic nerve hypoplasia, and she had a glass or two of wine before she knew she was pregnant. She felt guilty for maybe being the cause of Josh's blindness and she felt that her husband blamed her as well. To make matters worse, Josh hasn't responded to her like their first child, his older sister, did. Josh doesn't seem to be interested in his mother or father. He is 2½ months old now and isn't smiling back when his mother smiles at him. He seems to want to avoid looking at her. "He looks at anything but me," she sobbed. "It's like he's punishing me for what I did to him. There are days I can't stand to feel the rejection and the guilt. It's easier to let my mom come and take care of him, and he doesn't seem to care if I am there or not."

Bryon quickly processed and prioritized what Anna just shared on the first visit. He was going to have to be flexible and not pull out all of the forms he brought for Anna to sign first thing. He understood that she was grieving. He knew from his experience and training that he didn't need to fix things or tell her he knew how it felt or not to worry. Anna needed someone to listen to her fears and concerns, so Bryon did. Then, Bryon proceeded to ask Anna if she would like to know about the behavior of infants with visual impairments and what can be done to help their vision and development. Anna said she would like to learn about that. Bryon said he had also brought some information from the Blind Babies Foundation about optic nerve hypoplasia. They could go over it together and he would leave it so Anna and her husband and other family members, friends, or professionals who saw Josh could read it. Bryon explained that the information on the Internet was posted by anyone who wanted to post it and it could be difficult to know what was true and what wasn't. The Blind Babies Foundation is a nonprofit home-based organization that serves families with children with visual impairments, birth to 5 years. They have written resources for parents and professionals called "Pediatric Visual Diagnosis Fact Sheets" on difficult visual impairments.

Bryon told Anna that an infant's smile is vision driven. That is, the infant smiles back in response to seeing his mother smiling at him. Josh's lack of gazing at his mother's face, lack of eye contact, and lack of smiling at her smile is not because of his lack of feeling love for her; it is because Josh does not know where to look anymore and he doesn't know that his beautiful mother is smiling at him or that her expression is communicating "I love you." Josh doesn't read facial expressions.

Bryon showed Anna how Josh is communicating: "Look, Anna, see how Josh arches his back and fusses when I hold him? I'm going to hand him to you now. See how I tell him, 'Here's your mom. She wants to hold you!' Look, say something and use his name. That was great. 'Hi, Josh,' you said. Look how he quieted and stopped fussing when you took him in your arms and kissed his head. He knows your voice. He knows your smell. Josh doesn't smile at you now when you smile because he doesn't see it when you smile. He recognizes a lot of things that he does get excited about when you come close, and eventually he will smile. It will just be later than when your daughter first smiled. There are some things that you and other family members can do during your everyday activities that can help Josh smile at you. Do you want to hear some suggestions?

- *Wear a bright lip color to help Josh focus on your lips as you talk and smile, helping him with imitation of mouth movements.*
- *Hold Josh close to your face as you smile and talk to him, letting him feel your lips, touching Josh's lips and talking softly to him.*
- *You and the rest of the family turn Josh to face you as you speak to him, or position yourselves in front of Josh when you speak to him.*
- *Touch, tickle, talk, and imitate back Josh's sounds so that Josh may smile back at you and other family members."*

Bryon knew that touch and increasing the circle of communication between Josh and Anna as well as helping Anna understand how Josh is communicating will help Anna bond with Josh. Bryon also offered infant massage as a service for Anna and Josh, knowing that this also strengthens the parent–child bond and is excellent sensory input for Josh. Bryon will share other supportive resources for the family and Anna, as well.

Babies who don't see objects/toys clearly far away or babies who see very little to nothing are not interested in being on their tummy. In fact, usually they resist it, feeling more secure on their back. Putting an infant on his or her tummy or shaking a toy with sound about his or her head to encourage the infant to lift his or her head will help. The infant may be more passive and uninterested in what is around him or her—not being motivated to reach or crawl for objects that he or she does not see.

Cognitive skills that depend on interaction, vision, motor abilities, and experience are delayed by vision loss. Cause-and-effect relationships, for example, take much repetition and practice for the infant to understand that he or she made it happen. It is important to wait for a child to respond and to give the child time.

Much of the information that a visually impaired child takes in about his or her environment is fragmented. For example, a baby who is fed a mashed banana has no idea that the banana was from a bunch, was a certain size and shape, and was peeled. The banana magically appears on the infant's plate, and that is his connection with the word banana—a mushy paste or mashed pieces, however it is presented to him or her. As a home visitor brings the nubbie glitter ball for a child to play with, the child learns the word *ball*. The glitter ball is the child's experience with *ball*. Will she understand football, baseball, golf ball, basketball, or Ping-Pong ball and how each looks when she hears "ball"? No, she will need to feel each ball in order to learn the concept that each ball is a ball but is different. She won't learn this by looking at pictures of balls or symbols of balls but by feeling the real objects to put the experiences with the sensory perception and language.

A question that is frequently asked of vision specialists and home visitors is whether a child who avoids eye contact and is finger flicking, light gazing, hand waving, and/or eye poking has autism. These behaviors are behaviors of children with visual impairment. Self-stimulating behaviors can develop at an early age, but not all children with visual impairment develop self-stimulating behaviors. The behaviors serve a purpose. They provide movement stimulation, electrical stimulation, or some other kind of stimulation. Children will engage more in these behaviors when there is nothing else to occupy their hands, eyes, or mind. In other words, they are often just plain bored and have found something more entertaining to do than staring into space. The challenge is to keep these entertaining behaviors from interfering with development. Once a pattern is set, it can be very difficult to break. Often, the objective will be to decrease the behavior, not to stop it altogether.

Language Development with Children with Visual Impairment

To encourage language development and communication with a child who is visually impaired, turn off the television and music when playing or talking. It is important for the child to learn to identify sounds and to locate sounds in the environment. Background noise makes it difficult for the child to distinguish differences. Being able to hear and distinguish sounds is especially important when children's primary mode of learning is other than vision.

Encourage communication by turn taking and using physical prompts and cues. Talk to the child, identify by name anyone who comes into the room or leaves. Identify by name anyone who is talking. Use touch to get attention, cue, or prompt. Let the child know when something is going to happen. Describe what is going on. A child with a vision loss may have no idea that it is time for him or her to drink from a bottle until it is suddenly thrust into his or her mouth. Instead, as the child hears the refrigerator door open, the milk pouring, and the warming of the milk, an adult can describe this process in short sentences. Mom can shake the bottle to let the child hear it, move it to help him or her see it, and perhaps put red tape on the bottle to really help her child see it. Then, she can say, "Matty, its time for your bottle. I'm going to pick you up now."

It is important for adults to use and model personal pronouns. Adults usually use the child's name rather than correctly using the personal pronoun (e.g., "It's time for Chance's nap" rather than "It is time for your nap"). Use directional words such as *up, down, underneath, behind, in front of, in, out, on the side of, rather than, here,* and *there* to describe where to look or put things.

How the Home Visitor Can Help

During the home visit, the following can be modeled and explained:
- Give the child time to process information. Allow the child time to respond. When you think you have waited long enough, take a breath and wait some more.

- Repeat, repeat, repeat. You will be tired of repetition long before the child. Repetition is helpful to the child. Use the same objects and the same way of presenting.
- Give the child frequent breaks. Processing and using vision is very tiring, especially if the child has other disabilities.
- Use objects from the kitchen or the house that encourage comparing and contrasting objects that are very similar but have differences (e.g., plastic measuring cups, stainless measuring cups; see Toys Cleverly Disguised as Household Objects in the Appendix). Favorites include objects with textures and weight (e.g., curlers; nail brushes; different size whisks; measuring spoons and cups; dog, cat, and bird toys).
- Offer toys with lights, sounds, and music. Electronic toys can quickly become boring to children unless they are multifunctional. Look for toys that require more than pushing a button.
- Use bright colors such as red, yellow, pink, or orange. Plastic Slinky toys come in these colors.
- Pay attention to lighting. After the TV, the next most difficult physical obstacle for working with a child with a visual impairment is poor lighting. Many homes have the drapes drawn and the lights off during the day. This makes it very difficult for the child to see. It can be awkward to have to ask the parent or caregiver to open the drapes or turn on the lights, as many are very reluctant. The home visitor must explain how light will help the child see better and then ask if they will turn on the lights or open the drapes. The other problem can be glare. Make sure the light source (e.g., the sliding glass door, the window) is behind or to the side of the child. Make sure that light is not reflecting off a glass coffee table or tile floor.
- Make sure that the child has good head support. People cannot use their vision if their head slumps forward on their chest.
- Check the visual distance of the object that the child is being asked to view. Is it being presented in the child's best area of viewing? If the child has poor central vision as with albinism, the object should be in the child's peripheral vision field. If the child has retinopathy of prematurity (ROP) and has poor peripheral vision, the object should be placed in the child's central area of vision.

- Use real/familiar objects. Keep it simple and familiar.
- Try slowly moving an object in the child's field of vision. Often a child will see an object if it is moving rather than still.
- Remind the child to "look me in the eyes." Children with vision loss will often need help with such social skills in order to engage in conversation.
- Teach toddlers with a visual impairment to keep their distance, another social skill. Some children get right in the face of other children because they cannot see them well.
- Help children with cues about body language and gestures that they miss in social situations. Extra help is needed for children with visual impairment to understand others' emotions and facial expressions.
- In new environments, take the child with a visual impairment for a walk and talk about the physical layout of the child's surroundings, especially outside. Remind the child to use his or her vision by looking down and up. Have him or her look around and scan for specific things in the environment. To help with corners or stair edges, use colorful electrician's tape to call attention to these areas while the child is learning.

HEARING DISABILITIES

Today, most children are born in hospitals and have the advantage of universal newborn hearing screening. It can identify children who have profound hearing loss, as well as identify children with hearing loss in only one ear (Irwin, 2007). Hearing loss is usually described as slight, mild, moderate, severe, or profound depending on how well the child can hear the intensities or frequencies most associated with speech. Even very mild losses make it difficult to hear the higher, softer sounds in speech and may interfere with a child's ability to learn language.

There are four types of hearing loss. Diseases or obstructions in the outer or middle ear cause *conductive* hearing losses. Infants and toddlers are especially susceptible to fluctuating conductive hearing losses from ear infections that result in fluid in the middle ear throughout the preschool years. These losses usually affect all frequencies of hearing and usually do not result in severe losses. Children with conductive hearing loss can usually be helped medically or are able to use a hearing aid. *Sensorineural* hearing losses result from damage to some parts or all of the hearing nerves in the inner ear. Sensorineural losses can range from mild to profound and are often not helped by hearing aids. A *mixed* hearing loss results with a combination of conductive and sensorineural loss. Finally, a *central* hearing loss results from damage to the nerves or nuclei of the central nervous system.

Hearing specialists, preferably a team led by an otolaryngologist, should serve children with severe or profound hearing losses. If a cochlear implant is recommended, the home visitor must be sure that the parents have all of the information they desire, including information about important follow-up after the procedure. Generalist home visitors may serve children with mild to moderate losses that are often conductive in nature and, thus, fluctuate. It is important to remember that early developmental milestones will be similar to those of children with normal hearing. The impact of a hearing impairment is most obvious in language development. Cognitive ability is hindered only to the extent that performance depends on language comprehension and use. Children with hearing impairments may exhibit inappropriate behavior due to frustration from not being able to hear properly or lack of understanding.

How a Home Visitor Can Help

For the child with a known hearing loss, ask for a speech-language pathologist to follow the child to make the best use of his or her hearing and to prevent secondary speech and language disorders. Such children should have frequent hearing checkups. Check with the family to see that hearing aids are working and in use.

For the child who does not have an identified loss but who has frequent ear infections, watch for signs of temporary or fluctuating hearing loss (e.g., confusion about the source of a sound, non-response to a sound). The family should report frequent ear infections to their health provider.

For the child with even slightly smaller ear canals, such as children with Down syndrome, recommend that they be checked periodically for hearing loss because they are prone to ear infections.

For the child who has developmental delay, cerebral palsy, or multiple disorders, recommend that they receive hearing testing and monitoring. Research suggests that 40% of children who are deaf or hard of hearing have an additional disability (Wiley & Moeller, 2007). It is vital that children with other disabilities have intervention for hearing loss (usually hearing aids) because they need all of their sensory systems to function at the optimum level.

The delays of speech and language as a result of hearing loss are well known to home visitors, so all children who exhibit speech and language delay should have a hearing evaluation by an audiologist. If the hearing loss does not place the child in the eligibility category for services for the deaf and hard of hearing, a speech-language pathologist can help the child. The child's hearing loss may be undetected because the primary disorder has been the focus of intervention.

SUMMARY

No child or family served by home visitors in early intervention is typical. However, some reasons for eligibility are more common than others. Children usually come to the attention of the home visitor because of their primary disorder. Secondary disorders develop over time as a consequence of the primary disorder, and intervention prevents or reduces their occurrence. This chapter summarizes some general intervention strategies meant as a starting point for the most common disorders. In all cases, the family's culture and how that culture views disorders must be considered. Many common-sense approaches work best with disorders of behavioral regulation, and the home visitor can help the family to adjust the environment and reactions to aberrant behaviors. With speech and language disorders, the home visitor can begin with simple imitation, turn taking, and shared regard, but the speech-language pathologist should be consulted if a child is eligible. By the same token, the home visitor collaborates with the occupational or physical therapist to help children gain functional motor strategies. Children with Down syndrome respond well to emphasizing strengths and visual modalities, whereas in other genetic disorders the opposite may be true. Home visitors are cautioned against overidentification of ASD, but they may be the provider who guides a parent to find a diagnosis and appropriate intervention. Research does indicate that children who begin treatment early achieve their highest potential significantly more often than those who begin later. Parents of children with FASD may be helped to change their perspective from *won't* to *can't*. The most important aspect of service to children who are medically fragile and have multiple disabilities and their families is to keep the child from infectious disease and to manage the many services that come into the home. Low-incidence disorders (e.g., visual impairment, hearing impairment) may co-occur with other problems, and the home visitor must be vigilant to their possibility.

In general, the home visitor is advised to emphasize strengths (child and family) and understand that relationships are of primary importance. The home visitor's most important task is to help every child function to their fullest potential within the family and within the larger world.

7

Special Family Challenges

"It's not how many people there are in a family that counts, but rather the feelings among the people who are there."

–Fred Rogers

Central to the principles of family-centered intervention is the idea that home visitors and families are in an equal partnership. Parents are thought to be resilient entities capable of raising a child with special needs. Such is the model on which home visitors strive to build a relationship; however, that is not always the case when a home visitor may encounter parents with mental illness, with developmental disabilities, or who are teens. In these situations, families have unique challenges that go beyond those of other families of children with disabilities. Special challenges are also characteristic of families with children who are being raised in foster or adoptive homes or by their grandparents. This chapter addresses some of these challenges as well as those presented to parents who must cope with significant medical issues.

The home visitor may be tempted to retreat into child-centered intervention and not deal with the anticipated complexities of working with at-risk families. It may seem easier to let social workers and psychotherapists contend with these families and let the home visitor work with the child. In following this strategy, the home visitor will develop only a superficial relationship with the family and will be unable to determine what the parents' main concerns are for their child. Thus, the home visitor may be more likely to recommend interventions that parents are unable to implement.

PARENTS WITH MENTAL HEALTH PROBLEMS

Mental health is an envelope term that can encompass mild disorders to extreme pathology. Postpartum depression is the mental health issue that home visitors most often see. Home visitors who understand the grieving process can support family members who are experiencing transient mental health problems. In some instances, however, the mental health of a family member has a serious impact on the mental and physical health of the child in his or her care. Home visitors are directed to Guidelines for Referral: Red Flags in the Appendix and are referred to Chapter 5 for those instances in which the family member has not been identified as needing mental health services and the home visitor is expected to facilitate the referral.

How a Home Visitor Can Help

The following suggestions are for those situations in which a caregiver has been identified as having a mental illness and is receiving help while the child is also receiving visits from the home visitor.

1. **Respect confidentiality.** Conversations during the home visits should not be shared with any other agency unless specific permission is given by the parent. The parent should be assured of that. It is a temptation to learn as much as possible about the parent's mental health condition, thus raising ethical concerns of privacy and confidentiality. Vacca and Feinberg (2000) recommended that all early interventionists working with the family limit their information-seeking efforts to the following questions when speaking with referring psychiatric personnel:

   • What are the parents' strengths, and how can these be utilized in developing and maintaining a relationship with a home visitor?

   • How can the early intervention team effectively support the parent? Are there useful strategies for working with the parent, and are there strategies that should be avoided?

2. **Don't be a mental health practitioner.** The establishment of trust and discussion of the purpose of early intervention is the overriding task during the first visit when a parent has been in the mental health system. The parent may fear that the professional is going to be judgmental and take the child away. The home visitor should assure the parent that the early intervention system is different from the mental health system. The home visitor may provide emotional support to families, but psychotherapy is beyond the purview of the home visitor.

3. **Help parents to be empowered about their children.** Most parents who have been in the mental health system do not perceive that they have been active partners in the decisions made about their own treatment plans. They have been rewarded for being compliant rather than for participating in decisions on goals and objectives. The home visitor needs to emphasize that parents are essential in the formulation of individualized family service plan outcomes, trusting relationships in the same way that they would with any other family.

4. **Ensure that boundaries are established.** Transitions out of the program and discontinuation of services may be traumatic because the parent will be losing a source of emotional support. Considerable preparation and gradual termination of the relationship with the parent are important components of the ending of early intervention services for parents who may be especially vulnerable (Vacca & Feinberg, 2000).

PARENTS WITH DEVELOPMENTAL DISABILITIES

Home visitors will likely have among their clients mothers with developmental disabilities. Home visitors must keep in mind all that has already been said about developing partnerships because they work with parents who, themselves, have developmental delays. Of course, mothers with low cognitive skills love their children with the same intensity as other mothers. This love can provide a powerful motivating force to learn and be as responsible as possible. Home visitors not only will want to assist parents with developmental delays to develop solid parenting skills but also will be ever mindful of monitoring the progress of the child and the home in terms of child safety.

How a Home Visitor Can Help

Listed next are some of the primary points for home visitors to keep in mind when working with parents who have developmental delays.

1. **Determine what is really important.** Parents with developmental delays cannot be expected to focus on the development of parenting skills if they have not yet learned to manage their basic needs. The home visitor may have to begin with helping these parents to plan budgets and connect with available community resources in order to secure transportation and attend to medical needs. Safety for themselves and their child should be at the top of the priority list. Is food being prepared and stored properly? Are doors and latches secured? Are toxic cleaning materials stored away from little fingers?

2. **Coordinate help.** Find out which agencies are extending help to these families. If there are several, assist in the development of a collaborative intervention plan. Be mindful that these parents may not want to be labeled in a way that promotes special services for them.

3. **Make frequent, brief contacts.** Telephone calls will be more effective than written notes or e-mails to these families. Consider that the attention span and memories of the parents may be briefer than those of others.

4. **Avoid lengthy explanations.** Be brief and clear. Parents with developmental delays may have difficulty with abstract thinking, problem solving, and exercising good judgment. Demonstrate, model, and repeat the behaviors that you want the parents to

learn. Use concrete methods. Whenever possible, have the parents practice in front of you so that you can correct any mishaps and make positive comments about their progress. Break down tasks, and use visual cues such as pictures and charts.

5. **Require little or no reading.** Get to know the literacy level of the parents in order to provide resources that can be useful to them. Help them ask their questions, and answer them in short sentences.

6. **Model appropriate parent–child interaction.** Physically point out infant cues and model responsive behavior. Teach parents simple games such as Peek-a-boo so that they can more readily become involved with their child.

7. **Help parents interpret their child's behavior.** It is easy for parents with developmental disabilities to misinterpret their children's behavior and see them as "bad children." They may abuse their children without realizing that they are doing so.

8. **Build social networks.** Find appropriate social support groups, and encourage parents to become involved. Mothers with cognitive delays often have smaller friendship networks and rely more on family for social support.

9. **Consider how much family support is available.** If the parents are from a background of poverty, fewer family resources may be available to offer assistance. Never assume that just because there is a large, extended family, resources are available. A family's potential network might be "worn out" or dysfunctional.

TEENAGE PARENTS

Chapter 2 offered insight into the myriad feelings that parents may have when coping with the stresses that accompany raising a child with disabilities. One can only imagine what challenges might confront a single, teenage mother in this circumstance. In fact, infants of teenage mothers are considered to be among the largest percentage of children who have characteristics that place them at risk (March of Dimes, 2004). These at-risk factors include low birth weight, neurodevelopmental delays, and difficult temperament. These at-risk factors are complicated by environmental factors such as low level of maternal education, social isolation, single parenthood, and low socioeconomic status.

Home visitors should consider what teenage parents may be experiencing in their own lives. For example, Flanagan (2005, p. 33) acknowledged the following common situations that can be characteristic of teen parents:

- Past experiences of abuse, educational failure, and chaotic or poor parenting influence teens' parenting behaviors.

- Immature thought processes and cognitive difficulties are typical of all young teens but may have a major impact on how adolescents perceive themselves, their children, and their parenting role.

- Feeling unable to change anything in their lives is common among very young mothers. Life "happens" to them; they are powerless to alter their circumstances.

- Multigenerational families offer support, but they may also be the sources of complexity, confusion, and stress.

Korfmacher (2005) reviewed five successful early intervention programs involving teen parents. This research concluded that teen parenting is just one of many risk factors for healthy development. Korfmacher also found that interventionists must work harder to engage teen parents in the relationships and activities that will make notable positive differences in their lives and in the lives of their infants.

Although public schools offer programs for teenage mothers, they usually have a curricular agenda that assumes that all children are typical. These programs may or may not support the development of positive early relationships between mothers and their infants (Wells & Thompson, 2004). Given the co-occurring risk factors typically associated with teenage parenting, a critical task for home visitors is to assist these mothers in developing a loving and responsive relationship with their child. Strong mother–infant attachment is more likely to create positive motivation on the part of the mother to follow through and develop essential parenting skills. (See Attachment Intervention in Chapter 5.)

Inexperienced teen parents are likely to have unrealistic expectations of themselves and their child. Home visitors must strive to understand how the infant's disabilities may impact development of the bond of affection so critical to healthy infant development. Home visitors who understand how infants and their parents influence each other will be able to support the reciprocal nature of the development of bonds of affection. For example, teenage parents may not realize that children with visual or hearing impairments may not smile or reach out when a parent approaches. An infant who is hyperirritable may cry or turn away when his mother brings her face close or talks to him. The usually nurturing experience of feeding a young child may turn into a period of frustration that can be exacerbated by a young mother's need for instant gratification.

Home visitors must be patient in developing a collaborative, trusting relationship with the young parents that builds confidence in one another and in the parents. Understanding what the pregnancy and the child mean to a teenage mother is thought to be one of the first steps toward providing education and developmental guidance that will meet the needs of teen parents and their babies (Korfmacher, 2005). Home visitors just cannot expect to immediately engage in direct, sustained interaction with the infant and formal teaching activities with mothers.

How a Home Visitor Can Help

Home visitors must keep in mind that helping young parents respond appropriately to their infant or toddler's needs requires a developmental approach. After all, 15-year-olds are still 15-year-olds. They think concretely and live in the present. It may not be easy for them to think of alternative solutions to solve a problem or take another's perspective. If the teenage parents have learning disabilities or developmental delays, then the home visitor must take into consideration the parents' disabilities.

Mike and Jennifer qualified for visits from the At-Risk Parenting Program because they were 15 and 16 years old when their baby, Joe, was born full term and healthy. As soon as Jennifer was 16, her parents signed a permission form for them to marry, which they gladly did. Jennifer stayed home with the baby in their modest apartment, and Mike went to high school and kept his position on the football team. Until they married, Jennifer qualified for Temporary Assistance for Needy Families (TANF) for housing and WIC for supplemental food and baby formula. They did not realize that all of the services that Jennifer received as a single mother would be terminated upon getting married. Their home visitor, Marlene, suddenly became a resource provider. The couple could not pay their rent, and their heat was cut off at the beginning of winter. Mike would have to at least quit the football team and perhaps high school and get a job. That was clear. The strong bond of their love for each other was strained. Their dream of being together and forming a family was off to a rocky start.

Although home visitors should focus on supporting teenage mothers and sometimes fathers in perceiving themselves as the primary nurturing relationship in their child's life, home visitors must realize that extended family members have often assumed the primary caregiving role.

Virginia made her appointment to visit Rosa, age 16, and her baby when Rosa came home from her job at the hardware store. Rosa's mother took care of the baby, Teresa, while Rosa worked. Rosa had to walk several blocks home from the bus stop, and she looked hot and tired when she arrived after Virginia did. Baby Teresa was awake in her crib in the room that she and Rosa shared in Rosa's parents' house. Teresa lay on her back quietly while Virginia and Rosa talked. Rosa's mother was within earshot in the next room, but she did not enter the conversation until Virginia asked her to join them. Rosa gave monosyllabic answers to Virginia's questions about Teresa. She didn't know much about Teresa's routine except that she was up most of the night feeding her and trying to keep her quiet so Rosa's father wouldn't be disturbed. She said Teresa slept most of the day and was awake at night. Virginia reflected that Rosa must be exhausted, and Rosa nodded. She also asked if Rosa would like to pick up Teresa because she hadn't seen her all day. Rosa said she would just like to rest right now. She would have to tend to the baby all night. Virginia noted that Rosa and baby Teresa were at risk for serious attachment issues. The focus of her intervention would have to be on the relationships of mother and child and grandmother and child before she could do anything else to help this family.

Home visitors should seek to assist young parents to under-stand what their children are capable of developmentally while they help them to reinterpret their infant's behavior. They can help these young parents realize that their babies get to know them through touch, smell, voice, and sight. Holding, talking, and singing to their infants should be encouraged. Healthy interactions including play behavior can be modeled and reinforced by home visitors. Infants' signals need to be directly pointed out to the young parents. The home visitor needs to be patient and ready to praise young parents who may have had little acknowledgment and praise while they were growing up.

Teenage fathers should be encouraged to be involved as well. Fathers tend to play more roughly and be more tactile, more physi-cal, and less physically constraining than mothers. They need concrete suggestions for physically interacting when children have disabilities. They may be especially fearful of infants who are tiny or medically fragile. Fitzgerald and McKelvey's (2005) research found that teen fathers tend to be less empathic to their children's developmental needs than are older fathers. Nevertheless, this research also found that teenage fathers are more likely to be highly invested in their chil-dren, enjoy interactions more, and often participate more in their chil-dren's daily care when compared with older fathers. Home visitors need to reach out to include young fathers who have stayed connected to their child and his or her mother.

FOSTER AND ADOPTIVE PARENTS

Foster and some adoptive parents have some unique issues to consider no matter what disabilities are characteristic of the child in their care. Generally, there are always issues related to attachment. Dozier, Dozier, and Manni (2002) discussed several reasons why children in foster care may have difficulty forming secure attachments with their foster parents. These children often have experienced compromised early environments. They may have been abused or neglected or have suffered a disruption in the primary attachment relations as discussed in Chapter 5. Children develop strategies for coping with these realities. It is not unusual for children to act as if they do not want or need caregiving. They avoid or reject nurturing, especially if they have been placed in foster or adoptive care after 10 months of age (Stovall & Dozier, 2000). Home visitors must be alert to help foster and adoptive parents realize that a resistant child needs them regardless of how resistant the child might act. Foster and adoptive parents must be helped to reinterpret children's behavioral signals.

Home visitors can begin to understand the nature of the child's attachment by very carefully observing or asking about the child's behavior when he or she is distressed. Children who regularly seek out their primary caregiver when they are hurt or anxious display secure attachment. Children with insecure attachments may never seek out the caregiver's attention or they take much longer to quiet as they are less able to use the caregiver's attention to help them relieve their stress. Caregivers who are inconsistent may create resistant attachments resulting in children who are fussy and inconsolable as illustrated in the following vignette. Foster and adoptive parents must be encouraged to understand how essential consistent and loving nurturance is to foster children even if these children are fussy or act as if they do not want any nurturing.

Bridget, along with public health nurses, made home visits to Lauren and her two children, Oren and Margo. The nurses determined that Lauren was an unfit mother because of her addiction to alcohol and the unsavory people who were constantly in her apartment that might pose a danger to the children. Little Oren, age 11 months, was placed in a foster home with Thelma who had had dozens of foster children throughout many years. Thelma's home was neat and well run, and Thelma, although she was not what Bridget would call a warm person, was efficient in caring for the children in her home. She kept the children warm and dry and well fed. On Bridget's first visit to the foster home, Thelma told her that Oren had cried in the night but she had left him alone so he would learn that crying did not work to get attention. During Bridget's visit, Oren did not smile. His face displayed anxiety and he whimpered throughout the session. Bridget was inexperienced. On later reflection, she thought, "I should have just hugged that child for an hour. That was what he needed."

Dozier, Dozier, and Manni (2002) offered several intervention strategies worthy of our consideration. They referred to their recommended approach as Attachment and Biobehavioral Catch-up, or the ABC Intervention. Component A focuses on the caregiver's need to recognize that the child needs him or her, regardless of how that need is communicated. Caregivers are helped to see the child's behavior in a new light. Component B recognizes that some caregivers find it difficult to provide nurturance, especially when children are distressed or resistive. Caregivers are encouraged to consider any issues or thoughts they may be having that make it difficult to provide nurturance when children appear to be unreceptive. They are urged to understand how important touch is and to play touchy games such as "This little piggy." Of course, they are helped to understand the cues used by the child to signal that he or she wants to terminate the touching. Component C realizes that infants and toddlers may need help in developing trust through the creation of a predictable, responsive interpersonal environment. Caregivers continue to learn to read their child's communicative signals while allowing him or her to take the lead during play. It is believed that when young children begin to feel that they have some effect on their environment, they will more readily develop behavioral, emotional, and physiological regulation.

How a Home Visitor Can Help

Home visitors and most parents are well aware of the importance of play in fostering the development of young children. However, home visitors may assist foster parents in understanding that infants and toddlers placed in their care may have experienced play deprivation. Children who enter foster care or are adopted may have had little experience with play. Their development may have suffered from lack of playful stimulation. They may have spent long hours alone in cribs or infant seats. Many will not have experienced the secure, safe environment that frees children to pursue their play. Children who lack positive early relationships may become withdrawn from interactions. Then, add a disability to environmental deprivation and children experience double jeopardy. Comfort (2005) described some of the behaviors that suggest early play deprivation. These include the tendency to avoid playing with others, the lack of initiative in exploring toys, not knowing what to do with a toy, having no interest in books, playing repetitively with toys, having short attention spans during playtime, and desiring to play with toys designed for younger children.

Encouraging foster parents to understand why their children may not know how to play with toys or to interact with them will help

them to play more patiently and effectively with their foster children. Home visitors can help foster parents understand that play-deprived children may be spontaneously aggressive with toys or other children, may be easily frustrated when they do not know how to play, may lose self-control, may not seem appreciative when they receive a new toy, and may even ignore or break a toy. In fact, some children in foster care may not play appropriately with others or share play equipment until they are 7 or 8 years old (Comfort, 2005).

Home visitors should model and encourage foster or adoptive parents to introduce play time gently and within daily routines whenever possible. Some children haven't even experienced laughter while their diaper is being changed or the simple game of Peek-a-boo. With a consistent, trusting, and safe relationship with their caregivers, reluctant children can begin to feel the safety necessary to explore and take risks with the toys in their environment. Adults should avoid surprises and should not push children into play that involves being messy (e.g., sand, paint, paste) if children appear to be uncomfortable. Children should be given some toys of their own that they are not expected to share. Home visitors can help foster and adoptive caregivers realize that they can really make a difference. Once their children feel safe and secure, their children are likely to demonstrate the curiosity and joy that play brings to life.

GRANDPARENTS IN THE ROLE OF PARENTS

It is not unusual for home visitors to visit homes in which the parenting role is being fulfilled by grandparents. In 2000, roughly 2.4 million grandparents had responsibility for raising their grandchildren (U.S. Bureau of the Census, 2000). In many of these homes, single grandmothers are raising the children. Few studies have been concerned with the reasons for grandparents assuming the role of caregiver for children with disabilities. Janicki, McCallion, Grant-Griffin, and Kolomer (2000) did find that substance abuse by the child's parent(s) was the primary reason for grandparents assuming the role of caregivers in New York City. Some of the other factors include incarceration of the child's parents, death or absence of parents, unemployment of parents, child abuse/neglect, and finances.

Home visitors must be aware of the challenges that face grandparents above and beyond those faced by other parents of children with disabilities. Fuller-Thomson and Minkler (2000) reported that close to one third of grandmother caregivers suffer from depression and more than half have at least one limitation that makes fulfillment of their own daily living activities difficult. This is true even when their grandchild does not have disabilities. Grandparents may be placed in an uncomfortable situation, at times, because they want to allow their own child to be present in their grandchild's life but worry that the child's parents may be irresponsible. Sometimes, grandparents feel like they have failed in their own parenting role if their own daughter or son is unable to cope with adult responsibilities. Grandparents may not have legal authority to be the guardian of their grandchildren, which makes it difficult for them to obtain needed medical care, public assistance, or even early intervention services. Finally, one cannot overestimate the fatigue factor and the impact that extra physical and emotional stresses have on the caregiver's health and stamina.

Mavis had a full house. She still had three of her own children at home, including one in elementary school, when her oldest daughter dropped off her daughter Nicole, almost 3 years old, for her to keep and didn't come back. Mavis's husband wasn't working, and the family was in survival mode. Nicole was fearless. She would climb trees to the top and run through the outside gate in their rural setting. She had to be watched constantly, and the discipline Mavis used with her own children didn't work with this child. It seemed that "no" meant nothing to her. She told Beverly, her home visitor, that she just couldn't cope with it all. Mavis knew that her daughter was heavily into drugs and alcohol, and she feared that she would never see her again. Beverly's task was to help Mavis cope with Nicole's behavior and to educate the family about the possible effects of fetal alcohol spectrum disorder while keeping Nicole safe. She also had to have help as she searched for resources for this family. Mavis was the glue that held the family together, and she needed support quickly.

How a Home Visitor Can Help

Support, support, support—grandparent families need all of the support they can get. Grandparents may feel isolated and feel that they do not fit into traditional parent support groups. Their own friends may be traveling and enjoying the leisure that comes with having an "empty nest." Grandparents not only will need emotional support and support that addresses their own physical limitations but also may need assistance with legal and financial issues. Listed next are helpful tips for the home visitor to consider when working with grandparents who are being parents to young children with disabilities. Some of these were adapted from the work of Rowan (2006):

1. **Create a partnership with grandparents that conveys and develops trust.** Given the usual age difference between the grandparents and the home visitor, building a relationship may seem a little daunting to the home visitor. Acknowledging and respecting the grandparents' knowledge and encouraging them to express their opinions will go a long way in establishing a productive relationship. Keep in mind all that has been said about being culturally sensitive because some grandparents may be less assimilated into the mainstream culture than the child's parents.

2. **Carefully explain the services that are available, and help grandparents to have access to them.** Grandparents may never have heard of respite and may need to be encouraged to accept services for themselves as well as the child.

3. **Encourage grandparents to join grandparent support groups or help them to organize a playgroup.** Such groups may help grandparents to avoid isolation and to realize that others also have parented children who are unable to fulfill their adult responsibilities.

4. **Simplify the delivery of services as much as possible.** As grandparents may be less mobile and more easily fatigued, minimizing the number of professionals and appointments involved will relieve stress and save energy. Grandparents may also lack sufficient transportation to agency offices.

5. **Become aware of grandparents' physical limitations and health challenges.** Arranging for a physical therapist to assist grandparents when lifting their grandchild may prevent injury or pain to the caregiver.

6. **Be prepared to find services that can address legal issues.** Each state is different in how grandparents' legal status is handled in relation to the child's biological parents. Providing grandparents with the ability to make medical decisions and enrolling them in educational services may depend on addressing their legal status. Besides referral to local attorneys, home visitors should be prepared to make referrals to law clinics and others who provide pro bono or low-cost assistance.

7. **Be knowledgeable about how financial assistance is obtained.** Grandparents may need assistance in obtaining such services as social security disability insurance and Medicaid, home energy assistance and weatherization, food stamps, WIC (a special food program for children under 5 years old), and opportunities for tax credits.

Table 7.1. Resources for grandparents

AARP Grandparent Information Center
601 E Street, NW
Washington, DC 20049
Telephone: 888-687-2277; 202-434-6466
Web site: http://www.aarp.org/families/grandparents/gic/
    a2004-01-16-grandparentsinfocenter.html

National Center on Grandparents Raising Grandchildren
Georgia State University
College of Health and Human Sciences
Post Office Box 3995
Atlanta, Georgia 30302
Telephone: 404-413-1074
Web site: http://chhs.gsu.edu/nationalcenter

Grandparents Raising Grandchildren
Telephone: 1-800-333-4636
Web site: http://www.usa.gov/Topics/Grandparents.shtml

8. **Be prepared to assist interested grandparents in using the Internet and contacting national resources.** Remember, finding information electronically does not come as naturally to the current generation of grandparents as it will to future generations of grandparents. Included in Table 7.1 are a few helpful resources. In addition, a national list of family resource centers is included in the Appendix.

SUMMARY

If raising a child with disabilities doesn't bring enough stress for any family, certain circumstances can make it even more difficult to provide a nurturing environment. Home visitors must be prepared to build trust and provide the resources necessary to support and enhance the lives of those whose lives are already complicated. This chapter intends to assist home visitors to be better equipped to handle the challenges present when parents have mental health problems or developmental disabilities, are teenagers, are foster or adoptive parents, or who have taken on the parenting role as grandparents.

8

Expanding the Early Intervention Team

with contributions from Carole Osselaer

"One does not worship, display, or teach culture: One acknowledges it as a whole way of life grounded in the past, and one necessarily lives a culture."

–Houston A. Baker, Jr. (1990)

Home visitors are in an unusual situation. In order to adequately serve families, they are called upon to work with a large variety of professionals. These include physical, occupational, psychological, and speech-language therapists. Collaboration with these professionals is often addressed during their training to become home visitors. However, they are rarely trained to work effectively with interpreters or translators. Nevertheless, in order to be culturally sensitive and to offer services in the dominant language of the family as required by law, effective involvement of interpreters or translators may be required. Home visitors may or may not accompany families on visits to their pediatricians or other medical specialists. Even so, families may expect guidance and advice in how to work with or find qualified medical service providers. However, only nurses receive instruction in how to work collaboratively with medical specialists. This chapter is designed to assist home visitors who may need to work closely with interpreters or translators. It is also designed to assist home visitors in preparing parents to become partners with their health care providers (Kuo & Inkelas, 2007).

Avoiding Communication/Cultural Barriers with Effective Interpreters/Translators

Although we have addressed the critical importance of cultural sensitivity throughout this book, we believe that special attention needs to be given to the role of effective use of interpreters. Interpreters are employed by a number of institutions to act as communication mediators between individuals who do not share a common language. If they have received any training at all, interpreters traditionally have been trained for settings such as hospitals or courtrooms. Rarely has educational interpretation received attention in training programs. In fact, there is no certification required or even any consistent requirements from state to state for interpreters. There are no federal or national agencies or organizations that certify interpreters to serve in health care or educational settings, neither are there any professional organizations for educational interpreters (Hwa-Froelich & Westby, 2003). This discussion is offered as guidance to help both home visitors and interpreters work together in the best interest of the families. It is hoped that potential communication and cultural barriers to collaboration among families and professionals will be avoided.

WORKING WITH INTERPRETERS AND TRANSLATORS

It is important to understand the role of both interpreters and translators. *Interpreters* are those who provide an oral translation between speakers of different languages. A *translator* is one who translates the same ideas in a different language from the original. The subtle distinction between interpreter and translator is that the interpreter does *more* than translate word for word orally. There is an obligation for the interpreter to explain whatever might be misunderstood to all parties in the communication. On the other hand, a translator is expected to translate ideas from the words of the communicator without clarifying and explaining (Hwa-Froelich & Westby, 2003). Certainly, the same person can fulfill both roles, such as translating a written IFSP document and interpreting during IFSP meetings. We use I/T to designate a person acting as an interpreter and/or a translator.

Interpretation may be thought of along a continuum from neutral to active. A neutral interpreter merely passes messages back and forth from one person to another; he or she is passive and does not develop a relationship with the participants. In comparison, an active interpreter does more than a word-by-word translation of messages back and forth (National Council on Interpretation in Health Care, 2001).

The *neutral* interpreter serves as a conduit of the message. He or she has no personal involvement in the process. The conduit interpreter focuses on the linguistic translation of the message. Thus, the responsibility for effectiveness rests with the home visitor rather than the interpreter.

The *minimally active* interpreter is usually a member of an educational team—a team that has received training in working with an interpreter. The interaction involves more than linguistic translation of an oral message. It involves operating within the cultural communication framework that is associated with the message and the speaker. For example, an Asian interpreter may use a more respectful approach when speaking to an older Asian man or a highly educated person but use a more equal-power communication style with someone who is the same gender, age, and/or education level. It does not mean that the interpreter becomes an advocate for either party.

The *maximally active* interpreter is an advocate for clarity in communication and understanding in the interaction. Interpreters who are maximally active assume even more involvement in the process. The interpreter facilitates the understanding of and communication between participants who speak different languages. The focus is on communication clarity. In addition to using communication styles appropriate to the situation and speakers, like the minimally active interpreter, the maximally active interpreter intervenes when a misunderstanding occurs. The maximally active interpreter may assume different roles, such as sharing personal opinions, asking for clarification, checking for understanding, sharing cultural information, and making sure that each participant is aware of what has been said to the other participant. Both the minimally active interpreter and the maximally active interpreter work best when they are viewed as integral members of the early intervention team.

According to Hwa-Froelich and Westby (2003), active interpreters can negotiate between two cultures and establish ties of trust and respect. Interpreters and home visitors must adjust their behavior to avoid the problems with cultural norms and expectations that might negatively affect communication. For example, an active interpreter can help home visitors to understand that it is culturally customary to accept some refreshment from a mother when she receives a service provider in her home before discussion may begin about her child. The two concepts of neutral and active interpreting form opposite ends of an interpreter perspective as illustrated in Figure 8.1.

Neutral interpreter Passes messages back and forth and has no relationship with the participants

(+) The translation is accurate without bias, and there are no conversations with the family that the provider does not hear.

(–) Clarity and understanding can be compromised if the neutral interpreter is not concerned with them.

Minimally active interpreter Facilitator for communication and understanding between two parties; a member of a team

(+) The interpreter takes an active interest in the family and in helping them to understand the provider and the process.

(–) The provider may feel left out as the interpreter engages the family. The interpreter may assume too much responsibility while trying to be helpful.

Maximally active interpreter Advocate for clarity in communication and understanding in the interaction; an integral member of the team

(+) This interpreter intervenes when he or she thinks a misunderstanding has occurred. He or she may assume different roles in the same session and is more of an equal partner with the provider.

(–) Provider may be uncomfortable with so much active participation by the interpreter. Interpreter may become advocate for the family.

Figure 8.1. Interpreter perspective continuum. *Key:* + = advantages, – = disadvantages. (*Source:* Hwa-Froelich & Westby, 2003.)

When interpreters assume roles other than as a conduit and move into becoming more active, there is a risk of misunderstanding among all the parties involved. Some participants in the interaction may assume that the interpreter will be only conduit. Other participants may expect the interpreter to be an advocate, whereas the interpreter may view him- or herself as a conduit, minimally or maximally active. Furthermore, interpreters may change roles several times during an interaction. Home visitors must work with their agencies in determining where an interpreter fits along the continuum of involvement.

With hope, agencies will recruit and assign skilled interpreters. The following list is modeled from the Ohtake, Santos, and Fowler (2002) list of the minimal skills interpreters need for a successful interpretation process:

1. The interpreter has knowledge of both English and the language or languages that the family uses.
2. The interpreter has knowledge of the culture, values, and traditions of both parties.
3. The interpreter has basic knowledge of terms and concepts in special education.
4. The interpreter has knowledge of the roles of individuals in special education.
5. The interpreter has knowledge of the roles of individuals in the special education process (e.g., IFSP meeting).
6. The interpreter has good interpersonal skills.
7. The interpreter understands the necessity for a professional role in the process (e.g., remembering that he or she works with the provider for the same agency as the provider). This means that the interpreter should not keep information from the service provider, even if asked to do so by the family member.

There are basically three types of content changes that I/Ts can make. These changes may alter the intended meaning of what the person is saying a little bit, a lot, or not at all. If the change results in a significant difference in the meaning of the message, then it may be considered an error, particularly in neutral translating. The three types are

1. *Omissions.* This is when the I/T leaves something out. It might be one word, a phrase, or an entire sentence. This could because
    *   The I/T does not think that extra words are important (e.g., instead of saying "rather difficult," the I/T might say "difficult"). However, a small word can make a major difference sometimes (e.g., "mild" versus "moderate" retardation)
    *   The I/T does not understand what was said
    *   The words cannot be translated
    *   The I/T cannot keep up with the speaker
    *   The I/T forgot what was said
2. *Additions.* This is when the I/T adds extra words, phrases, or sentences that were not actually said. This may happen because
    *   The I/T wishes to be more elaborate as in the case of active translators
    *   The I/T needs the extra words to explain a concept that is difficult to translate
    *   The I/T adds his or her own thoughts to what was said
3. *Substitutions.* This occurs when the I/T uses other words, phrases, or entire sentences in place of the actual words used. This occurs because
    *   The I/T does not remember the specific word, phrase, or grammatical construction
    *   The I/T confuses words that sound almost the same
    *   The I/T uses a faulty reference (e.g., uses the word "he" to describe one of the student's parents when the service provider was actually talking about the mother)
    *   The I/T simply did not understand the speaker
    *   The I/T is lagging too far behind the speaker and misses part of what was actually said. The I/T then substitutes the part that was not actually heard. The I/T should request that the service provider either repeat or rephrase what was said to allow for better interpreting, when he or she is not sure what

has been said. This is more likely to occur when both I/T and service provider know each other and have a comfort level as team members.

Interpreters come to the job with a variety of backgrounds. It is up to home visitors as well as the agency to inform interpreters of what is expected. The following is a minimal list of ways by which home visitors may prevent misunderstandings in the interpreter–home visitor relationship.

Before the session,

1. If at all possible, have a meeting with the interpreter before the session.
2. Include the interpreter in team meetings. Pertinent information about the agency's philosophy, practices, and purposes should be offered.
3. Provide the interpreter with a glossary of terms used in special education.
4. Discuss the expectations you have for the interpreter with this family (e.g., do you want a neutral translator or do you want the interpreter to clarify concepts and help both parties understand each other?).

During the interpreted session,

1. Avoid idiomatic words, slang, and metaphors that are difficult to translate.
2. Use simple sentences.
3. Speak slowly and clearly.
4. Be sensitive to reactions shown by the interpreter to identify possible problems with interpretation.
5. Maintain eye contact with the family member (unless culturally inappropriate), or speak to the family member, not the interpreter.

After the session,

1. Encourage the interpreter to advise you if you and other team members communicate with the family in a culturally inappropriate manner.

2. Identify problems that the interpreter may have encountered during the meeting. The script found in Figure 8.2 may be given to interpreters to assist them when they introduce themselves at IFSP or individualized education program meetings.

INTERPRETERS' RELATIONSHIP WITH THE HOME VISITOR AND AGENCY

Home visitors may want to share with their interpreter the following guidelines for situations that may cause some confusion:

1. If the family asks you to attend family functions and birthday parties for their child for whom you have been interpreting, the family may like you and want to spend more time with you. To maintain your professional identity, it is generally not a good idea to become integrated with the family. However, in special circumstances you may attend social functions with them, remembering that this is a social event and that you do not discuss the child's problems or anything about the service providers with whom you work.

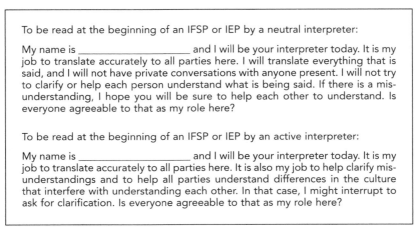

To be read at the beginning of an IFSP or IEP by a neutral interpreter:

My name is _____ and I will be your interpreter today. It is my job to translate accurately to all parties here. I will translate everything that is said, and I will not have private conversations with anyone present. I will not try to clarify or help each person understand what is being said. If there is a misunderstanding, I hope you will be sure to help each other to understand. Is everyone agreeable to that as my role here?

To be read at the beginning of an IFSP or IEP by an active interpreter:

My name is _____ and I will be your interpreter today. It is my job to translate accurately to all parties here. It is also my job to help clarify misunderstandings and to help all parties understand differences in the culture that interfere with understanding each other. In that case, I might interrupt to ask for clarification. Is everyone agreeable to that as my role here?

Figure 8.2. Introductory scripts.

2. If a family member wants to talk with you about events of the session with their child, tell him or her that you will be happy to ask the home visitor and get back to him or her or that you will ask the home visitor to talk about it with him or her.

3. If the family member asks you to keep something confidential and not tell the home visitor, remember that you are a member of the agency's team, even though you share a culture and affection for the family. Tell him or her that you cannot keep confidences and ask permission to tell the home visitor what you have just been told. If permission is not given, you must make a decision as to the importance of the information. If it is vital to the case, such as not giving the baby prescribed medications or nutrition, you must tell the family member that the provider will understand and that you must tell. If it is of a personal nature, keep the confidence, but tell the family member that you are obligated to share all information in the future.

4. Do not ask questions that the home visitor does not ask. It is not considered culturally or professionally appropriate to ask questions that do not pertain to the child and what affects the child. Therefore, questions about a family member's job or financial status, living arrangements, marital status, or anything of a personal nature is considered off limits.

5. If the family member wants to talk with you in your language about things that are not asked by the home visitor, particularly as you arrive and leave, as a courtesy to the home visitor give a short interpretation of what was said, such as, "Maria was commenting about how awful the traffic was and she thought we might be stuck in it." You do not need to provide a word-for-word translation for small talk.

6. If the family asks you to interpret for them in other dealings they have, such as with their landlord, either you or the home visitor must tell the family that you can only provide interpreter service when you are working for the agency. Do not give your telephone number to the families with whom you are working. They must go through the home visitor to contact you.

ENHANCING COMMUNICATION
WITH MEDICAL SPECIALISTS

Given the number of medically related appointments parents must face, home visitors often find that they are the ones to whom parents turn when they need support. It is not unusual for a child with special needs to have three to five medically related visits weekly. The most effective early intervention occurs when there is a partnership among the family, health care professional, and home visitor. A doctor, who had a difficult time navigating language and the system of physician specialists for his own son, wrote this:

> One of the consultants spent so much time and effort with our son and us that I am compelled to write to you. We cannot say enough about how much we appreciate all she has done. Even though I am an ER doctor, I could not have navigated through the system without her help.

Parents hear and try to process news at the same time they are trying to understand medical terms that usually are only familiar to the doctor. To make matters more difficult, the child is tired and scared and is often crying or uncooperative, needing the parents' attention. It is not unusual for parents to wait several hours to see a specialist, only to have 10–15 minutes of time.

Van Dyck, Kogan, Heppel, Blumberg, Cynamon, and Newacheck (2004) provided the first data examining the extent to which pediatric health care professionals address parental concerns about their child's learning and development. Interviews of parents of 22,656 young children found that fewer than half (43%) reported being asked about their concerns during the past 12 months. In addition, about half of the parents reported not receiving all of the information they needed regarding their child's development. Early childhood specialists are increasingly being encouraged to help parents communicate their concerns to pediatricians (Kuo & Inkelas, 2007). Through education and guidance, home visitors can empower parents to tell doctors about their concerns. Medical professionals can not be expected to *discover* a problem. Not finding a problem does not mean it is not there. When parents become partners with their health care providers, they will get more thorough and efficient care.

How a Home Visitor Can Help

Listed below are some ways the home visitor can be supportive by offering strategies and guidelines to parents and caregivers to help them understand how to be good medical advocates for their child.

1. The home visitor needs to be prepared to assist parents in understanding the medical aspect of the child's special needs. The child's diagnosis should be understood, and the child's medical records should be up to date. It is helpful for the home visitor to have a medical dictionary and a list of web sites to look up reliable information. Encourage parents to have a binder or binders (three-hole punch) to store medical reports, records, doctor's cards, lists of medications, copies of eyeglasses or other prescriptions, and so forth all in one place. It is also important to have an understanding of what the medical diagnosis means to the parents (in the parents' own words).

2. The home visitor needs to be able to clearly explain basic health care rights, which include the right to a second opinion. The second opinion is not a second opinion if it is within the same group of doctors as the first opinion.

3. As a home visitor, you may want to offer to attend the first one or two critical appointments with the physician specialist and the family. The first two appointments when the family is hearing the diagnosis and treatment plans that are being established can be an especially supportive time for the home visitor to be present if the parent or caregiver desires. The home visitor can take notes (not babysit siblings), which then can be reviewed after the visit and discussed.

4. Home visitors may be asked to help coordinate educational and medical interventions with the parent, child, medical professional, and intervention team. Any action like this should be discussed with the parents to see if they would feel supported.

Riley was referred to an early intervention program for services when her low vision diagnosis required her to have one eye patched in an attempt to strengthen vision in her other eye. She had more than a 50% delay in three areas. Riley's delay in two areas was due to wearing arm restraints for most of her waking hours to stop her from tearing off her patch (secondary disorder). Riley's mother was under extreme stress. The specialist had referred Riley to the intervention program, being concerned not just about vision but about the loss of developmental skills and the mother's emotional state.

The home visitor worked with the family on behavior strategies to help them teach Riley to wear her glasses and patch. She supplemented the doctor's information by helping Riley's mother understand that by patching the stronger eye she was helping the brain use the vision in the weaker eye. She showed how, through fine motor play with highly motivating activities, she could distract Riley from removing the patch from her eye. One year later, Riley's skills were beyond her age level and she no longer qualified for special education services. She wears her patch and glasses as prescribed by the pediatric ophthalmologist, and her mother reports that Riley's last picture vision acuity test results made all the hard work worthwhile.

Her mother also learned that she could ask the doctor questions about Riley's treatment and be forthright with the doctor when she was unable to accomplish what he had prescribed, even though she was trying. The home visitor explained that if the doctor thought that she was following his directions and they were not working, then he might have an alternative method to accomplish the same result. She was encouraged to contact Riley's doctor and let him know what was happening rather than wait 6 months for the next appointment. After talking to the doctor, she was surprised to learn that nothing was an exact science, that the doctor was trying but wasn't certain that what he was prescribing was going to work. She did not know she had a choice to follow his suggestions. She appreciated being treated with respect as Riley's parent and being part of the decision-making team. Even though it was very hard and discouraging at times, she wanted to stick with the plan for treatment, even if there was a small chance of success. She knew that if the treatment did not work, she could say that she had given it her best.

5. Parents may need assistance in finding the right medical professional. As difficult as it may be, given all of the other changes, finding a pediatrician who has had some experience in caring for children with special needs is essential. It is important to consider personal style. Some doctors believe that they are in charge, that they are the decision makers. They share information only as needed and no more. Some families prefer this style. The parent may be very dependent on this type of doctor. He or she can be reassuring to the point of telling the parent that everything is fine, whether it is or is not. This can create a strain with the home visitor, who is trying to support the growth and development of the child, whereas the parent insists that the doctor has no concerns.

   When looking for a doctor, parents can be encouraged to talk to other parents, nurses, doctors, and professionals in the field. They might ask, "If your son or daughter had this problem, who would you see?" In this way, the parent is not asking for a referral but is asking for a personal opinion. There are good Internet sources such as www.bestdoctors.com, www.health-grades.com, and www.usnews.com. In addition, parents can call their state's medical board office to find out whether a doctor is board certified in the particular area of their child's needs.

6. Some parents might need help getting appointments. Home visitors can help them to realize that getting appointments often takes a lot of time on the telephone, so they should avoid calling on busy Monday mornings. Discuss the importance of building rapport with office staff who may control scheduling. However, if they encounter uncooperative staff, they should realize that the behavior of the staff does not reflect the competence or personality of the doctor. Tables 8.1, 8.2, and 8.3, developed by two home visitors, offer parents pointers on how to become empowered as advocates for their child, to be able to communicate their concerns and get the information they need.

Table 8.1. Setting the appointment

Get a physician's referral.

Have insurance approvals.

Have social security card number/medical coverage card.

Schedule the first morning appointment or first appointment after lunch. The doctor runs behind as the day progresses and restarts the schedule after lunch.

If you can't get an appointment as soon as you need it, ask if there is a cancellation list or when is the best time to call back to see if there is a cancellation, or ask if the doctor has another office location where he or she sees patients.

If needed, ask for an interpreter to be present; specify the language.

Ask if there is anything that you need to bring.

Ask how long you can expect to be there, so you will know what plans to make for work, siblings, and so forth.

Get parking and directions and any special considerations for traffic or construction.

Table 8.2. Getting ready

Arrange for child care for siblings and some one to pick up children from school, just in case.

Bring current pertinent medical records, MRIs, reports, studies, and so forth. Order and pick up copies of current reports that you do not have. Make a copy for the doctor.

Know both parents' health background. Write it down.

Make a list of all medications, supplements, vitamins, herbs, and so forth that your child is taking. Include the dose and frequency.

Bring any current aids (e.g., eyeglasses or contacts to the pediatric ophthalmologist).

Table 8.2. *(continued)*

Write down a list of questions and concerns beforehand that pertain to why you are seeing the specialist. Keep the list to three to four good questions; the doctor has a limited amount of time, even though you will have waited a long time.

Ask someone to come with you to take notes, or bring a tape recorder and have the doctor summarize the visit.

Take snacks, special toys, or music to keep your child entertained. Don't forget extra diapers and any special equipment, in case the visit is extended

Table 8.3. The visit

Inform the receptionist that you have medical records. If you didn't bring copies, they will want to make copies

If you have to leave by a specified time, inform the receptionist.

Pull out the list of questions so that the doctor sees it.

Ask questions if you don't understand what the doctor has said.

Ask the doctor to explain words or terms that are unfamiliar. Better yet, ask him or her to use simple, easy-to-understand terms.

To get better information, ask better questions. Do not ask the doctor to predict your child's future. He or she can not predict his own child's future.

Stick to the reason you are there. Do not ask the specialist to solve your child's behavior issues if you are seeing him or her regarding your child's vision.

Communicate clearly. Repeat back to the doctor what you heard him or her say about your child's condition.

If you still do not understand, you might try again with, "This is difficult for me to understand. Will you please explain it to me one more time? Will you give me an example?"

Before proceeding with any surgery or procedure, be sure that you take the time to research it and understand all that it involves. Ask the doctor the recommended timeline of what he or she suggests, the chances of success, how many procedures he or she has done, what will happen if you do not do what the doctor suggests, and if there a chance the surgery/procedure may not work or will have to be repeated.

Always seek a second opinion from a different medical group. Seek out a well-known specialist from bestdoctors.com, a referral, or thorough research. Depending on your child's condition and insurance coverage, a second opinion, in fact, may be worth paying for. A cash discount is usually offered, and the expense is not as expensive as often thought, especially when it might make a difference.

Get a written prescription for any actions or follow-through that the doctor wants you to do. This eliminates confusion after you leave the doctor's office.

Ask that a copy of the visit summary be sent to you and to other primary people involved with your child. Have their addresses with you.

Ask for referrals to other services in the community that might be available to help you and your child.

Ask the doctor the best way contact to him or her if you have questions. Does the doctor have e-mail? Doe he or she take and return phone calls? Does he or she have a nurse or an assistant to call?

Know the next step for follow-up or a return visit.

SUMMARY

Interpreters and translators have unique skills that can assist home visitors to avoid communication and cultural barriers to the creation of a truly family-centered approach to early intervention. However, home visitors rarely receive training in how to include interpreters and translators as essential members of the team. This chapter defines the responsibilities of these specialists and discusses the continuum of the roles they play, the skills they must have, and obligations that home visitors have in relation to their services. It also alerts the home visitor to possible problems in the I/T process that may change the meaning of the content being communicated. Home visitors are being urged to expand the early intervention team to include medical specialists. Therefore, strategies for helping families enhance communication with their health care providers have been included. It is hopeful that when parents become partners with their health care providers, they will have their concerns heard and their needs met.

9

Personal Concerns
of the Home Visitor

"You are in charge of your own attitude—
whatever others do or circumstances you face.
The only person you can control is yourself."

–Marian Wright Edelman

Throughout this book, we have endeavored to both instruct the early interventionist who is new to home visiting and to enhance the skills of those who are experienced home visitors. We have also attempted to bring about reflection on the nature of our work with children and families as we have progressed from personal philosophy to interacting with other professionals in our work. We work with families, but we must also work for our employers; we must be mindful of our safety; we must handle the rules and regulations and paperwork requirements of our agencies; and we must guard against giving so much that we cross into burnout. As we give of ourselves to families, the business of taking care of ourselves is sometimes forgotten. In this chapter, we address those issues that encompass personal and professional ethics, boundaries in family services, noncooperative families, personal safety, nurturing the nurturer, and personal organization.

ETHICAL ISSUES

Home visitors often encounter family values, customs, and beliefs that are different from their own. Sometimes these differences are between home visitors and their own agencies. Such conflicts are common in professions in which people differ on how to help others best. Because there is no national home-visiting organization with a set of professional ethical guidelines, we must look to other codes of ethics and adapt them for ourselves. (The American Association of Home-Based Early Interventionists, or AAHBEI, is an organization that provides networking opportunities, conferences, and a newsletter that can be found at http://www.aahbei.org.) Furthermore, there is little formal training that is focused on ethics in preservice programs. Ethical questions that home visitors commonly encounter include whether to intervene in a particular situation, how best to do so, and how to balance the needs of different family members. Sometimes, home visitors wonder whether to tell the truth in certain situations or when, if ever, they can share information given to them in confidence (Wasik & Bryant, 2001). The following sections discuss 1) some of the more common ethical issues faced by home visitors and how these issues affect home visitor–family relationships and 2) ethical issues of home visitor–agency or legal conflicts.

Home Visitor–Family Issues

Wasik and Bryant (2001) cited a framework for assessing values conflicts based on work by Reamer (1993).

1. The basic well-being of a person is more important than following rules or acquiring secondary benefits. In other words, a person's health or safety is more important than a home visitor's absolute honesty.

    Marian, a home visitor, knew where her client Kenny and his mother had moved to escape an abusive father. When the father called Marian to ask if she knew where they were, Marian lied and said that she did not know. Protecting the mother and child took precedence over telling the truth.

2. A client may freely choose to do something that we might consider self-destructive, unless the exercise of that freedom interferes with someone else's basic well-being.

Shirley visited the home of Madeline, a child with a hearing impairment. Madeline had hearing aids, but she could not wear them when her ears were discharging fluid, which was often. Shirley noticed that the small home was thick with cigarette smoke in the winter, with the windows closed. She mentioned to Stacey, Madeline's mother, that second-hand smoke could contribute to Madeline's nearly constant respiratory distress and ear infections. Stacey said that living with Madeline was so stressful that she needed the outlet of smoking and she did not believe that smoking was that harmful to Madeline. Stacey's stress level was a factor in her interaction with her child, and Shirley was well aware that any intervention to end her smoking was not welcome. Both Madeline and Stacey were her clients; however, she believed that the level of smoke in the house was harming Madeline. First, she gathered printed evidence of the effects of second-hand smoke on children's health, which she gave to Stacey to read. Then, she asked for a compromise: She had no objection to Stacey smoking, just not smoking in the house on the first floor where it could affect Madeline. This was hard for Stacey as the house was very small and she would need to be outside in the cold or in the basement, but she agreed.

Home Visitor–Agency or Legal Issues

A different kind of ethical dilemma is raised when a law or policy seems to conflict with a home visitor's ability to help a family.

1. Home visitors are generally expected to obey the laws of society and the policies of their employer and their profession. The decision to report suspected child abuse is a classic example of such a dilemma. Most states mandate that professionals report cases of suspected abuse to state authorities. However, home visitors may sometimes believe that such reporting would impair their relationship with a parent, which they believe is more helpful to the family than the services the state agency might be able to deliver.

Jean accompanied two public health nurses on a visit to Doris, who had a 2-year-old daughter, Debbie, and an infant son. They were part of a program to help families with children under age 1 year affected by poverty and low parenting skills. The infant boy was suspected of having delays due to prenatal exposure to alcohol. When Jean and the nurses arrived at 11:00 a.m., Doris was in bed with the children. Bottles of alcohol were all over the apartment, along with plates of partially eaten food. A man who was never identified slept on a sofa in the corner. Debbie wandered about eating food from the leftover plates, clad only in a shirt. Doris said the children wanted to sleep and to please go away for now.

Jean and the nurses saw real danger for Debbie if her mother went back to bed, leaving her alone with the man. Debbie was clearly hungry, so Jean suggested that they come in and fix breakfast for the family. Doris protested that it was not necessary but the three women cheerfully came in and began to clean up and cook—not usually part of a home visit. One found breakfast food for Debbie, one dressed her, and one fixed a bottle for the infant. They made coffee for Doris and kept her awake for the hour of their visit. They put the infant in her arms, and she fed him the bottle. Although they intervened for one day, there was still the dilemma of the children being in a dangerous environment when they left. They made an appointment for the next day to discuss options with Doris, which included a possible report to Child Protective Services. Once abuse is reported, how could these visitors continue to be effective with this family? Both children were attached to Doris, and if they were removed from her care, all three would suffer the consequences of interrupted attachment.

Jean had the advantage of having others with her, which is rare in home visiting. Early interventionists are not trained as mental health workers or substance abuse counselors, and making an appointment for the next day was appropriate so that Jean could get counsel from a supervisor in the interim. If Jean saw that the children were in clear danger and she had been alone, then she would have had to act quickly and call authorities to come immediately.

2. Agency rules prevail unless a client is in serious jeopardy. Such rules as consulting a supervisor before making a referral to an outside agency may hinder relations with the family, but the home visitor made the commitment to follow those rules as a condition of employment. A home visitor may work to change policies and rules, but until that time, the policy must be honored.

The main point is that no set of ethical principles can be followed rigidly in daily practice of home visiting. Rules can not cover every choice that a home visitor must make. Nevertheless, knowledge of ethical guidelines, thoughtful consideration of each situation, and consultation with other professionals can make difficult judgments easier (Wasik & Bryant, 2001).

BOUNDARIES IN FAMILY SERVICE

Once parents feel they have a trusting relationship with their home visitor, within the privacy of their own home, they may try to extend the discussion beyond the explicit goals and tasks of the program to include personal problems that are preoccupying them. These topics may involve family conflict such as with a spouse or parents, internal stresses (e.g., depression), or external problems (e.g., inadequate housing, income, or employment; Klass, 2008). An ethical issue can arise because the professional relationship that evolves between the home visitor and the family begins to look like a personal friendship. Positive feelings that the home visitor and family strive for and are necessary to a good working relationship should not be confused with friendship. In rare instances, a friendship existed before the professional relationship was established. This is particularly problematic. A balance between genuine professional concern and maintaining distance is necessary, although it can be hard to achieve.

Rosa, a Spanish-speaking home visitor, was assigned to Beatriz and her son Jorge. Beatriz was delighted to have someone in her home who spoke her language, and she began to lean more and more on Rosa in her efforts to navigate an alien culture. She asked Rosa to go shopping with her, which Rosa did in order to bring Jorge into a natural environment and to encourage a new experience. Then Beatriz asked Rosa to talk to her landlord for her and tell him the rent would be late. Rosa then had to define and clarify her role in the home. She regretted that she had not done this early in the relationship. She was there to help Beatriz and Jorge, and she was bound by the rules to limit her involvement with the family to that relationship. Beatriz was hurt that Rosa put limits on their relationship. When she asked Rosa to attend Jorge's birthday party, Rosa declined, as it was on a Saturday when she had to attend to her own family.

NONCOOPERATIVE FAMILIES

Home visitors must sometimes discontinue home visits because the family, particularly the primary caregiver, appears to be uncooperative. When the home visitor knocks and hears movement in the house, yet no one comes to the door, can intervention really be effective in that family? Before terminating services, the home visitor is obligated to consider reasons for the lack of cooperation and have a talk with the mother about them. Perhaps the mother does not feel a part of the goal setting or feels unable to follow through with recommendations. Perhaps other concerns of the family have overwhelmed her and she does not trust the home visitor enough to confide in her. If the talk does not improve the situation, the home visitor, after consulting with her supervisor and making sure that no dangers exist for the child, must tell the mother that there are other clients who can use her time and that she will need to terminate the service. The door should always be left open with a number to call (the agency, not a home number) when the family is ready to resume services (Wasik & Bryant, 2001).

PERSONAL SAFETY

Children and families who need and are eligible for home visitations, of course, live in all neighborhoods in the country. Crimes occur everywhere, so the issue of personal safety must be in the back of the mind of every home visitor. Occasionally, program directors may deem some areas too unsafe for home visitations to occur. In those situations, alternative sites can be chosen for family members and professionals to meet (e.g., parks, restaurants, coffee shops, the home of a relative or friend where security and safety is the norm). Program directors often work with local law enforcement agencies to determine whether any areas are off limits. Home visitors are not expected to make visitations in areas in which they feel unsafe. Table 9.1 lists essential safety tips.

NURTURING THE NURTURER

Home visitors face challenges unique to their profession. Their involvement with families is intense. Much must be accomplished in a relatively short period of time. This intensity makes it necessary for home visitors to have a broad and secure base of support. These nurturers must be nurtured themselves in order for them to provide the daily care and attention children and families deserve. Following are some strategies based on those that supervisors and administrators have found useful in nurturing home visitors so they can, in turn, nurture families and children (Infant Development Association of California, 2004).

1. *Formal supervision* that is nonjudgmental and supportive may take place in the field, with the supervisor visiting the home with the home visitor, or a regularly scheduled conference may take place elsewhere. The goal is for the supervisor to understand the challenges faced by the home visitor and to be in a position to offer support, help, and reflection. (True *reflexive supervision* is beyond the scope of this book to address. It is a skill adapted by practitioners of infant mental health as best practice.) To be truly helpful, the supervisor must be someone the home visitor views as experienced, knowledgeable, and safe. For their part, supervisors should recognize when a home visitor is close to burnout or is exhausted physically or mentally. If so, the supervisor should allow the home visitor to have a time out or day off from the difficult work of home visiting.

Table 9.1.   Don't let it happen to you: Safety tips for the home visitor.

Be alert to high-risk situations:

    Isolated areas, no telephone, dirt roads

    Different people in the home each week

    People loitering outside

    Dangerous dogs

    Families who often will not let you into the house or ask you to wait outside for a while before letting you in

    Individuals in the home appearing to be under the influence of drugs

    Drug paraphernalia in the home

    Indications of drug traffic in the home

    Your instincts tell you "This is a high-risk situation"

Precautions to prevent problems:

    Before going on a high-risk visit, let someone else know and put into writing where you are going, when you are leaving, and when you expect to return.

    Visit in pairs.

    Make early morning appointments.

    Avoid visits on days when welfare checks arrive.

    Plan your route in advance.

    Do not circle the block looking for the home (someone may think you are looking for drugs).

    Meet in a well-peopled place such as a popular restaurant.

    Keep a cell phone within easy reach.

    Do not carry a purse, wear jewelry, or take valuables with you.

    Ask to be introduced to all people in the house.

    Introduce yourself to apartment complex managers.

    Research the area ahead of time—learn the gang colors of any existing gangs and do not wear them.

    Do use cars marked as county or state vehicles.

    Carry identification on your person.

    Ask families about the safety of their neighborhoods.

    Park in front of the home if at all possible.

    Keep car doors locked and windows rolled up.

    Do not hide an extra key anywhere in or on your car.

    Be aware of avenues of escape.

    Always stand to the side of the door when knocking.

    Assess the situation before entering; give preliminary information outside; ask permission to enter; ask who is home (watch body language).

    Do not walk in when someone yells, "Come in."

    Make other plans to visit if anyone in the household appears to be under the influence of alcohol or drugs.

    Position yourself where no one can come in behind you.

    Avoid isolating yourself in a room without a second exit.

    Project an air of authority—keep your eyes direct and scan the environment with your head up; wear pants and flat shoes.

    If there is an altercation outside, leave when you assess it is safe and ask someone from the house to accompany you.

From Cook, R., Klein, M.D., & Tessier, A. (2008). *Adapting early childhood curricula for children with special needs.* Upper Saddle River, NJ: Prentice Hall; reprinted by permission.

2. In many situations, *informal peer support* is the only strategy that is open to a home visitor. If at all possible, home visitors should have the opportunity to come together to share the challenges of home-based intervention with colleagues.

3. Having regular opportunities—that is, *ongoing training*—to think intellectually about home visiting and to learn new information about families and techniques to work with them helps home visitors to become and feel more competent.

4. It is important to have *interdisciplinary case conferences,* scheduled and structured discussions of specific families that allow all of the professionals involved with the family to share their perspectives with their colleagues.

5. Home visitors should have *standard protocols for family crises and high-risk situations.* They should receive explicit information on handling emergencies and crises as part of their orientation to the agency (e.g., information about boundaries, what to do if a child becomes ill during a home visit, when a family has no food or place to live, when the home visitor is exposed to violence in the home, when the home visitor suspects or witnesses child maltreatment).

6. The work and efforts of home visitors should be constantly recognized through staff recognition programs/celebrations (e.g., providing praise when staff share meals and have opportunities for relaxation).

Angela dreaded going to see Sam and his mother, Jane. Despite Angela's best efforts, Sam was not learning or improving. Jane did not voice any concerns, but Angela had seen other children change with her visits and she was frustrated that she was not helping Sam and Jane. She needed another strategy and she did not see it coming from the newly hired director of the program, who did not have as much experience as she had. She hadn't seen Margaret for a long time. Margaret had been a student in the same university program as Angela. Margaret was also a home visitor. Angela called Margaret to meet her for lunch. She spilled out her frustrations about Sam and Jane to Margaret, who listened carefully and then asked some questions. Margaret did not offer any solutions, however, until Angela asked what Margaret thought she should do. Margaret said she did not know what Angela should do, but maybe she should share her concerns with Jane. Was Jane satisfied with the progress? Did Jane have any ideas about how to move things along? If not, did anyone else who was involved, such as Jane's husband or mother, have any ideas? Angela had not thought of that, and she was not sure she wanted to admit to a mother that she was stumped. It might make her look incompetent. So Margaret suggested that Angela consult with her team; perhaps someone in another discipline was having the same perceptions of progress. Angela liked that idea and decided to call for a case conference.

As Angela drove away from the lunch with Margaret, she reflected on why this time with Margaret had been so helpful. First, Margaret had really listened to her without interruption. She had been empathetic and shared some similar experiences of her own. She had not hurried to a solution until she had gathered all of the information. And she had not offered to fix anything for Angela by giving

advice until Angela asked for it. She had offered several options and was not judgmental about Angela's rejecting her first option. She did not insist that she knew the answers but treated Angela like a colleague with whom she was trying to solve a problem, not as if she had superior knowledge. Then, Angela had a flash: "That's how I want to solve problems with families." Margaret had done some active listening with her without either of them being aware of it. In fact, if Margaret had gone into obvious active listening mode, Angela would have resented it because Margaret would have been in the "expert" role. Instead, they were two colleagues with mutual respect. Next time it might be Margaret's turn to talk things over with Angela. Angela began to rethink sharing her concerns with Jane and doing some problem-solving together.

PERSONAL ORGANIZATION

It has been said that when we are not in control of a situation, we are most likely to feel anxious and frustrated. Our professional lives may spin out of control when we feel behind in paperwork, when we feel unprepared for our home visits, and when we feel inadequate to be effective with our families. The scenario with Angela and Margaret addresses the home visitor's feelings of inadequacy when we do not perceive our role as effective with a family. Home visitors often complain that they can not keep up with the required paperwork and do not have enough time to prepare for home visits.

In Chapter 4, we refer to the Home Visit Record (see Appendix) as a tool for efficiency of paperwork and to help preparedness. This record (in triplicate) can be used effectively for three purposes:

1. The home visitor records what has happened on that day, but most important, she writes the next steps on the record before she leaves the house, including what materials to bring to the next visit. If there is no time to plan for the next visit until it is imminent, at the very least, the home visitor has her lesson plan, materials to take to the visit, and a record of the conversation with the parent in the "What's New" section of the Home Visit Record.

2. A copy of the record goes to the agency as a record of the visit and may be read by anyone else who goes into the home.

3. A copy of the record is left with the parent to refer to during the time between visits. As the records accrue, a documentation of progress is obtained for both the home visitor and the parent.

The Home Visit Records are kept in each child's folder and carried by the home visitor, along with other pertinent information regarding that child (e.g., individualized family service plans, test protocols, reports from other professionals). Many home visitors keep the folders in the trunk of their car in a locked box (for confidentiality). Many home visitors have elaborate color-coding systems that serve them well and would be a good subject for an agency get-together or staff meeting.

AGENCY GUIDELINES

Throughout this book, we referred to agency policies that guide home visitors, and we addressed problems that occur when agency policies seem to differ from personal philosophies. We suggest that an agency that employs home visitors provide them with a written guide, often a handbook of agency policies, when they are hired. It is much easier to refer to the guidelines when a home visitor is violating an explicit or implicit rule than to have a personal confrontation. For example, appropriate dress for the home visitor, on rare occasions, can become an issue. Home visitors should dress for comfort and for messes. We are often spilled on, drooled on, and sneezed on and are often sitting on the floor. The words "dress modestly" may mean different things to different people, so explicitly stating "no spaghetti straps, short shorts, bare midriffs, or underwear showing" may be needed. The following list of considerations is meant as a beginning for agencies to use in formulating guidelines. Some of these policies have been addressed previously:

1. Suspected child abuse and whether to consult a supervisor
2. Collaboration with interpreters
3. Safety

4. Terminating services for the family
5. Whom to ask for help
6. What services are paid for or reimbursed
7. Protocols for high-risk situations (e.g., when a child becomes ill during a visit)
8. All paperwork requirements
9. Appropriate dress for visits

SUMMARY

This chapter addresses personal issues of the home visitor. Home visitors have no formal national organization and must rely on other disciplines for guidance in ethics. Standard protocols can allay many issues that distress home visitors and can be established as part of an orientation to the work setting, such as what to do when confronted with unusual situations within a home. Ethical issues may be a source of stress when personal ethics clash with those of one's employer or government regulations. Establishing boundaries can be critical in the relationship with a family. Above all, home visitors must be safe, and home visitors and agencies must take precautions to be sure that they are safe. We must not forget that as nurturers of children and families, we also need to be nurtured lest we give so much that we burn out. A safe person who will listen as we would listen to a family can be most helpful, whether it is a supervisor or colleague. A Home Visit Record can be used to fill several organizational purposes and saves time, therefore cutting down on stress and feelings of inadequacy. Agencies may find it helpful to provide guidelines to home visitors concerning ethics and agency policies.

References

Ainsworth, M.D., Blehar, M., Waters, E., & Wall, S. (1978). *Patterns of attachment: A psychological study of the Strange Situation.* Hillsdale, NJ: Lawrence Erlbaum Associates.

Bailey, D., Bruder, M.D., Hebbeler, K., Carta, J., Defosset, M., Greenwood, C., et al. (2006). Recommended outcomes for families of young children with disabilities. *Journal of Early Intervention, 28*(4), 227–251.

Bailey, L., & Slee, P. (1984). A comparison of play interactions between nondisabled and disabled children and their mothers. A question of style. *Australia New Zealand Journal of Developmental Disabilities, 10*(1), 5–10.

Baker, B.L., Blacher, J., Crnic, K., & Edelbrock, C. (2002). Behavior problems and parenting stress in families of three-year-old children with and without developmental delays. *American Journal on Mental Retardation, 107,* 433–444.

Baker, H.A., Jr. (1990). *Long black song: Essay in Black American literature and culture.* Charlottesville: University of Virginia Press.

Banks, R.A., Santos, R.M., & Roof, V. (2003). Sensitive family information gathering. *Young Exceptional Children, 6*(2), 11–18.

Barnard, K.E., Morisset, C.E., & Spiker, S. (1993). Preventive interventions: Enhancing parent–infant relationships. In C.H. Zeanah, Jr. (Ed.), *Handbook of infant mental health* (pp. 386–401). New York: Guilford Press.

Barnett, D., Clements, M., Kaplan-Estrin, M., & Fialka, J. (2003). Building new dreams. *Infants and Young Children, 16*(3), 184–200.

Bartlett, D.J., & Palmisano, R.J. (2002). Physical therapists' perceptions of factors influencing the acquisition of motor abilities of children with cerebral palsy: Implications for clinical reasoning. *Physical Therapy, 82,* 237–248.

Bernheimer, L.P., & Weisner, T.S. (2007). "Let me just tell you what I do all day. . ." *Infants & Young Children, 20*(3), 192–201.

Bernstein, V.J. (2002). Supporting the parent–child relationship through home visiting. *IDA News, 29*(2), 1–4.

Bernstein, V.J. (2007). *Using a relationship-based approach to strengthen families: The nature of nurturing.* Presentation at the Children's Hospital and Research Center, Oakland, CA.

Bernstein, V.J., Campbell, S., & Akers, A. (2001). Caring for the caregivers: Supporting the well-being of at-risk parents and children through supporting the well-being of programs that serve them. In J. Hughes, J. Close, & A. La Greca (Eds.), *Handbook of psychological services for children and adolescents* (pp. 107–131). New York: Oxford University Press.

Berry, J.O., & Hardman, M.L. (1998). *Lifespan perspectives on the family and disability*. Boston: Allyn & Bacon.

Bhavnagri, N.P., & Krolikowski, S. (2000, Spring). Home–community visits during an era of reform (1870–1920). *Early Childhood Research and Practice, 2*(1). Retrieved March 28, 2008, from http://ecrp.uiuc.edu/v2n1/bhavnagri.html

Bidder, R.T., Gray, P., Newcombe, R.G., & Evans, B.K. (1989). The effects of multivitamins and minerals on children with Down syndrome. *Developmental Medicine and Child Neurology, 31*, 532–537.

Brandt, K. (2001). Toys cleverly disguised as household items. *IDA News, 28*(3), 12–13.

Brazelton, T.B., & Greenspan, S.I. (2000). *The irreducible needs of children: What every child needs to grow and flourish.* Cambridge, MA: Da Capo Press.

Brazelton, T.B., & Sparrow, J.D. (2006). *Touchpoints: Birth to 3: Your child's emotional and behavioral development* (2nd ed.). Cambridge, MA: Da Capo Press.

Bridges, W. (2003). *Managing transitions: Making the most of change.* Cambridge, MA: Perseus Books.

Bromwich, R. (1997). *Working with families and their infants at risk.* Austin, TX: PRO-ED.

Bronfenbrenner, U. (1979). *The ecology of human development.* Cambridge, MA: Harvard University Press.

Brooks-Gunn, J., & Lewis, M. (1984). Maternal responsivity in interactions with handicapped infants. *Child Development, 55*, 782–793.

Bruder, M.B. (2000). Family-centered early intervention: Clarifying our values for the new millennium. *Topics in Early Childhood Special Education, 20*, 105–115.

Cadigan, K., & Estrem, T. (2007). Identification and assessment of autism spectrum disorders. *Impact.* Retrieved August 8, 2007, from http://ici.umn.edu/products/impact/193/over4.html

Capone, G.T. (2004). Down syndrome: Genetic insights and thoughts on early intervention. *Infants & Young Children, 17*(1), 45–58.

Casey, P.H., Barrett, K., Bradley, R.H., & Spiker, D. (1993). Pediatric clinical assessment of mother–child interaction: Concurrent and predictive validity. *Developmental and Behavioral Pediatrics, 14*(5), 313–317.

Center for Immigration Studies. (2007). *Immigrants in the United States: A profile of America's foreign-born population.* Retrieved March 2008 from http://www.cis.org

Centers for Disease Control and Prevention, U.S. Department of Health and Human Services. (2007, February 8). *CDC releases new data on autism spectrum disorders (ASDs) from multiple communities in the United States* [Press release]. Atlanta, GA: Author.

Ciaramicoli, A.P., & Ketcham, K. (2001). *The power of empathy: A practical guide to creating intimacy, self-understanding and lasting love in your life.* New York: Dutton.

Coe, R., and Priest, J. (2002, September). *Finding out what works: Collaborative experiments in education.* Paper presented at the Annual Conference of the British Educational Research Association, University of Exeter, England.

Comfort, R.L. (2005). Learning to play: Play deprivation among young children in foster care. *Zero to Three, 22*(5), 50–53.

Cook, R.E., Klein, M.D., & Tessier, A. (2008). *Adapting early childhood curricula for children with special needs* (7th ed.). Upper Saddle River, NJ: Prentice Hall.

Crais, E.R., Douglas, D., & Campbell, C. (2004). The intersection of gestures and intentionality. *Journal of Speech, Language, and Hearing Research, 47,* 678–694.

Crais, E.R., Roy, V.P., & Free, K. (2006). Parents' and professionals' perceptions of the implementation of family-centered practices in child assessments. *American Journal of Speech-Language Pathology, 15,* 365–377.

Crnic, K., Hoffman, C., Gaze, C., & Edelbrock, C. (2004). Understanding the emergence of behavior problems in young children with developmental delays. *Infants & Young Children, 17*(3), 223–235.

Cromwell, J., Belgum, E., and Kohnert, K. (2005, July). Diversity in autism: Perspectives on language learning and education. *American Speech-Language-Hearing Association Division 1, 12*(2), 2–5.

Cullinane, D., & Ausderau, K. (2001). Practical strategies for the complex process of feeding. *IDA News, 28*(2), 1–2.

Cutspec, P.A. (2004, December). Bridging the research-to-practice gap: Evidence-based education. *Centerscope, 2*(3), 1–8.

Daley, T. (2002). The need for cross-cultural research on the pervasive developmental disorders. *Transcultural Psychiatry, 39,* 531–550.

Division for Early Childhood. (2001). *Developmental delay as an eligibility category.* Retrieved February 26, 2008, from http://www.dec-sped.org/pdf/position papers/ConceptPaper_DevDelay.pdf

Division for Early Childhood. (2005). *Identification of and intervention with challenging behavior* [Concept paper]. Retrieved February 26, 2008, from http://www.dec-sped.org/pdf/positionpapers/ConceptPaper_ChallBeh.pdf

Dozier, M., Dozier, D., & Manni, M. (2002). Attachment and biobehavioral catch-up: The ABC's of helping infants in foster care cope with early adversity. *Zero to Three, 22*(5), 7–13.

Dunst, C.J., Bruder, M.B., Trivette, C.M., & Hamby, D.W. (2006, March). Everyday activity settings, natural learning environments, and early intervention practices. *Journal of Policy and Practice in Intellectual Disabilities, 3*(1), 3–10.

Dunst, C.J., Trivette, C.M., & Cutspec, P.A. (2002, September). Toward an operational definition of evidence-based practices. *Centerscope, 1*(1), 1–10.

Dunst, C.J., Trivette, C.M., Humphries, T., Raab, M., & Roper, N. (2001) Contrasting approaches to natural learning environment interventions. *Infants & Young Children, 14,* 48–63.

Dyches, T., Wilder, L., Sudweeks, R., Obiakor, F., & Algozzine, B. (2004). Multicultural issues in autism. *Journal of Autism and Developmental Disorders, 34,* 211–222.

Edelman, M.W. (1992). *The measure of our success.* New York: HarperCollins.

Eisenberg, S. (2004). Structured communicative play therapy for targeting language in young children. *Communication Disorders Quarterly, 26*(1), 29–35.

Family-guided Approaches to Collaborative Early-intervention Training and Services (FACETS). (2007). Retrieved March 15, 2007, from http://www.parsons.lsi.ku.edu/facets

Fenichel, E. (2001). From neurons to neighborhoods: What's in it for you? *Zero to Three, 21*(5), 8–15.

Fey, M.E. (1986). *Language intervention with young children.* Boston: Allyn & Bacon.

Fidler, D.J. (2005). The emerging Down syndrome behavioral phenotype in early childhood. *Infants & Young Children, 18*(2), 86–103.

Filipek, P.A., Accardo, P.J., Ashwal, S., Baranek, G.T., Cook, E.H., Jr., Dawson, G., et al. (2000). *Practice parameter: Screening and diagnosis of autism: Report of the Quality Standards Subcommittee of the American Academy of Neurology and the Child Neurology Society.* Neurology, 55(4), 468–479.

Fitzgerald, H.E., & McKelvey, L. (2005). Low-income adolescent fathers: Risk for parenthood and risky parenting. *Zero to Three, 25*(4), 35–41.

Flanagan, P. (2005). Caring for the children of teen parents. *Zero to Three, 25*(4), 31–34.

Fuller-Thomson, E., & Minkler, M. (2000). The mental and physical health of grandmothers who are raising their grandchildren. *Journal of Mental Health and Aging, 6*(4), 311–323.

Gallagher, P.A., Fialka, J., Rhodes, C., & Arceneaux, C. (2002). Working with families: Rethinking denial. *Young Exceptional Children, 5*(2), 11–17.

Gillespie, L.G. (2006). Cultivating good relationships with families can make hard times easier! *Young Children, 61*(5), 53–55.

Goldstein, H., Walker, D., & Fey, M. (2005, November). *Comparing strategies for promoting communication of infants and toddlers.* Paper presented at the annual convention of the American Speech-Language-Hearing Association, San Diego.

Gomby, D.S., Culross, P.L., & Behrman, R.E. (1999). Home visiting: Recent program evaluations—analysis and recommendations. *The Future of Children, 9*(1), 4–26.

Gomby, D.S., Larson, C.S., Lewit, E.M., & Behrman, R.E. (1993). Home visiting: Analysis and recommendations. *The Future of Children, 3*(3), 6–19.

Graham, M.A., White, B.A., Clarke, C.C., & Adams, S. (2001). Infusing infant mental health practices into front-line caregiving. *Infants and Young Children, 14,* 14–23.

Greenspan, S. (2002). *The secure child: Helping our children feel safe and confident in an insecure world.* Cambridge, MA: Perseus Books.

Greenspan, S., & Wieder, S. (1999). A functional developmental approach to autism spectrum disorders. *Journal of the Association for Persons with Severe Handicaps,* 24(3), 147–161.

Guralnick, M.J. (2004). Family investments in response to the developmental challenges of young children with disabilities. In A. Kalil & T. Deleire (Eds.), *Family investments in children's potential: Resources and parenting behaviors that promote success* (pp. 119–137). Mahwah, NJ: Lawrence Erlbaum Associates.

Guralnick, M.J. (2005). Early intervention for children with intellectual disabilities: Current knowledge and future prospects. *Journal of Applied Research in Intellectual Disabilities,* 18, 313–324.

Gutterman, N. (1997). Early prevention of physical child abuse and neglect: Existing evidence and future directions. *Child Maltreatment,* 2(1), 12–34.

Hanson, M.J., & Lynch, E.W. (2004). *Understanding families: Approaches to diversity, disability, and risk.* Baltimore: Paul H. Brookes Publishing Co.

Harris, R.A. (2002, Summer). Preferred practice patterns for speech-language pathologists in service delivery to infants and toddlers and their families: Guidelines for intervention planning and delivery. *California Speech Hearing Association (CSHA) Magazine,* 31–34.

Harris, S., & Handleman, J.S. (2000). Age and IQ at intake as predictors of placement for young children with autism: A four- to six-year follow-up. *Journal of Autism and Developmental Disorders,* 30(2), 137–142.

Hebbeler, K., Spiker, D., Bailey, D., Scarborough, A., Mallik, S., Simeonsson, R., et al. (2007, January). *Early intervention for infants and toddlers with disabilities and their families: Participants, services, and outcomes. Final report of the National Early Intervention Longitudinal Study (NEILS).* Menlo Park, CA: SRI International.

Heffron, M.C. (2000). Clarifying concepts of infant mental health: Promotion, relationship-based preventive intervention, and treatment. *Infants & Young Children,* 12(4), 14–21.

Hodapp, R.M., DesJardin, J.L., & Ricci, L.A. (2005). Genetic syndromes of mental retardation: Should they matter for the early interventionist? *Infants & Young Children,* 16(2), 152–160.

Hotelling, B.A. (2004). Newborn capabilities: Parent teaching is a necessity. *Journal of Perinatal Education,* 13(4), 43–49.

Hwa-Froelich, D.A., and Westby, C.E. (2003). Considerations when working with interpreters. *Communication Disorders Quarterly,* 24(2), 78–85.

Individuals with Disabilities Education Act (IDEA) Amendments of 1997, PL 105-17, 20 U.S.C. §§ *et seq.*

Individuals with Disabilities Education Improvement Act of 2004, PL 108-446, 20 U.S.C. §§ 1400 *et seq.*

Infant Development Association of California. (2004). Nurturing the nurturer. *IDA News,* 31(2), 7.

Irwin, L. (2007). *"Minimal" hearing loss: What does it mean?* Retrieved February 26, 2008, from http://www.handsandvoices.org/articles/tech/minimal.html

Janicki, M., McCallion, P., Grant-Griffin, L., & Kolomer, S.R. (2000). Grandparent caregiver I: Characteristics of the grandparents and children with disabilities for whom they care. *Journal of Gerontological Social Work, 33,* 35–55.

Kaczmarek, I., Pennington, R., & Goldstein, H. (2000). Transdisciplinary consultation: A center-based team functioning model. *Education and Treatment of Children, 23,* 156–172.

Keilty, B. (2008). Early intervention home-visiting principles in practice: A reflective approach. *Young Exceptional Children, 11*(2), 29–40.

Klass, C.S. (2007). *The relationship between the parent and the home visitor.* Retrieved June 17, 2007, from http://www.aahbei.org/files/forms/Klass.pdf

Klass, C.S. (2008). *The home visitor's guidebook: Promoting optimal parent and child development* (3rd ed.). Baltimore: Paul H. Brookes Publishing Co.

Klein, M.D., & Chen, D. (2006, Spring). Home visiting in early intervention: Serving infants with special needs and their families. *American Association for Home-Based Early Intervention, News Exchange, 11*(2), 1, 4–6.

Klein, M.D., Chen, D., & Haney, M. (2000). *Promoting learning through active interaction: A guide to early communication with young children who have multiple disabilities.* Baltimore: Paul H. Brookes Publishing Co.

Korfmacher, J. (2005). Teen parents in early childhood interventions. *Zero to Three, 25*(4), 7–13.

Kuo, A.A., & Inkelas, M. (2007). The changing role of pediatric well-child care. *Zero to Three, 27*(3), 5–11.

Landa, R.J., Holman, K.C., & Garrett-Mayer, E. (2007). Social and communication development in toddlers with early and later diagnosis of autism spectrum disorders. *Archives of General Psychiatry, 64*(7), 853–864.

Lavin, J.L. (2001). *Special kids need special parents.* New York: Berkley Books.

Law, J. (1997). Evaluating intervention for language-impaired children: A review of the literature. *European Journal of Disorders of Communication, 32,* 1–14.

Lessenberry, B.M., & Rehfeldt, R.A. (2004). Evaluating stress levels of parents of children with disabilities. *Exceptional Children, 70*(2), 231–244.

Lord, C., & McGee, J.P. (Eds.). (2001). *Educating children with autism.* Washington, DC: National Academies Press.

Mahoney, G., Boyce, G., Fewell, R., Spiker, D., & Weeden, C.A. (1998). The relationship of parent–child interaction to the effectiveness of early intervention services for at-risk children and children with disabilities. *Topics in Early Childhood Special Education, 18,* 5–17.

Mahoney, G., Robinson, C., & Perales, F. (2004). Early motor intervention: The need for new treatment paradigms. *Infants & Young Children, 17*(4), 291–300.

Manolson, A. (1992). *It takes two to talk: A parent's guide to helping children communicate.* Toronto: The Hanen Centre.

March of Dimes. (2000). *Lives in the balance: 2000 annual report.* White Plains, NY: Author.

March of Dimes. (2004). *Facts you should know about teenage pregnancy.* White Plains, NY: Author.

Martland, N.E.E. (2001). *Expert criteria for evaluating the quality of Web-based child development information.* Unpublished doctoral dissertation, Tufts University, Boston.

McCollum, J.A., Ree, Y., & Chen, Y.J. (2000). Interpreting parent–infant interactions: Cross-cultural lessons. *Infants & Young Children, 12,* 23–33.

McDonough, S.C. (2004). Interaction guidance: Promoting and nurturing the caregiving relationship. In A.J. Sameroff, S.C. McDonough, and K.L. Rosenblum (Eds.), *Treating parent–infant relationship problems* (pp. 79–96). New York: Guilford Press.

McWilliam, R.A. (2003). Giving families a chance to talk so they can plan. *AAH-BEI News Exchange, 8*(3), 1, 4–6.

McWilliam, R. (2005). *Home visiting.* Presentation to The Division for Early Childhood Conference, Portland, OR.

McWilliam, R., & Scott, S. (2001). A support approach to early intervention: A three-part framework. *Infants & Young Children, 13*(4), 55–66.

McWilliam, R.A., Snyder, P., Harbin, G., Porter, P., & Munn, D. (2000). Professionals' and families' perceptions of family-centered practices in infant–toddler services. *Early Education and Development, 11*(4), 519–538.

Miller, J., & Rosin, P. (1998). *Improving communication skills: Research to practice.* Retrieved February 26, 2008, from http://www.ndss.org/index.php?option= com_content&task=view&id=206&Itemid=235

Minde, K. (1993). Prematurity and serious medical illness in infancy: Implications for development and intervention. In C.H. Zeanah, Jr. (Ed.), *Handbook of infant mental health* (pp. 87–105). New York: Guilford Press.

Moore, M.L., Howard, V.F., & McLaughlin, T.F. (2002). Siblings of children with disabilities: A review and analysis. *International Journal of Special Education, 17*(1), 49–64.

Mundy, P., & Neal, A.R. (2001). Neural plasticity, joint attention and autism. In L.M. Glidden (Ed.), *International review of research in mental retardation* (Vol. 23; pp. 139–168). San Diego: Academic Press.

National Council on Interpretation in Health Care. (2001). *Guide to initial assessment of interpreter qualifications* (NCIHC Working Paper Series). Retrieved June 8, 2007, from http://www.ncihc.org

National Research Council. (2001). *Educating children with autism.* Washington, DC: National Academies Press.

Noyes-Grosser, D.M., Holland, J.P., Lyons, D., Holland, C.L., Romanczyk, R.G., & Gillis, J.M. (2005). Rationale and methodology for developing guidelines for early intervention services for young children with disabilities. *Infants & Young Children, 18*(2), 119–135.

Ohtake, Y., Santos, R.M., and Fowler, S. (2002). It's a three-way conversation: Families, service providers, and interpreters working together. *Young Exceptional Children, 4*(1), 12–18.

Pawl, J.H., & St. John, M. (1998). *How you are is as important as what you do... in making a positive difference for infants, toddlers and their families.* Washington, DC: ZERO TO THREE: National Center for Infants, Toddlers and Families.

Pehlman, L. (2007). *The home visitor's role in working with the child with autism and the family.* Retrieved April 27, 2007, from http://www.aahbei.org/files/forms/Pehlman.pdf

Pilkington, K. (2006, Summer). A secure attachment: A birthright for every baby. *American Association for Home-Based Interventions (HBEI) News Exchange, 11*(3), 1,4, 6.

Poulson, C.L. (1988). Operant conditioning of vocalization rate of infants with Down syndrome. *American Journal of Mental Retardation, 93*(1), 57–63.

Poulson, M. (2003, Summer/Fall). Infant–toddler assessment: Clinical procedures and interpretations. *IDA News, 30*(2).

Prelock, P. (2006, October). Working with families and teams to address the needs of children with mental retardation and developmental disabilities. Perspectives on Language Learning and Education. *American Speech-Language-Hearing Association Division 1, 3*(13), 7–11.

Rapport, M.J.K., McWilliam, R.A., & Smith, B.J. (2004). Practices across disciplines in early intervention: The research base. *Infants & Young Children, 17*(1), 32–44.

Reamer, F.G. (1993). *Ethical dilemmas in social service: A guide for social workers* (2nd ed.). New York: Columbia University Press.

Reichle, J. (2007). *Beginning communication approaches with young children who have ASD.* Retrieved February 26, 2008, from http://ici.umn.edu/products/impact/193/over14.html

Reinhartson, D.B. (2000). Preverbal communicative competence: An essential step in the lives of infants with severe physical impairment. *Infants & Young Children, 13*(1), 49–51.

Reschly, B. (1979). *Supporting the changing family: A guide to the parent-to-parent model.* Ypsilanti, MI: High/Scope Press.

Richmond, M.E. (1912). *Friendly visiting among the poor: A handbook for charity workers.* New York: Macmillan.

Rimmerman, A. (1989). Provision of respite care for children with developmental disabilities: Changes in maternal coping and stress over time. *Mental Retardation, 27*, 99–103.

Rogers, F. (2003). *The world according to Mister Rogers: Important things to remember.* New York: Hyperion.

Rossetti, L. (2001). *Communication intervention: Birth to three* (2nd ed.). Albany, NY: Singular.

Rowan, L. (2006, Fall). Tips for providing services to grandparent families: Lessons learned. *News Exchange, 11*(3), 1–2, 7.

Sallows, G.O., & Graupner, T.D. (2005). Intensive behavioral treatment for children with autism: Four-year outcome and predictors. *American Journal of Mental Retardation, 110,* 417–438.

Sanz, M.T., & Balana, J.M. (2002). Early language stimulation of Down's syndrome babies: A study on the optimum age to begin. *Early Childhood Development and Care, 172,* 651–656.

Sanz, M.T., & Menendez, J. (1995). A study of the effect of age of onset of treatment on the observed development of Down's syndrome babies. *Early Childhood Development and Care,* 93–101.

Saxon, T.F. (1997). A longitudinal study of early mother–infant interaction and later language competence. *First Language, 17*(51), 271–281.

Scarborough, A.A., Hebbeler, K.M., & Spiker, D. (2006, March). Eligibility characteristics of infants and toddlers entering early intervention services in the United States. *Journal of Policy and Practice in Intellectual Disabilities, 3*(1), 57–64.

Scoby, J. (2000, July). *The critical needs of children.* Paper presented at the Attachment Parenting Symposium, Harvard Medical School, Boston.

Shonkoff, J.P., & Phillips, D.A. (Eds.). (2000). *From neurons to neighborhoods: The science of early childhood development.* Washington, DC: National Academies Press.

Shriberg, L., & Kwaitkowski, J. (1982). Phonological disorders II: A conceptual framework for management. *Journal of Speech and Hearing Disorders, 47,* 242–256.

Siegel, C. (n.d.). *Guidelines for referral: Red flags.* Minneapolis, MN: Center for Early Education and Development, College of Education and Development, University of Minnesota; adapted by permission.

Siegel, D.I. (1999). *The developing mind.* New York: Guilford Press.

Sileo, T.W., & Sileo, A.P. (1996). Parent and professional partnerships in special education: Multicultural considerations. *Intervention in School & Clinic, 31*(3), 145–154.

Simpson, R.L. (2007). *Effective practices for students with ASD.* Retrieved February 26, 2008, from http://ici.umn.edu/products/impact/193/over10.html

Smith, T.B., Oliver, M.N., & Innocenti, M.S. (2001). Parenting stress in families of children with disabilities. *American Journal of Orthopsychiatry, 71,* 257–261.

Smith, T.E., Gartin, B.C., Murdick, N.L., & Hilton, A. (2006). *Families and children with special needs.* Upper Saddle River, NJ: Merrill/Prentice Hall.

Spagnola, M., & Fiese, B.H. (2007). Family routines and rituals: A context for development in the lives of young children. *Infants & Young Children, 20*(4), 284–299.

Sparks, S. (1993). *Children of prenatal substance abuse.* San Diego: Singular.

Sparks, S., (n.d.). *HOPE Homestart: Early start program* [form]. San José, CA: HOPE Homestart.

Spiker, D., Malik, S., & Hebbeler, K. (2007, March). *Challenge: How can we describe the disability-related characteristics of children in EI?* Paper presented to the Infant Development Association of California, San José, CA.

Stovall, K.C., & Dozier, M. (2000). The development of attachment in new relationships: Single subject analyses for ten foster infants. *Development and Psychopathology, 12*(2), 133–156.

Streissguth, A. (1997). *Fetal alcohol syndrome: A guide for families and communities.* Baltimore: Paul H. Brookes Publishing Co.

Summers, J., Hoffmann, L., Marquis, J., Turnbull, A., & Poston, D. (2005). Relationship between parent satisfaction regarding partnerships with professionals and age of child. *Topics in Early Childhood Special Education, 25*, 48–58.

Tarbell, M. (2003). *Weaning children from gastrostomy tubes: Treating the whole child.* Presentation to the American-Speech-Language-Hearing Association annual convention, Chicago.

Thompson, T. (2007). *Autism spectrum disorders: Definitions and implications.* Retrieved February 26, 2008, from http://ici.umn.edu/products/impact/193/default.html

Tomasello, M. (2003). *Constructing a language: A usage-based theory of language acquisition.* Cambridge, MA: Harvard University Press.

Toomey, K.A. (1999). Gastroesophageal reflux and breastfeeding. *Colorado Breastfeeding Update, 7*(2), 3–5.

Toomey, K.A. (2002). Feeding strategies for older infants and toddlers. *Pediatric Basics, 100,* 2–13.

Trout, M.A., & Foley, G. (1989). Working with families of handicapped infants and toddlers. *Topics in Language Disorders, 10*(1), 57–67.

Turnbull, A.P., & Turnbull, H.R. (2006) *Families, professionals and exceptionality: A special partnership.* Upper Saddle River, NJ: Merrill/Prentice Hall.

U.S. Bureau of the Census. (2000). *Marital status by sex, unmarried-partner households, and grandparents as caregivers.* Retrieved November 16, 2007, from http://factfinder.census.gov

Vacca, J.J. (2001). Promoting positive infant–caregiver attachment: The role of the early interventionist and recommendations for parent training. *Infants and Young Children, 13*(4), 1–10.

Vacca, J., & Feinberg, E. (2000). Rules of engagement: Initiating and sustaining a relationship with families who have mental health disorders. *Infants & Young Children, 13*(2), 51–57.

Valvano, J., & Rapport, M.J. (2006). Activity-focused motor interventions for infants and young children with neurological conditions. *Infants & Young Children, 19*(4), 292–307.

Van Dyck, P., Kogan, M.D., Heppel, D., Blumberg, S.J., Cynamon, M.L., & Newacheck, P.W. (2004). The national survey of children's health: A new data resource. *Maternal and Child Health Journal, 8,* 183–186.

VandenBerg, K., Browne, J.V., Perez, L., & Newstetter, A. (2003). *Getting to know your baby*. Oakland, CA: The Special Start Training Program, Department of Education, Mills College.

Vigil, D.C. (2002). Cultural variations in attention regulation: A comparative analysis of British and Chinese-immigrant populations. *International Journal of Language and Communication Disorders, 37,* 433–458.

Vigil, D.C., & Hwa-Froelich, D.A. (2004). Interaction styles in minority care-givers: Implications for intervention. *Communication Disorders Quarterly, 25*(3), 119–126.

Wasik, B.H., & Bryant, D.M. (2001). *Home visiting: Procedures for helping families* (2nd ed.). Newbury Park, CA: Sage.

Weitzman, E. (2005). *Routines: Powerful ways to promote interaction and language learning.* Paper presented at the American Speech-Language-Hearing Association Convention, San Diego.

Wells, R., & Thompson, B. (2004). Strategies for supporting teenage mothers. *Young Exceptional Children, 7*(3), 20–27.

Westby, C., Burda, A., & Mehta, Z. (2003). Asking the right questions in the right way: Strategies for ethnographic interviewing. *The ASHA Leader, 8*(2), 4–5.

Wickerson-Kane, K.S., & Goldstein, H. (1999). Communicative assessment and intervention to address challenging behavior in toddlers. *Topics in Language Disorders, 19*(2), 70–89.

Wiggin, K.D. (1923). *My garden of memory: An autobiography.* Boston: Houghton Mifflin.

Wilcox, M.J., Kouri, T.A., & Caswell, S. (1990). Partner sensitivity to communication behavior of young children with developmental disabilities. *Journal of Speech and Hearing Disorders, 55,* 679–693.

Wiley, S., & Moeller, M.P. (2007). Red flags for disabilities in children who are deaf/hard of hearing. *The ASHA Leader, 12*(1), 8–9, 28–29.

Winton, P., & Winton, R. (2005). Family system. In J. O'Brien & J.W. Solomon (Eds.), *Pediatric skills for occupational assistants.* Philadelphia: Mosby.

Wolfe, P. (2000, May 11–13). *Revisiting effective teaching.* Paper presented at the Brain Research and Practices Conference, San Francisco.

Woods, J.J., & Wetherby, A.M. (2003). Early identification of and intervention for infants and toddlers who are at risk for autism spectrum disorder. *Language, Speech and Hearing Services in Schools, 34,* 180–193.

Zaidman-Zait, A., & Jamieson, J.R. (2007). Providing web-based support for families of infants and young children with disabilities. *Infants & Young Children, 20*(1), 11–25.

Zeanah, C.H., Jr. (Ed.). (2000). *Handbook of infant mental health* (2nd ed.). New York: Guilford.

Appendix

Infant Development from Birth to 3 Years—Heads Up

Sense of self	Physical changes	Relationships	Understanding the world	Communication
Expresses different needs and moods (fussy, hungry, tired, wet, wanting to be held) through variations in tone and intensity of crying Comforted by voice, if held closely or wrapped in a blanket Has own personality Is developing a sense of trust	Newborn reflexes: • Startles at a sudden light or noise • May startle when touched unexpectedly • Will follow a rattle with eyes for a short distance • Arms, legs, and body move, wiggle, and shake at the same time • Turns to suck on breast or bottle nipple Will lift head when placed on stomach Looks at objects (mobile, picture, fuzzball) placed in line of vision Grasps a finger when placed in infant's hand "Prereaches": simple reach and grasp movements exist but then fade Head unsteady; needs support Can bring fingers to mouth to suck	Snuggles, cuddles Recognizes Mom's voice Looks directly at a familiar adult face Looks away from strangers (yawns, shows signs of anxiety) Responds to rhythm of adult speech by body movements, looking alert, dozing off, and so forth Needs the closeness of holding for stimulating bonding	Tuned in to speech from birth Learning grows out of reflexes (e.g., child first sucks air, then learns to suck food) Learns about objects through looking Looks at bright objects Follows a slow-moving bright object Will ignore something that disturbs infant the first time infant hears it	Cries Responds to sounds (e.g., ringing bell, music, dog barking)

From Reschly, B. (1979). *Supporting the changing family: A guide to the parent-to-parent model.* Ypsilanti, MI: High/Scope Press; adapted by permission.

Infant Development from Birth to 3 Years—The Crawler-Creeper

Sense of self	Physical changes	Relationships	Understanding the world	Communication
Shows delight with self Gets others to "play" by actively expressing affection Stops eating to play Feeds self simple finger food (e.g., crackers) Still takes everything into mouth Holds out arms to be held or picked up Discovers parts of body (puts feet into mouth)	Balances on a lap Has coordinated seeing and grasping; reaches and grasps for objects (e.g., dangling objects) Rolls over Sits in high chair Bears weight on legs Crawls; may creep Rakes (makes sweeping, uncoordinated reaches) to attain objects; works to get toys that are out of reach Sits alone Will hold a cube in each hand Practices motor skills: first sitting, then pivoting, rolling, crawling, pulling self up to knees, and standing while holding on to something Passes cube hand to hand Learns to get self into sitting position	Receives and shows pleasure in being with mother Coos; makes sounds to get comfort, help, or people to play with Can pick out mom from others May show anxiety at strangers Will smile at own reflection in the mirror May start a game with an adult (e.g., drop the rattle, tickle me, catch the object)	Infant's world widens; horizons expand; exploring by looking continues Recognizes familiar objects; can select favorite toy if placed in front of infant Repeats enjoyable activities and actions over and over Likes to make things happen; explores by feeling, tracing, tasting Experiments with objects by shaking, banging, pushing, dropping Shows interest in external environment by • Searching for dropped objects • Recognizing partly hidden objects • Acting, then waiting for effect to occur • Trying to repeat actions accidentally discovered • Picking out cues that may help in recognizing a known place (Grandma's, babysitter's, nursery)	Develops syllables (e.g., *b, d, m*) Recognizes own name Turns toward voices and interesting sounds

From Reschly, B. (1979). *Supporting the changing family: A guide to the parent-to-parent model.* Ypsilanti, MI: High/Scope Press; adapted by permission.

Infant Development from Birth to 3 Years—The Cruiser

Sense of self	Physical changes	Relationships	Understanding the world	Communication
Begins to sense that he or she is a separate being	Can hold two cubes and bang them together	Behaves differently with different people	Continues to play Peek-a-boo as a way of learning things exist when they cannot be seen	Says "mama" or "dada" but doesn't understand meaning
Expresses feelings:	Can grasp small objects (e.g., raisins, cherries) between thumb and finger	Shows separation anxiety	Understands that he or she can get a toy that is out of reach	Imitates speech sounds
• Demonstrates affection		Waves bye-bye		Differentiates expressive vocalizations
• Listens with pleasure to sounds	Creeps, if has not before	Masters separation anxiety	Searches actively for hidden objects	Associates "ba" with bottle, "mama" with Mom, "dada" with Dad, "ma" with more, and so forth
• Has a sense of humor	Holds furniture and pulls self up to stand		Throws, retrieves, loses, searches, and finds	Engages in reciprocal baby talk; babbles back at parents
• Expresses aggression by throwing things	Walks when led, holding on to adult's thumb		Understands that something has to be done to get what infant wants	Understands simple statements such as, "Bring me the shoe"
	Handles objects with more ease		Intentionally chooses appropriate actions to carry out with a variety of toys	
	Able to coordinate eye-hand movements more easily		Begins to solve simple problems	
	Picks up small objects but will choose large over small		Can make things happen	
	Easily sits up without support		Often gets distracted when pursuing goals (e.g., if intent is to use the string to pull toy, then infant may end up playing with the string)	
	Enjoys emptying and filling			
	Discovers genitals		Can anticipate an immediate happening (e.g., the sound of footsteps means "Mom")	

From Reschly, B. (1979). *Supporting the changing family: A guide to the parent-to-parent model.* Ypsilanti, MI: High/Scope Press; adapted by permission.

Infant Development from Birth to 3 Years—The Walker

Sense of self	Physical changes	Relationships	Understanding the world	Communication
Imitates housework	Scribbles	Explores parents' hair, faces, glasses, and so forth	Pursues new and different activities for their own sake	Knows a few words other than "Mama" and "Dada"
Fights diaper changing	Builds tower of two or three cubes	Runs to be picked up, cuddled	Continues to be curious about objects	Expresses desires verbally
Expresses a variety of emotions, including much affection	Neat pincer grasp	Enjoys roughhousing, tossing games	Tends to experiment with different objects and things	Follows verbal cues
Will "make a scene" to get what is wanted; protests loudly	Imitates complex motor tasks (e.g., stirring, sweeping)	Will obey "no"	Expands range of explorations; empties cupboards, pokes into shelves and drawers, pulls out pots and pans	Knows own name and turns around when infant hears it
Shows off	Climbs stairs	Teases	Demonstrates skill in making things happen:	Uses words and gestures to get adult's attention
Conveys a variety of messages with ease (e.g., shakes head for "no," points)	Stands alone	Initiates games of give and take	• Nests toys	Asks "What?" or "What's that?" frequently
Is "into everything"	Walks	Likes to be within sight and hearing of adult	• Puts in, takes out	May try to sing
Has a firm sense of self as a separate being	Stoops to pick up objects	May stop playing for a little while to make sure parent is nearby	• Pulls, pushes	Enjoys rhymes and tries to join in
	Tears papers, magazines		• Rolls, rocks	Echoes important words or last words addressed to infant
	Climbs: gets on top of or under tables, desks, counters, and so forth		Active in trial-and-error exploration	Uses first sentences
	Rocks in rocking chair		Seeks new ways to get what he or she wants and to solve problems	
	Can get up on furniture; bounces on furniture		Identifies body parts	
	Uses both hands freely but may show preference for one hand		Recognizes existence of objects apart from self	
	Picks up small objects			

From Reschly, B. (1979). *Supporting the changing family: A guide to the parent-to-parent model.* Ypsilanti, MI: High/Scope Press; adapted by permission.

Infant Development from Birth to 3 Years—The Doer

Sense of self	Physical changes	Relationships	Understanding the world	Communication
Strives for autonomy; wants to do things on own: • Takes off clothing • Helps with simple household tasks • Begins to clean up • Shows independent streak (e.g., "do it myself"; often refuses help with dressing, bathing) • Acts possessive (me, mine) • Can be negative (says "No no"); has temper tantrums • Becomes aware of who he or she is by mastering skills, opposing people and situations, asserting self, making choices, protesting, and cooperating • Demands sameness of routine yet dislikes pressure that training places on infant	Actively explores as large and small muscle skills and eye-hand coordination are mastered and fine tuned: • Builds towers of three to five blocks, then knocks them down, rebuilds, and so forth • Dumps items from containers • Kicks large ball • Throws ball • Opens and closes containers • Tries hopping, somersaults, walking backward • Carries several toys at once • May be ready for toilet training • Climbs on furniture to look out window, get to counter, and so forth Will spontaneously make circular scribbles and dots when given paper and crayon (will do this on walls—watch out!)	Plays near other children, not with them Pats and hugs house pets affectionately, though can be rough Punches, slaps Imitates parents Bossy—gives orders Increases range and frequency of interaction with adults Resists demands of adults either playfully or seriously	Learns to master many aspects of the environment through observation, exploring, trial-and-error testing, problem-solving Combines toys in more complex ways Has favorite toys, foods, books; makes selections Struggles; gets frustrated when learning new skills Invents new ways to solve problems Memory develops: holds images (e.g., parents' faces) in mind; begins to use these images Understands that infant or another person can "picture" what has to be done to cause something to happen Firmly grasps concept of object permanence (understands objects exist when they cannot be seen) Watches and understands TV shows Begins to engage in "make-believe" activities	Uses two or three different words in sentences Points to and names body parts with help Names familiar items (e.g., ball, cat, truck) in pictures Follows simple directions: "Show me your nose," "Get your coat" Likes to listen to stories; pages through magazines with adults "Talks" on phone Imitates animal sounds (e.g., cat's meow) Hums; may sing Understands more words and ideas than can be expressed Is taken with the power of words: • Refers to self by name • Asks names of objects over and over • Talks to self during play

From Reschly, B. (1979). *Supporting the changing family: A guide to the parent-to-parent model.* Ypsilanti, MI: High/Scope Press; adapted by permission.

Infant Development from Birth to 3 Years—The Tester

Sense of self	Physical changes	Relationships	Understanding the world	Communication
Begins to gain a sense of self as a small individual who can do things independently:	Continues to master motor skills:	Relies on routines (likes things arranged and done same way every day)	Continues to be naturally and actively curious	Improves language skills rapidly
• Develops self-help skills (e.g., washing hands, using toilet, undressing self)	• Stacks/builds towers with cubes or blocks	May get upset if mother stays away overnight	Continues to learn about people and things and to organize own findings	Uses plurals
• Has favorite foods and other preferences	• Puts in, takes out, puts together, takes apart	Has flashes of temper	Uses words with pictures	Understands more than infant can say
• Continues to demand independence	• Can copy simple shapes	Imitates adult activities (e.g., dusting, sweeping, drinking coffee)	Associates people with certain places; knows where neighbors live	Sings songs
• Feels part of the family; does not want to be left out—puts off going to bed	• Can throw a ball	Has difficulty sharing	Knows names of body parts	Uses phrases, simple sentences ("He go car," "Me want milk")
• Develops sense of humor	• Jumps, rides a tricycle	Will play by self	Begins thinking and expressing thoughts about things not directly involved with	Counts ("one, two")
	• Runs (lopsided)	Shows achievements to parents	Can name, identify, ask for, and describe objects, people	Enjoys rhymes, chants
	• Climbs	Likes running errands ("go get a spoon, please")	Begins to identify size relationships (e.g., which ball is bigger)	Understands and uses concept words (e.g., hot, cold, high, down, soft, no, hard)
	• Walks down stairs	Enjoys roughhousing	Can represent the world through mental images	Talks about events (e.g., trip to store, a book, spilled milk)
	• Feeds self (may be messy, awkward)	Likes to watch others play	Can recognize similarity and differences in objects	Follows a series of directions
	• Sleeps less—is usually awake for most of the day	Gradually is able to separate from parent	Can classify objects (put the puzzles on the shelf and the truck under the table)	Can express wants and needs (e.g., "more milk," "want candy")
	• Tries to work zippers, snaps, buttons, and other closures	Likes chances to do for self and others	Makes choices	Likes to talk and work with parents
	• Begins to master slides and swings		Has beginning understanding of time concepts ("After your nap, we'll go outside")	Responds to questions, simple statements
	• Begins to coordinate complex hand and eye movements (e.g., can work a four- or five-piece puzzle)		Shows animistic thinking	Can be engaged in simple conversations
	• Inserts shapes into shape box, pegs into pegboard; strings large beads		Sees objects in terms of one or two prominent features	Asks, "Why?"
			Learning is situation-bound	

From Reschly, B. (1979). *Supporting the changing family: A guide to the parent-to-parent model.* Ypsilanti, MI: High/Scope Press; adapted by permission.

Speech and Language Development
of Infants and Young Children

Stages of speech and language development	Developmental stages	How to stimulate speech and language development
Sounds	Heads Up The Looker The Crawler/Creeper The Cruiser	Look at the baby (eye contact) Smile at the baby, make faces Touch the baby—whole body receives messages Sing Encourage imitation games such as Peek-a-boo Imitate the baby's speech sounds Encourage the baby to imitate new sounds Read books with the baby
Single words	The Walker	Name objects for the baby Read books with the baby Recite nursery rhymes Imitate the baby's movements and vocalizations Encourage imitation games such as Peek-a boo Talk to the baby about what you are doing when you are together
Two- or three-word utterances	The Doer	Be a good speech model Repeat new words over and over Talk about what you are doing when you are together Read books with the child Listen to the child when he or she is talking to you Carry on conversations with the child
Sentences	The Tester	Frequently use words in your speech that the child has trouble with Talk about relationships of words, objects, and ideas Talk about similarities or differences between things Encourage the child to tell stories using books and pictures Allow the child time to play with other children Pay attention to the child when he or she is talking, remembering that repeating words and sounds is normal during this period of growth Extend the child's conversation

From Reschly, B. (1979). *Supporting the changing family: A guide to the parent-to-parent model.* Ypsilanti, MI: High/Scope Press; adapted by permission.

State Parent Training and Information Centers

Alabama

Special Education Action Committee
600 Bel Air Boulevard
Suite 210
Mobile, AL 36606
Telephone: 800-222-7322
http://www.iser.com/SEAC-AL.html

Alaska

PARENTS, Inc.
4743 E. Northern Lights Boulevard
Anchorage, AK 99508
Telephone: 800-478-7678

Arizona

Pilot Parents of Southern Arizona
2600 N. Wyatt Drive
Tucson, AZ 85712
Telephone: 877-365-3152
http://www.pilotparents.org

Team of Advocates for Special Kids
  (TASK)
2400 North Central Avenue, Suite 200
Phoenix, AZ 85004-1313
Telephone: 800-237-3007
http://www.taskca.org

Arkansas

Arkansas Disability Coalition
1123 S. University Avenue
Suite 225
Little Rock, AR 72204-1605
Telephone: 800-223-1330
http://www.adcpti.blueskywebsites
  .com/adcpti.html

California

Exceptional Parents Unlimited
4440 N. First Street
Fresno, CA 93726
Telephone: 559-229-2000
http://www.exceptionalparents.org

Matrix Parent Network and Resource
  Center
94 Galli Drive, Suite C
Novato, CA 94949
Telephone: 800-578-2592
http://www.matrixparents.org

Parents Helping Parents
3041 Olcott Street
Santa Clara, CA 95054-3222
Telephone: 866-747-4040
http://www.php.com

Rowell Family Empowerment of
  Northern California
3830 Rancho Road
Redding, CA 96002
Telephone: 877-227-3471
http://www.rfenc.org/NEWSITE

Support for Families of Children with
  Disabilities
2601 Mission Street
Suite 606
San Francisco, CA 94110-3111
Telephone: 415-282-7494
http://www.supportforfamilies.org

Team of Advocates for Special Kids
 (TASK)
100 West Cerritos Avenue
Anaheim, CA 92805
Telephone: 866-828-8275
http://www.taskca.org

Colorado

PEAK Parent Center
611 N. Weber
Suite 200
Colorado Springs, CO 80903
Telephone: 800-284-0251
http://www.peakparent.org

Connecticut

Connecticut Parent Advocacy Center
338 Main Street
Niantic, CT 06357
Telephone: 800-445-2722
http://www.cpacinc.org

Delaware

Parent Information Center
5570 Kirkwood Highway
Wilmington, DE 19808
Telephone: 888-547-4412
http://www.picofdel.org

District of Columbia

Advocates for Justice and Education
2041 Martin Luther King Avenue, SE
Suite 400
Washington, DC 20020
Telephone: 888-327-8060
http://www.AJE-DC.org

Florida

Family Network on Disabilities
2735 Whitney Road
Clearwater, FL 33760-1610
Telephone: 800-825-5736
http://www.fndfl.org

Parent to Parent of Miami
7990 SW 117th Avenue
Suite 201
Miami, FL 33183
Telephone: 800-527-9552
http://www.ptopmiami.org

Georgia

Parents Educating Parents and
 Professionals for All Children
3680 Kings Highway
Douglasville, GA 30154
Telephone: 800-322-7065
http://www.peppinc.org

Hawaii

Hawaii Parent Training and
 Information Center
200 N. Vineyard Boulevard
Suite 310
Honolulu, HI 96817
Telephone: 800-533-9684

Idaho

Parents Unlimited, Inc.
600 N. Curtis Road
Suite 145
Boise, ID 83706
Telephone 800-242-5884
http://www.ipulidaho.org

Illinois

Family Matters Parent Training and
 Information Center
1901 S. Fourth Street
Suite 209
Effingham, IL 62401
Telephone: 866-436-7842
http://www.fmptic.org

Family Resource Center on
Disabilities
200 E. Jackson Boulevard
Room 300
Chicago, IL 60604
Telephone: 800-952-4199
http://www.frcd.org

Indiana

INSOURCE
1703 S. Ironwood
South Bend, IN 46612
Telephone: 800-332-4433
http://www.insource.org

Iowa

Access for Special Kids (ASK)
321 E. Sixth Street
Des Moines, IA 50309-1903
Telephone: 800-450-8667
http://www.askresource.org

Kansas

Families Together, Inc.
3033 W. Second Street
Suite 106
Wichita, KS 67203
Telephone: 888-815-6364
http://www.familiestogetherinc.org

Parent Advocacy and Support Services
555 N. Woodlawn
Suite 3105
Wichita, KS 67208
Telephone: 316-685-1821
http://www.mhasck.org

Kentucky

Special Parent Involvement Network
10301-B Deering Road
Louisville, KY 40272
Telephone: 800-525-7746
http://www.kyspin.com

Louisiana

Project PROMPT
201 Evans Road
Building I, Suite 100
Harahan, LA 70123
Telephone: 800-766-7736
http://www.projectprompt.com

Pyramid Parent Training Program
2552 Philip Street
New Orleans, LA 70119
Telephone: 504-827-0610

Maine

Maine Parent Federation
Post Office Box 2067
Augusta, ME 04338-2067
Telephone: 800-870-7746
http://www.mpf.org

Maryland

Parents' Place of Maryland
801 Cromwell Park Drive
Suite 103
Glen Burnie, MD 21061
Telephone: 800-394-5694
http://www.ppmd.org

Massachusetts

Federation for Children with Special
Needs
1135 Tremont Street
Suite 420
Boston, MA 02120-2140
Telephone: 800-331-0688
http://www.fcsn.org

Michigan

CAUSE
6412 Centurion Drive
Suite 130
Lansing, MI 48917
Telephone: 800-221-9105
http://www.causeonline.org

Tri-county Partnership
18100 Meyers
Suite 305/307
Detroit, MI 48235
Telephone: 800-298-4424
E-mail: infodetroit@causeonline.org

Minnesota

PACER Center, Inc.
8161 Normandale Boulevard
Minneapolis, MN 55437-1044
Telephone: 800-537-2237
http://www.pacer.org

Mississippi

EMPOWER Community Resource
  Center
136 S. Poplar Street
Greenville, MS 38702-1733
Telephone: 800-337-4852
http://www.msempower.org

Missouri

Missouri Parents Act
8301 State Line Road
Suite 204
Kansas City, MO 64114
Telephone: 800-743-7634
http://www.ptimpact.com

Montana

Parents Let's Unite for Kids
516 N. 32nd Street
Billings, MT 59101
Telephone: 800-222-7585
http://www.pluk.org

Nebraska

PTI Nebraska
3135 N. 93rd Street
Omaha, NE 68134-4717
Telephone: 800-284-8520
http://www.pti-nebraska.org

Nevada

Nevada Parents Encouraging Parents
2355 Red Rock Street
Suite 106
Las Vegas, NV 89146
Telephone: 800-216-5188
http://www.nvpep.org

New Hampshire

Parent Information Center
Post Office Box 2405
Concord, NH 03302-2405
Telephone: 800-947-7005
http://www.parentinformation
  center.org

New Jersey

Statewide Parent Advocacy Network
  (SPAN)
35 Halsey Street, Fourth Floor
Newark, NJ 07102
Telephone: 800-654-7726
http://www.spannj.org

New Mexico

Parents Reaching Out
1920B Columbia Drive SE
Albuquerque, NM 87106
Telephone: 800-524-5176
http://www.parentsreachingout.org

New York

The Advocacy Center
590 South Avenue
Rochester, NY 14620
Telephone: 800-650-4967
http://www.advocacycenter.com

Advocates for Children of New York
151 W. 30th Street
Fifth Floor
New York, NY 10001
Telephone: 866-427-6033
http://www.advocatesforchildren.org

Resources for Children with Special
   Needs
116 E. 16th Street
Fifth Floor
New York, NY 10003
Telephone: 212-254-4070

United We Stand of New York
594 Bushwick Avenue
Brooklyn, NY 11206
Telephone: 800-496-9623
http://www.uwsony.org

North Carolina

Exceptional Children's Assistance
   Center
907 Barra Row
Suites 102/103
Davidson, NC 28036
Telephone: 800-962-6817
http://www.ecac-parentcenter.org

North Dakota

Pathfinder Family Center
1600 Second Avenue, SW
Minot, ND 58701
Telephone: 800-245-5840
E-mail: ndpath01@srt.com

Ohio

Ohio Coalition for the Education of
   Children with Disabilities
165 W. Center Street
Suite 302
Marion, OH 43302-3741
Telephone: 800-374-2806
http://www.ocecd.org

Oklahoma

Oklahoma Parents Center
4600 Southeast 29th Street
Suite 115
Del City, OK 73115-4224
Telephone: 877-553-4332
E-mail: okparentsctr@aol.com

Oregon

Oregon Parent Training and
   Information Center
2288 Liberty Street, NE
Portland, OR 97301
Telephone: 888-505-2673
http://www.orpti.org

Pennsylvania

Mentor Parent Program, Inc.
Post Office Box 47
Cole Hill Road
Pittsfield, PA 16340
Telephone: 888-447-1431
http://www.mentorparent.org

Parent Education Network
2107 Industrial Highway
York, PA 17402-2223
Telephone: 800-522-5827
http://www.parentednet.org

Rhode Island

Rhode Island Parent Information and
    Resource Center
175 Main Street
Pawtucket, RI 02860-4101
Telephone: 800-464-3399
http://www.ripin.org

South Carolina

Parent Training and Resource Center
1575 Savannah Highway
Suite 6
Charleston, SC 29407
Telephone: 843-266-1318
http://www.frcdsn.org

Parents Reaching Out to Parents of
    South Carolina
652 Bush River Road
Suite 203
Columbia, SC 29210
Telephone 800-759-4776
http://www.proparents.org

South Dakota

South Dakota Parent Connection
3701 W. 49th Street
Suite 102
Sioux Falls, SD 57106
Telephone: 800-640-4553
http://www.sdparent.org

Tennessee

Support and Training For Exceptional
    Parents
712 Professional Plaza
Greeneville, TN 37745
Telephone: 800-280-7837
http://www.tnstep.org

Texas

The Arc of Texas in the Rio Grande
    Valley
Parents Supporting Parents Network
601 N. Texas Boulevard
Weslaco, TX 78596
Telephone: 888-857-8668
E-mail: weslaco@gte.net

Partners Resource Network, Inc.
1090 Longfellow Drive
Suite B
Beaumont, TX 77706
Telephone: 800-866-4726
http://www.partnerstx.org

Partners Resource Network, Inc.
1001 Main Street
Suite 804
Lubbock, TX 79401
Telephone: 877-762-1435
E-mail: wtxpen@sbcglobal.net

Partners Resource Network
3311 Richmond
Suite 334
Houston, TX 77098
Telephone: 877-832-8945
E-mail: pmteam@sbcglobal.net

Special Kids
Post Office Box 266958
Houston, TX 77207-6958
Telephone: 713-734-5355
E-mail: speckids@aol.com

Utah

Utah Parent Center
2290 E. 4500 South
Suite 110
Salt Lake City, UT 84117-4428
Telephone: 800-468-1160
http://www.utahparentcenter.org

Vermont

Vermont Parent Information Center
600 Blair Park Road
Suite 301
Williston, VT 05495
Telephone: 800-639-7170
http://www.vtpic.com

Virginia

Parent Education Advocacy Training
    Center
6320 Augusta Drive
Springfield, VA 22150
Telephone: 800-869-6782

PADDA
813 Forrest Drive
Suite 3
Newport News, VA 23606
Telephone: 888-337-2332

Washington

Parent to Parent Power
1118 S. 142nd Street
Suite B
Tacoma, WA 98444
Telephone: 253-531-2022
http://www.p2ppower.org

Washington PAVE
6316 S. 12th Street
Suite B
Tacoma, WA 98465-1900
Telephone: 800-572-7368
http://www.washingtonpave.org

West Virginia

West Virginia Parent Training and
    Information
1701 Hamill Avenue
Clarksburg, WV 26301
Telephone: 800-281-1436
http://www.WVPTI.org

Wisconsin

Family Assistance Center for
Education, Training and Support
2714 N. Dr. Martin Luther King Drive
Suite E
Milwaukee, WI 53212
Telephone: 877-374-4677
http://www.wifacets.org

Wyoming

Parent Information Center
5 N. Lobban
Buffalo, WY 82834
Telephone: 800-660-9742
http://www.wpic.org

Home Visit Record Form

Child's name: _____ Date: _____

Location of visit (circle one):   home   day care

Other: _____

Present at visit: _____

Time in: _____ Time out: _____

Regular home visit: _____

Circle one: IFSP   IEP

annual   semi-annual   transition

Circle one: assessment   intake

full   speech   OT   PT   feeding

What's New?

Today's activities:

Recommendations:

What's coming up?

Materials/Information left over:	Materials/Information for next visit:

Date/Time next home visit:

Source: Sparks (n.d.).

The Art and Practice of Home Visiting: Early Intervention for Children with Special Needs and Their Families by Ruth E. Cook, Ph.D., & Shirley N. Sparks, M.S., CCC-SLP

Toys Cleverly Disguised as Household Items[1]

I have found it helpful to find materials that children at various developmental stages can use. These are some of my favorites from around the house, and most of them are easy to wash. The A-frame toys that I mention are those frames from which you can suspend toys. If you attach some of these toys with elastic, the toys are easier for some children to use. For each item, I give a basic sensory play strategy, more advanced play schemes, and language concepts that the toy can help develop. I have written it from the child's perspective. Have fun!

1.   Net mesh ball (and you thought it was for bathing!)

   My little hands can hold it easily. It makes an interesting texture to mouth, and it is great to attach to an A-frame toy.

   It makes a relatively safe ball to throw and kick.

   "Kick" and "throw" are good words for you to use when I play with the mesh ball.

2.   Large plastic drinking cups from fast food restaurants (Finally, something to do with *all* those cups!)

   They are easy to hold by the rim and look way down inside.

   I love to stack and nest these cups. They are *sooo* much easier than those tiny blocks. I like to put small blocks or toys into the cups. They make a great noise when they hit the bottom, and then I can pour the blocks from one cup to another. These can make good bowling pins, and you can cover up one of my favorite toys to see if I know it is still there. You can even stuff the net mesh ball part way into one of the cups and let me work to get it out.

   "In," "out," and "pour" are words I hear you say when I play.

---

[1]From Brandt, K. (2001). Toys cleverly disguised as household items. *IDA News, 28*(3), 12–13; adapted by permission.

3. Individual plastic soda bottles (Yet another way to recycle)

   Put some clear corn syrup or liquid glycerin, some food coloring, and some glitter in a bottle. Let me shake and look at it. I might even try to lift it. In another bottle, you could put oil and water with food coloring. You might even be able to put a bell in some of the wide-mouth bottles (then you don't have to put that liquid stuff inside).

4. Spatula

   I like to mouth the spatula and turn it different ways to see how it looks. It is easy for me to hold the handle. Be careful because I can use it as a tool (weapon) as I learn to bang it.

   It is fun to use it to "flip pancakes" (coasters) and move them from one container to another. You might want to put the pancake on the spatula when I am first learning. Later, I can slide the spatula under the block or pancake. Rubber (non-skid) materials make my job as chef much easier. I take great pride in not spilling the pancakes before they get to their destination. Some of my friends like to use the spatula as a croquet mallet or golf club. That mesh ball makes these sporting activities safer for the spectators and the furniture.

   "Pancakes" and "in" are words you can use while I play.

5. Wire whisks

   Wire whisks are *very* easy for me to grab and to put in my mouth. They are good to hang from an A–frame toy. If you put a large bell from a craft shop inside the whisk, I can use it as a rattle. It will even make more noise when I bang it on the floor, a drum, or a tambourine. The metal feels a little colder than those plastic toys you give me.

   Please be careful when you select a whisk for me, as some of them have kind of pointy things on the end and I might hurt myself.

6. Measuring spoons with a large ring holding them together (metal or plastic—or how about a set of each?)

A large ring lets me hold them more easily. I like the sound they make when I shake them. You can even hang them from the A-frame toy.

For pretend play and fine motor activities, I can use the spoons to feed my dolls. I can "lace" the spoons back on the ring. I can nest spoons from larger to smaller. I can scoop beans or other small objects (as long as you make sure I don't try to eat them) from one container to another. If you are really brave, how about letting me scoop water from one cup to another? Just know that I will get myself and the surrounding area wet.

Use the words "on," "spoon," "shake," and "scoop" while I play.

7. Milk container blocks

You have already probably washed some milk cartons, cut off the top, and put them together for me. But, have you thought of different size cartons? Egg substitute or milk containers, Pringles cans, and plastic baby food containers make different sized blocks. How about putting a bell inside or some rice or beans?

8. Plastic ketchup and mustard dispensers

I like red and yellow, so these really catch my eye. You can make these into rattles for me by putting some beans or rice in them.

I can use them to squirt air to push cotton balls across the table. That makes my hands stronger!

I can pretend I am cooking and squeeze some out onto food.

9. Velcro-type hair curlers (Please get me a couple different sizes— in different colors, too)

I like to reach for, feel, and mouth the curlers. You can put the curlers on my clothes or on the carpet and I will pull them off. Try putting one in my hair and see if I notice it and can take it off. Put a couple of curlers together and I can use both hands to separate them.

Let me put the smaller curlers inside the larger curlers. This way I learn about sizes and get a different feel than most of those plastic toys they make for nesting.

Use the words "in," "big," and "small" for this activity.

10. Toothbrush holders (different colors, different textures, and even some that are oblong instead of round)

Let me reach for and grab half of or the entire holder. It is a perfect size to put in my mouth. If you put beans in the holder (please make sure to tape it shut securely so I don't have a chance to eat the beans) I can use it as a rattle.

Let me pull the toothbrush holder apart and then try to put it together. Some of them make a great popping noise when I pull them apart. I wonder what I would do if you gave me two holders in different colors? Would I know which pieces went together? Let me try standing the two halves upright on a flat surface. I can also put things into the toothbrush holder and then pour them out!

Use comparison words such as "together–apart," "open–close," and "in–out"; use other words such as "pop," "pour," or references to the colors of the holders while I'm playing.

11. Heath Supplement Containers or Herb and Spice Containers

Please make sure to take the labels off before you give these containers to me so that I don't think it is safe to play with medicine. If you put some rice, beans, or bells in the containers, I love to shake them. If you make some rattles with round bottles and some with square containers (they are a little harder to find) I can learn about "roundness" and "squareness" as I touch and mouth them.

Turning the tops to take them off and put them on is hard, but when I am ready please let me try it. If you put a favorite small toy of mine in the bottle and then put the lid on, I might be even more motivated to open it up.

Use words such as "on–off," "turn," and "twist" during my play.

Guidelines for Referral: Red Flags[1]

Home visitors have the opportunity to observe parents and children interact repeatedly in their most familiar surroundings. If persistent difficulties are noted in the domains listed, a referral for more intensive treatment may be indicated. *Please remember to consider cultural variations in parenting as you are making your assessment.*

Parent's Mood/Behavior

Parent appears significantly depressed, as demonstrated by low energy, unresponsiveness to surroundings, or disinterest in the child's behavior or welfare.

Parent appears extremely anxious, nervous, stressed, or overwhelmed—beyond what is expected of other parents with same-age child.

Parent appears to have a serious lack of understanding of child development, resulting in unrealistic expectations for the child that may be harmful or dangerous.

Parent appears to have a serious mental disorder, such as schizophrenia or bipolar disorder, that may impair his or her ability to safely care for the child.

Parent appears to be abusing substances, such as alcohol or cocaine, that may impair judgment and interfere with his or her ability to safely care for the child.

Child's Appearance and/or Behavior

Child's physical needs are consistently neglected, as evidenced by dirty or unkempt appearance, poor nutrition, lack of dental care, or frequent untreated illness.

[1]From Siegel, C. (n.d.). *Guidelines for Referral: Red Flags.* Minneapolis, MN: Center for Early Education and Development, College of Education and Development, University of Minnesota; adapted by permission.

Child is not developing as expected, and underdevelopment is not due to a known medical condition. Signs include lack of weight gain, poor language and socialization skills, and inability to reach developmental milestones.

Child is frequently emotionally upset, more than is expected for the child's developmental level. Signs include displays of anger and aggression, tantrums, and inconsolable crying.

Child is frequently sad, anxious, or worried, more than is expected for children of similar age. Child smiles infrequently, does not show interest in playing, and/or reacts strongly to noise and movement.

Child is unresponsive to parent and/or environment, more than is expected for children of similar age. Child does not make eye contact with parent or others, does not engage in interaction with others, and shows little awareness of surroundings.

Parent–Child Relationship

Parent and child have difficulty connecting. Child does not respond to parent's presence. Parent is unable to engage or play with or set limits for child. Parent infrequently talks to child or holds child's hand. Parent and child have frequent miscommunications, or parent says he or she does not know how to relate to the child.

Parent consistently fails to protect the child, allowing child to touch, eat, play with, or climb on dangerous objects.

Parent is consistently cold or hostile to the child. Parent uses hard tone or offensive words or uses unnecessary force. Parent threatens to hit the infant or calls the child names.

Parent attributes malignant motives to child's behavior. Parent may say the child deliberately makes him or her angry by waking up at night or that the infant will turn out to be a mean troublemaker "just like his dad."

Index

Page numbers followed by *f* indicate figures; those followed by *t* indicate tables.